RECLAIMING HERSTORY

ERICKSONIAN SOLUTION-FOCUSED THERAPY FOR SEXUAL ABUSE

RECLAIMING HERSTORY

ERICKSONIAN SOLUTION-FOCUSED THERAPY FOR SEXUAL ABUSE

Cheryl Bell-Gadsby, M.A., R.C.C.

&

Anne Siegenberg, M.S.W., R.S.W.

BRUNNER/MAZEL *Publishers* • New York

Library of Congress Cataloging-in-Publication Data

Bell-Gadsby, Cheryl.
  Reclaiming herstory: Ericksonian solution-focused therapy for sexual
abuse / Cheryl Bell-Gadsby & Anne Siegenberg.
    p. cm.
  Includes bibliographical references and index.
  ISBN: 0-87630-777-2 (hardcover)
  1. Adult child sexual abuse victims—Rehabilitation.
2. Psychotherapy. 3. Hypnotism—Therapeutic use. 4. Erickson,
Milton H. 5. Erickson, Milton H. I. Title.
  [DNLM: 1. Child Abuse, Sexual—psychology. 2. Psychotherapy—
methods. 3. Survivors—psychology. WA 320 B4335r 1996]
RC569.5.A28B46 1996
616.85'83690651—dc20
DNLM/DLC
for Library of Congress   95-41587
                                                                  CIP

Published by
BRUNNER/MAZEL, INC.
19 Union Square West
New York, New York 10003

Manufactured in the United States of America

10   9   8   7   6   5   4   3   2   1

To my mother, Barbara, who always taught me that I could do anything I set my mind to. Your voice is what keeps me here.

All my love,
Cheryl

To Muz, for his continued support, love, and belief in me.

To my mother for providing the opportunity to create this book with her loving encouragement and dedication.

To my father for acknowledging that his ability to express unconditional love has helped nurture our relationship.

To my family whose mere existence has been an ongoing source of inspiration and joy to me.

Love always,
Anne

Contents

List of Metaphors, Exercises, and Rituals

Stage One

Stage Two

Stage Four (Part B)

Metaphors, Exercises, and Rituals

Foreword

I hated reading this book. At least part of me did.

Now I know that's a strange opening to a foreword for an important and hope-filled book written by two friends and former students, now esteemed Canadian colleagues. But, the subject of the book is violence and part of me just didn't want to think about that topic. I've encountered too much violence in my years as a therapist. I've seen too much resultant devastation. I just wanted to put it out of my mind. Thinking about violence is like thinking about cancer.

The Nobel Laureate, Elie Wiesel, wisely suggested that violence begins when one behaves disrespectfully to another. I suspect he is correct; disrespect is a form of violence.

Violence is a cancer, whatever form it takes. In cancer, it is as if a part of an organism "goes berserk" and inexplicably invades other parts, causing a decrease in total viability. The organism has trouble defending itself against the aberration which operates in cloaked secrecy and cannot be recognized as an insidious invader; mindlessly it replicates itself. Moreover, the unchecked growth of the tumor is inexplicably self-reflexive and eventually causes its own demise.

Similar to cancer, the effects of violence are especially virulent when they take hold in children. Youngsters exposed to violence can suffer enormous social/psychological/physical consequences. As adults, self-esteem is especially affected.

Novel approaches to violence and the sequelae must be developed. *Reclaiming Herstory* is a book about remedying the stultifying affects of violence, especially the violence perpetrated on women who have been the subject of early sexual abuse.

Cheryl Bell-Gadsby and Anne Siegenberg have done admirable jobs of simplifying and codifying an approach, so that clinicians unfamiliar with the territory can improve their therapeutic efficacy. They're especially strong in identifying the stages of treatment and healing. They elucidate an Ericksonian-inspired use of metaphors and rituals. As master storytellers they provide protocols which can be easily modified and applied. Both individual and group approaches are emphasized.

The authors are diligent workers whose inspired compassion has undoubtedly aided many. Herein they make their wealth of experience available to the professional public. This is not a manual or text. It is an evolving story of helping survivors reclaim their lives.

I've seen few cases where early sexual abuse and subsequent dissociation are primary issues; it is not my specialty. The spectacular nature of these events are such that they catch our attention and tug on our heart strings. Yet, there is need to be rational and not sensationalize. The tempered methods of Bell-Gadsby and Siegenberg will help us be more effective with future patients, and they may renew our interest in the therapeutic use of fables. Over the years and similar to Erickson, I tend to use real stories with patients. Now I can muster more courage to be inventive.

There is still much to be written about approaches to violence and one only can hope that the authors further elucidate their methods. We are shown how they set up and follow through in order to improve the response to their stories and their strategies for interactionally utilizing the patient's natural groups, including families and environmental circumstances. But there is so much more that needs to be discovered about halting and reversing violence and its sequelae; one needs to understand the historical and interpersonal meaning of violent events on the victim—why some are so affected and others adapt.

Readers will find within immediately applicable methods. It will be easy to garner a humane perspective to an inhumane problem. Careful study of this book will help clinicians of all persuasions discover artful approaches to resurrecting self-esteem and reversing the effects of traumatic violence. Bell-Gadsby and Siegenberg are to be commended for their illuminating efforts. More importantly, they force us to come to terms with the topic often shrouded in denial. They irradiate broken lives with hope and power.

Jeffrey K. Zeig, Ph.D.
Director
The Milton H. Erickson Foundation

Acknowledgments

We would like to thank Jeffrey K. Zeig, Ph.D. for all of his mentoring and inspiration over the years. His continued belief and encouragement have helped us to remain focused on the exploration of future possibilities both personally and professionally.

A special thank you to all of the courageous survivors we have worked with over the years who have sparked the inspiration to write this book. It is our honor to share in your healing journey. Always remember that you *can* acknowlege your "herstory" and strive toward the future at the same time.

Thank you to my husband Chris for all of his love, patience, and support before, during, and after the writing of this book. A special message of appreciation to Robert Trowhill for all of his creative and technical assistance. Thank you also to Kate Blassnitz, M.S.W. for her special contributions and insights that helped formulate many of the questions used in the book.

C.B.G.

Introduction

Reclaiming Herstory: Ericksonian Solution-Focused Therapy for Sexual Abuse evolved out of our many years of working with survivors of sexual abuse and also out of our struggle as therapists in assisting these clients to reframe and transcend their traumatic historical events without retraumatizing or continuing to anchor them in that abusive past. We have found Ericksonian techniques and a solution-focused, future-oriented approach to be invaluable in working with this vulnerable clientele.

We view the role of the therapist as one who assists clients in the acquisition and retrieval of the adaptive skills and tools with which they can end their victimization and realize their true potential. The healing process is thus a collaborative partnership in which the therapist co-creates with the client a positive context for healing. This is achieved by identifying and assessing the individual needs, and by tailoring and developing tools such as therapeutic metaphors, exercises, and rituals that can help facilitate the healing process outlined in the four stages a survivor must traverse toward her ultimate empowerment and transformation.

The client and the therapist each guide the other along this path and there is continual reassessment of the client's healing process, at her individual pace, considering her particular history, until the acquisition of more adaptive and healthier skill sets are realized.

In as much as we have characterized the therapist-client alliance as a co-creative process, we have worked together co-creatively to bring this book into being. We have entered into a unique partnership, where the inspiration to write and the support to see this through from its conception to its birth have come from one another—and also from the many courageous survivors of sexual abuse with whom we have worked over the years: these circumstances and people have made this book possible. The constant encouragement mutually generated from one another during the process of writing this book has assisted us in breaking the isolative process of writing and helped us to negotiate any obstacles that came our way. Our regular meetings together were a source of inspiration and encouragement, affording us the ability to maintain a sense of humor and providing us with the courage to nurture our creation through to its ultimate birth.

The bulk of our experience comes from working over the past decade with hundreds of female survivors of sexual abuse, which accounts for our use of the pronoun "she" throughout this book. Although we have not worked with as many male survivors of sexual abuse, most of the Ericksonian methods discussed throughout this book, and the healing stages described, can equally be applied to the experience of the male population.

It is our view that counseling survivors of ritual abuse is a very distinct and different mindset to the clinical interventions presented in this book and, therefore, we would suggest that reference be made to material specifically designed for working with the ritually abused population.

In preparation for reading this book, and utilizing the methods of practice described, we suggest that it is the ethical responsibility of the therapist and therapist-in-training to seek further specialized instruction in the clinical issues surrounding sexual abuse and in Ericksonian applied theory and techniques.

This book caters to a wide range of therapists, including graduate students who have chosen to work with survivors of sexual abuse as a subspecialty, Ericksonian therapists who have identified sexual abuse as an area of specialty, sexual abuse therapists who are looking to expand their repertoire of tools with the creativity of the Ericksonian approach, and generalist therapists who are seeking a more precise understanding of the healing stages of the survivor. This book also provides general information for therapists desiring to familiarize themselves with different issues that arise from each stage of treatment.

It is our hope that when you, the therapist, are working with a client who identifies herself as a survivor of sexual abuse and who presents with a certain collection of issues, you can use our book as a reference guide—a guide to assist you in honing in on the particular healing stage that your client is currently in and in utilizing the appropriate therapeutic methods suggested. Hopefully, this book will expand your repertoire of skills and thus enhance your therapeutic effectiveness at each juncture of the healing journey.

This book began as a twinkle in our eyes—a collection of clinical issues and our own uniquely designed therapeutic interventions, which we sorted into five distinct healing stages that the survivor, in our experience, journeys through, before she is able to enjoy a certain quality of life that comes out of an increased sense of freedom from the effects of sexual abuse.

In creating a section on self-care for the therapist (see Chapter 8), we hope to impart the message that wherever you are developmentally in your clinical practice, it is both acceptable and mandatory to take time out of your busy schedule to put into practice creative methods of self-care. The actual process of recording what we do in the pages of this book has afforded us the opportunity of appreciating and honoring the way in which we work with our clients, and we encourage you, the reader, to do the same.

RECLAIMING HERSTORY

ERICKSONIAN SOLUTION-FOCUSED THERAPY FOR SEXUAL ABUSE

PART I

PROCESS AND PRACTICE

CHAPTER 1

Trauma and Memory

Fragments of life pieces...scattered over time...retrieved...then let go...retrieved again...and then let go again...and so the ebb and flow of memory besieged by trauma continues, until the pieces begin to fit together in some cogent way—creating a life-size jigsaw puzzle of human experience. In our clinical practice, persons having undergone such traumas as childhood sexual abuse often do not have clear memories of the event(s) until they are well into their 30s. Conversely, there are some trauma survivors who have a clear memory that spans back to when the abuse first began and before.

The focus of this chapter is to assist the therapist and the therapist-in-training in gaining a clearer understanding of the biological, mental, and emotional effects of trauma on memory. In addition, it seems appropriate to address the phenomenon of "false memory" in order to provide the reader with our particular understanding of the consequences of this phenomenon for both survivors of sexual abuse and the therapists who work with them.

For the purposes of this book, we define *memory* as a faculty that has the capacity to retain thoughts from the more recent past, all the way back to the past of long ago, that is, the historical past. In addition, we define *trauma* as a psychic injury caused by emotional shock, which continues to remain unhealed and sometimes dissociated from the conscious memory, often resulting in a behavioral and emotional disorder. Furthermore, we understand *dissociation* as the vehicle utilized by the brain under severe stress to carry a fragmented form of the trauma, which is often expressed by the survivor through flashbacks, dreams, anxiety, panic attacks, self-mutilation, and/or somatization.

It is our belief, supported by Bessel van der Kolk and Onno van der Hart (1991), that forgotten traumatic memory is not repressed, that is, pushed down and out, but rather it is dissociated, that is, contained in an alternate stream of consciousness where the narrative form of the memory becomes inaccessible and instead, is often expressed on a visceral and emotional level. Therefore, we will be using the term *dissociation* rather than *repression* or *suppression* to describe the impact of trauma on memory. *Posttraumatic Stress Disorder* is the term used in the *Diagnostic and Statistical Manual of Mental Disorders, Fourth Edition* to describe the reaction of a human being to such a traumatic event. The DSM-IV (APA, 1994) describes Posttraumatic Stress Disorder as a reaction to a situation that is outside of the realm of usual human experience. Such reactions include fear, terror, and a sense of helplessness, coupled with a behavioral component that is often characterized by emotional numbing, hypervigilance following the trauma, with the traumatic event commonly reexperienced through recurrent and intrusive recollections, distressing dreams, along with the development of dissociative states as a further reaction to the traumatic event.

I. THE BIOLOGICAL, MENTAL, AND EMOTIONAL EFFECTS OF TRAUMA ON MEMORY

When early traumatization occurs, in this case sexual abuse, the memory is often blocked to the extent that only very small fragments of experience are released into the conscious mind by the unconscious mind—creating a sort of protective covering for the person not yet ready to deal with her past abusive experience. Canadian lawyer Susan Vella (1994) speaks of the phenomenon of false memory as a sexual assault defense theory, citing a large study performed by Linda Meyer Williams that supports the belief that traumatic memory is dissociated. In a follow-up study of 200 adults treated as children for sexual abuse, 1 in 3 did not recall the abusive experiences documented in their hospital records 20 years prior.

According to Mary Sykes Wylie (1993), it is only in the last decade that the law and society are acknowledging and giving credence to the premise that traumatic memory is, by its very nature, often dissociated, and, as a result, the statute of limitations has been extended in 21 states in the United States as well as in Canada in order to take this premise into account.

From our experience in working with hundreds of survivors of sexual abuse, the clustering of the following factors tends to create a greater degree of dissociation from the traumatic event(s): the earlier the occurrence of the abuse, the more intense and violent the abuse, the more threatening the abuse, and the more closely related the victim is to the abuser. The extreme expression of dissociated memory can result in multiplicity, also known previously as Multiple Personality Disorder and now referred to as Dissociative Identity Disorder in the DSM-IV. Clients labelled "borderline," who were previously considered untreatable, are finally being recognized for who they have often been all along—survivors of sexual abuse. In a study conducted by Saxe, van der Kolk, Beckowitz, Chinman, Hall, et al. (1993), 100% of 110 psychiatric inpatients, who were previously diagnosed with schizophrenia, mood disorders, and borderline personality disorder were, in fact, individuals with dissociative disorders. They had not been asked such crucial diagnostic questions as whether they had experienced losing track of time, had partial or complete amnesia for certain events, and/or had experienced feelings of detachment or unrealness, that is, the determinants of dissociation. This is a strong indication that dissociated memory is not always recognized as traumatic—until the dissociated fragments are pieced together to create a full narrative of the event(s).

As therapists, it is of primary importance that we have some understanding of the chemical and biological effects of traumatization on the brain, and hence on memory. The breakthrough work of Pierre Janet (1886–1935) and, more recently, van der Kolk and van der Hart (1984–1993) on the brain and trauma, substantiates what we have learned from our clinical practice and further enhances our understanding of the mechanism of memory under stress. Van der Kolk and van der Hart (1991) discuss the fact that the combination of the arousal and autonomic nervous response, the secretion of neurotransmitters with resultant nerve stimulation, and the patterns and pathways of the nervous system play a vital role in the mechanism of memory retrieval. Although these factors must play an important role in the adolescent and adult survivor of sexual abuse, the mechanism in children is much more complex and less understood. This would stem from the fact that in infants and young children important parts of the nervous system related to memory are not yet myelinized. This constitutes the covering of the nerves with a specialized myelin sheath that protects the nerves, preventing disruption of impulses travelling within them. It is hypothesized that without this sheath, important parts of the brain associated with memory storage and retrieval are vulnerable to disruption. This may explain how most survivors, in our experience, recall sexual abuse from the age of about 5 years and older, with earlier narrative memory of trauma often only available in a more visceral, emotional form.

· Janet (1909b) has assisted us in understanding that "the healthy response to stress is mobilization of adaptive action." However, in the event of severe stress, such as childhood sexual abuse, van der Kolk and van der Hart acknowledge that "actual experiences can be so overwhelming that they cannot be integrated into existing mental frameworks, and instead, are dissociated, later to return intrusively as fragmented sensory or motoric experiences" (1991, p. 447). Traumatic memory gets fixed to resist further change, so that trauma victims continue to relive traumatic experiences in an unmodified, repetitive manner until, as Janet (1909) and more recently van der Kolk and van der Hart (1991) believe, flexibility is introduced in order to lessen the power of the memory. This is where horrific scenarios are unfrozen and replaced by alternative scenarios composed of more positive elements, resulting in the softening of the original experience of the trauma. In the creation of our metaphors, exercises, rituals, and practical techniques, we have attempted to help the survivor reintegrate those fragmented memories and experiences, in order to increase the mobility and flexibility of previously frozen behaviors and maladaptive patterns.

II. THE FALSE MEMORY BACKLASH: IMPACT ON THE SURVIVOR AND IMPLICATIONS FOR SEXUAL ABUSE THERAPISTS

With the recent media attention on False Memory Syndrome, whose premise is based on the belief that therapists can plant traumatic memory into the minds of unsuspecting clients, the very tenet of Posttraumatic Stress Disorder is challenged and brought under fire. Unfortunately, in our experience, recent clients in the process of recovering traumatic memory have begun to question their own newly retrieved fragments— wondering if perhaps they just made it up for some unknown reason: this is a tragic consequence of the false memory backlash.

The medical and legal professions have lent credence to the impact of war and physical trauma on memory, but very little credibility has been afforded the impact of child sexual abuse on memory until more recently. This newly acknowledged awareness was gaining momentum until the False Memory Syndrome Foundation brought forth their beliefs, backed by certain psychiatrists and psychologists who were prepared to state that repressed memory was a fallacy, and that if past trauma occurred, the memory of it in the present would be a clear, full one. As a result, the so-called false memory "experts" have done much to discredit survivors of sexual abuse, who recalled in adulthood traumatic memory that had been blocked from the conscious mind since childhood. The survivor is finally ready to speak out, based on her emerging belief in herself, only to receive the same message from the proponents of False Memory Syndrome that she received from her perpetrators and family members who supported them—"You're making it up," "It never happened."

As a result of the increased visibility and recognition in the media afforded victims of sexual abuse, survivors have come to view themselves as credible witnesses to the trauma they suffered, often at the hands of other family members. As the victim of such heinous acts, the survivor has begun to emerge from the shadows of denial and disbelief and find her own voice for the first time. The mighty and powerful voice of the perpetrator has finally been challenged, and the phoenix victim has arisen from the ashes to undergo a dramatic transformation. In order for this transformation to take place, the majority of therapists who work with survivors are a group of professionals dedicated to the healing process and invested in assisting their clients in leading active, healthy, productive lives. The false memory debate has come into the political arena to the extent that therapists who work with survivors of sexual abuse need to take a stand collectively and lobby for the rights of their clients, so that the survivor continues to get the message that she is believed and that she can trust her own memory—that is, she can trust herself.

The False Memory Syndrome Foundation is perpetuating another backlash, that is, the undermining of the therapist's role with survivors of sexual abuse, by suggesting that some therapists plant false memories into the minds of their clients. In order for a therapist to work with sexual abuse survivors, they should be required to meet such criteria as a professional degree in social work, psychiatry, or psychology, membership in a professional association; and specialized training in the area of sexual abuse. The silver lining to the False Memory Syndrome cloud is that it is forcing therapists to reexamine with a critical eye the way they practice, in order to determine how ethical it truly is. It is, therefore, a prudent and ethical practice to go at the client's pace, and if there is dissociated traumatic memory, it will eventually bubble in the conscious mind when the client is ready to reintegrate the memory in a way that is meaningful and healing for her.

Priscilla* was a 37-year-old client who was in therapy for a number of years before she was ready to remember her sexually traumatized past. Until that time, the fragments of memory that had been surfacing were too scattered to allow conclusions to be drawn, and Priscilla was encouraged by the therapist to express those memories through artwork. It was only when the client was ready to piece together in a retrospective therapy session all the artwork she had created over the years that she was able to tell the story of her sexual abuse.

It is our belief that dissociated traumatic memory can not only be retrieved in the therapist's office, but also can surface at different times in the person's life; for example, when facing a stressful situation at work or following the birth of a child, marriage, or divorce—all these milestones can evoke traumatic memory. For a fuller description of the impact of these milestones on the traumatized individual, please refer to Section V, titled "Issues That Often Trigger Memory" in this chapter.

It is becoming more evident that claims made by proponents of the False Memory Syndrome are highly questionable and according to Wylie (1993) are supported by powerful, wealthy perpetrators who are looking toward society to sanction their criminal behavior. Another silver lining to this cloud, however, is that in coming forward, the accused are themselves lifting the cloak of secrecy that has enshrouded their identity, even though the vehicle they have utilized to express themselves, the False Memory Syndrome Foundation, is an organizational expression of their collective denial. In fact, the founding members of The False Memory Syndrome Foundation, Dr. Pamela Freyd and her husband, Peter Freyd, were accused by their daughter, Jennifer Freyd, Ph.D., of sexually abusing her as a child. In an article where she refutes her parents' claims that she falsely accused them, Dr. Jennifer Freyd (1993) describes the False Memory Foundation as not just about memory research, but also as a collection of dysfunctional family members in emotional pain who have created a societal sanction to support their denial—a common characteristic of perpetrators.

Claims made by the False Memory Syndrome Foundation have done much to foster and encourage survivors to question and ultimately recant their stories. However, from sexual abuse therapists-in-training to the well-seasoned contingent, we need to assume an advocacy role as well as a clinical one with the survivors with whom we work, in order to

---

* All names and identifying characteristics of clients have been changed throughout this book to protect their privacy and confidentiality.

preserve and validate their traumatic truths and to maintain our own integrity. Otherwise, the groundbreaking work over the last two centuries by certain members of the medical profession including such notables as Janet, van der Kolk, van der Hart, and Herman, which substantiates and supports the experiences of sexual abuse in the lives of survivors, will be for naught. Further, there is no reasonable evidence to support the claim that False Memory Syndrome is clinically acceptable enough to be considered a *syndrome*, that is, implying something that is common, as Susan Vella (1994) indicates in her article on "False Memory Syndrome." Therefore, we believe that the personal testimony of those brave individuals who have survived these traumatic ordeals and with whom we work will prevail.

III. MEMORY AND THERAPEUTIC APPROACH

The current controversy surrounding False Memory Syndrome has, in our opinion, both positive and negative implications for therapists. We view this as an opportunity to clarify and concretize our methods and approach to doing therapy with adult survivors of child sexual abuse. The current research and literature available on memory as it pertains to trauma is sketchy and itself controversial. It is therefore important to be aware of how the use of methods such as hypnosis and guided imagery, group therapy, and the relationship with and approach of the therapist in general, affect the memory experience of the survivor.

There is no question that any client entering a therapist's office for help is in a very vulnerable and suggestible state. By the time a survivor of sexual abuse comes into therapy, she is usually at an extremely low point in her life and often desperately searching for answers and explanations for her traumatic past. The therapist therefore is in a very powerful and influential position in relation to the client. We believe it is important for the therapist to carefully think through his/her own beliefs and views concerning sexual abuse and how these values and beliefs are or are not communicated to the client. There is often a fine line between validation and suggestion.

It is, in our opinion, vital to be clear about one's theoretical and philosophical perspective regarding therapy in general and issues of sexual abuse in particular. For example, we clearly practice from both an Ericksonian and a feminist perspective and therefore include material and information that reflects and focuses upon abuse issues within a societal, political viewpoint as well as on individual experience. We are always very open with clients about our approach and theoretical orientation, and it is important to us to incorporate a feminist perspective into our work as it is both consistent with who we are as individuals as well as therapists. We believe it is necessary to communicate this to our clients and to find out their views and definitions of a feminist perspective. We each come into the room with our own experience defined in our own unique way and we are continually aware of how our biases concerning gender, politics, race, culture, and so on affect how we relate with each client. It is important to be as honest as possible about how these issues and beliefs affect the way we work and also to be aware of their moral and ethical implications for the therapeutic relationship.

One of the clear advantages of working from an Ericksonian perspective (see Chapter 2 for further details) is that this approach does not impose one particular view or theory of sexual abuse onto the client. The therapist does not have a rigid view but instead maintains as open and flexible an orientation as possible, which assists the client in putting together the fragments of her past in order to reach her *own* conclusions and "truth."

Any client entering therapy has a need to make sense of what she has experienced. There is however greater potential danger in doing therapy with abuse survivors as they begin to reconstruct their often splintered past and fill in the blanks of their personal history. The therapist must be very careful and as nondirective as possible in his/her approach at this time, to allow the client to draw her own conclusions about the details of her experience.

We see our role as one of providing as safe and supportive an environment as possible while facilitating, awakening, and utilizing the client's own resources and skills to understand her own story. It is natural for the survivor's story to change over time as her awareness of what is, or is not, abusive is more clearly understood. She may then look back at the past and realize that what she thought was "normal" was actually quite injurious and destructive. In our experience, as the client feels supported and safe in the therapeutic relationship, more memory and details from her past begin to surface. The danger of the False Memory Syndrome phenomenon is that this shift in perspective may be viewed as the survivor creating or fabricating memories to corroborate her story.

The task of the therapist at this stage is to provide an open forum for investigating the possibilities. We do this via a variety of techniques, which include various therapeutic exercises, metaphors, and other tools which will be described in detail later in this book. The content and integration of facts and experience are material from the client, not from the therapist. We collaborate with the client to help facilitate her own healing process, which is as unique as each client is unique.

We view memories, feelings, various body symptoms, and dreams as messages from the unconscious. Only the client can determine whether they are valid or not. We can offer our experience in dealing with these issues as well as educational information about sexual abuse in general, but the client herself must draw her *own* conclusions about the validity of her experience.

IV. MEMORY AND THE EVOLUTION OF THE SURVIVOR'S STORY

One of the disturbing effects of the False Memory Syndrome stance is that it can seriously undermine the natural evolution and belief of the survivor's story. Recently, we have had many clients with very clear and concrete memories who suffered setbacks as a result of the current media coverage surrounding this issue. The self-blame, self-doubt, and guilt a survivor experiences as a result of sexual abuse is negatively reinforced by this current topic.

Samantha, a 24-year-old incest survivor, has struggled for several years with the very real memories of her physical, emotional, and sexual abuse and their current impact on her life. There are two very distinct and diverse versions of her family history. Her father and grandfather (the offenders) live an outward life of highly respected, socially conscious individuals who have always considered themselves spiritually and philosophically superior in their approach to life. Indeed, this was the view and belief system Samantha grew up with. It was also a very powerful tactic that enabled the secrecy and silence of this particular family to be maintained. When Samantha disclosed her abuse and later confronted her father and grandfather, she was seen as the "crazy one" in the family. Her grandfather phoned her therapist at the time and demanded that he be able to come in and straighten out this lie about himself and his family.

The result of this dual reality upon Samantha has, needless to say, been extremely damaging. She struggles constantly with the part of herself that knows she experienced the abuse and with the self-doubt surrounding the family myth that she grew up with, which told her that hers was an "enlightened, superior" family with the highest standards possible.

In a situation like this, the current false memory debate only succeeds in further confusing and polarizing the situation. Samantha is even more anxious about her own "truth" and being able to place the responsibility for her abuse where it belongs, and her perpetrators have a politically correct and powerful rationalization for their innocence. Samantha is seen as the "crazy" one who is fabricating false memories to destroy her family.

In our experience in working with sexual abuse issues, it is essential that the therapeutic community acknowledge the fact that the survivor's story does and should change as the healing process progresses. As the survivor is able to assimilate the fragments of her traumatic history—and understand her problematic behavior and the often overwhelming feelings and reactions from which she may have previously been dissociated or numb to—she has the opportunity to integrate formerly traumatic frozen experience fragments into a meaningful context. Therefore, she can begin to reflect on and understand her past with a new more integrated meaning. At this point, in our experience, she is able to live in the present in a more integrated way, which allows her to accommodate to her environment rather than becoming constricted and triggered into old patterns.

Although this may seem disconcerting to those outside the therapeutic community, it is a clarification that needs to be made and understood, as do many other complex and often confusing issues related to sexual abuse. It is only natural that as one becomes less numb and isolated and more aware of self and others that the lens with which one views anything will change. It is not our job to pass judgment on the evolution of the client. But it is our responsibility to provide the support and safety for that evolution to unfold. One of our clients eloquently described this process after having done one of the exercises described in Chapter 3.

> Constructing the first doll helped me to clarify and to be specific about the person I was: my hair, my eyes, my body language, my clothing and my overall appearance. Not only did I see myself as a child, but I saw myself as others might have seen me. Much of it seems now to have been a mask, but a necessary mask. A lot of what I see is truly who I was, but I now understand all of the unseen, unspoken stuff going on below the surface. Mostly I see the innocence and vulnerability. One of the changes in my perspective is that I see myself as having been a "good" child who probably did mostly what was ex-

pected of her. My memory has always told me I was bad, rebellious and difficult. My experience of the event is changed in that I see now how innocent and vulnerable and truly not to blame I was.

Ellie

The nature of traumatic memory is as individual as each client is individual. Some survivors come into therapy with many clear visual and visceral memories, while others may only have one or two sketchy memories. And then there are the clients who come in for therapy without any concrete memories but are sure they have been abused.

Under the latter circumstances it is prudent for the therapist to determine why the client believes she has been abused and then to let her decide whether sexual abuse is the primary focus of therapy or not. There is a delicate balance between supporting and validating the client's experience and automatically assuming abuse is the main issue. We always try to be as honest as possible with the client about our ethical dilemma, while offering therapy as a forum for self-discovery and hopefully solutions to the pain the client is experiencing when she enters therapy. Thus, we leave the door open to all possibilities while not jumping to any hasty conclusions.

As part of a discussion of our approach to healing from sexual abuse and our therapeutic focus in general, we also explain our belief that healing is not directly linked to remembering everything about one's childhood (whether abuse is the issue or not) or every detail of every incident of abuse that has taken place.

Many clients assume that if they don't remember their childhood clearly, they may have been abused and have blocked out or "repressed" the traumatic memories. We stress that healing from trauma or anything else is an individual and unique process that is different for each of us. There is no way to predict exactly how that process will unfold. But based on our past experience, we can help the client be more familiar with the healing process as we understand it and together we can explore healthier and happier future possibilities.

At this point we would usually discuss how every individual interacts with his/her environment in his/her own way. Some of us are more auditory, some more visual, and some more kinesthetic (see Chapter 2 for further explanation). It may be that this affects how we remember material as well as how we interact with our surroundings. This may account for why some survivors experience more visceral or body flashbacks, while others experience vivid and disturbing visual memories.

The key message here is that healing is not directly linked to how plentiful or how vivid one's memories are, but in overcoming the effects of the abuse as defined by the client with the help of information and tools which are co-created by the client and the therapist.

V. ISSUES THAT OFTEN TRIGGER MEMORY

Over many years of dealing with sexual abuse survivors, we have identified some common psychosocial stressors that often trigger memories of sexual abuse:

1. *Pregnancy and childbirth are frequently powerful triggers of memory.* Many women begin to experience flashbacks and memories when they have children of their own. There is often an urgent need to understand their own past so they can protect their children.

Kelly, a 28-year-old woman, began having flashbacks toward the end of her pregnancy and had a series of nightmares concerning the safety of her unborn child. After the birth of her daughter she began remembering several incidents of sexual abuse between herself and her brother. These memories were triggered by a visit from her brother and sister-in-law who also had a newborn baby. Kelly realized that she was fearful for the safety of her nephew as well as her own daughter and that she needed to disclose her own abuse in an effort to protect her child and her brother's infant from what she strongly felt was a potentially dangerous and abusive environment.

Survivors often fear they may repeat the cycle of abuse themselves and find it difficult to bond with their infants. For some, this is the impetus for initiating therapy and can be an ideal time to use the opportunity to sort out many of the confusing and frightening feelings being sparked by this new and powerful relationship.

2. *Marriage and divorce can also be powerful triggers of memory.* The experience of transition, whether it is positive or negative, often awakens unconscious and conscious reactions and can activate the need to deal with recurring patterns and issues such as abuse.

3. *Another powerful event that may elicit memory previously out of conscious awareness is the death of the perpetrator.* Many survivors have strong and mixed reactions to the death of their offenders. Often for the first time the survivor feels safe enough to explore the complex relationship with the offender and is thus able to disclose or deal with the abuse suffered.

4. *Experiencing another traumatic event may also provoke memory of past abuse.* Helen, at 35, moved to a new apartment on the top floor of an

old house. Several days after moving in, a neighbor in the apartment below her was attacked and seriously assaulted. Helen began having flashbacks and dreams of her own abuse at the age of 5. Her anxiety, fear, and panic attacks immobilized her to the point where she was unable to leave the house at all and thus sought help to explore and deal with her past abuse.

VI. ETHICAL CONSIDERATIONS FOR THE THERAPIST WHO WORKS WITH SURVIVORS OF SEXUAL ABUSE

The following are some guidelines and issues we continually consider when doing therapy with survivors.

- Anything you say or any technique you use will impact the client; therefore you need to be clear and honest with regard to your intent and integrity within the therapeutic relationship.
- As a therapist, it is not your role to determine whether or not sexual abuse is the focus of therapy. That is up to the client.
- You need to be careful about the way you elicit information from clients. That is, the use of leading questions or questions in the form of presuppositions can lead clients to conclusions they may not arrive at by themselves.
- Respect for the client's timing is essential in order to allow each individual's healing process to unfold. The timing and the agenda are a collaborative process.
- Objective history taking is important. You need to be aware of and check your own biases regarding issues of sexual abuse, gender, race, politics, and so on.
- You may have your own history of abuse and it is important to be aware of how those issues affect your work and belief systems.
- Always be aware and honest about the power imbalance between you and your client and how that impacts the therapeutic relationship.
- Be clear about how and why you use techniques such as hypnosis or guided imagery. We are very specific about our intent with regard to the use of hypnosis or imagery:
- Hypnosis is not used for fishing expeditions or for the sole purpose of retrieving repressed memory. Rather, it is a tool and means of learning to listen to the needs of the "self," both physical and psychological, and to access inner resources and strengths. We

use hypnosis as a resource for self-soothing, control over panic reactions, and to help reintegrate fragments of the self. It is our experience, however, that when clients learn to control previously overwhelming reactions and emotions, memories and details of abuse often surface during relaxation exercises or guided imageries. Therefore, the therapist must be prepared for and experienced enough to handle the possible material and responses that may emerge.

- In our opinion, it is the therapist's responsibility and the client's right to know how the legal system in their home province or state views the use of hypnosis in therapy with sexual abuse issues. In some places, the use of hypnosis is viewed negatively and can result in evidence being disallowed. In the event a survivor may want to press charges at some future point, she should be aware of how the use of hypnosis and other techniques in treatment may affect her legal options.

- The issue of confidentiality and the content of client records and files is a complex one. You must decide how to handle the issues of the detail, tone, and content of the records kept in the client's file. These records may be subpoenaed in the event of legal action, or in cases when financial compensation is issued, the institution granting financial aid for therapy may require written reports and details of the client's history. In the latter cases, we would recommend allowing the client to be in control of what information is shared and would ask the client to read and approve any release of such information.

- In view of these issues, it is thus important for you to be aware of the legal requirements of freedom of information laws in one's home state or province so that informed decisions about such matters can be made.

- When leading groups for sexual abuse survivors, it is important that those attending have at least one concrete memory of the abuse before entering the group process and that appropriate screening has taken place. (See Chapter 2 for further details.)

VII. MEDICAL REFERRALS

Many of the survivors we see have been referred by family doctors or psychiatrists. Some women come in as a result of word of mouth referrals from friends, family members, or the media. Because there are many physiological effects resulting from sexual abuse, survivors generally have a wide range of somatic symptoms that have plagued them for years. It is always ethical and prudent to suggest that any physical symptoms be checked out by a physician. However, many women have already been the medical route and have found no tangible physical explanations for their symptoms. A great many women come into therapy with very negative experiences of consulting doctor after doctor who have not validated any of their physical experiences.

There is little literature or research on the subject of traumatic body memory. In our experience this is an area where survivors are grossly invalidated. The result is an implicit message that the survivor is imagining things, is complaining, and/or is hypochondriacal. Over time, the therapist is usually able to establish professional referral sources who are both educated in and validating of the many physiological responses to sexual abuse. These alliances can help defuse and normalize the often "crazy-making" symptoms that are difficult to clearly or concretely relate to the sexual abuse.

Ernest Rossi in his book, *The Psychology of Mind–Body Healing: New Concepts of Therapeutic Hypnosis* (1986/1993), explains how one's experience and behavior are encoded in the brain, and that in times of stress or trauma, certain informational substances are released throughout the body. Therefore, many of our life experiences or memories may be state-dependent, "that is, what we remember, learn and experience is dependent on the different psychological states encoded in the brain by information substances" (p. 357). Rossi thus addresses the mind–body connection and the hypotheses that body symptoms and body memory are related to these information substances that exist in the body on a molecular level. These new theories are quite controversial and require much more research; however, given our experience with survivors and their many unexplained symptoms and body experiences, this new research is exciting and makes a great deal of sense.

We feel very strongly that the treatment of sexual abuse needs to be viewed in the context of a holistic approach. There is a danger in the traditional medical establishment view of symptoms resulting from sexual abuse as being dysfunctional rather than understanding these behaviors and symptoms as coping skills that have been vital to the client's survival in the context of her abuse experience. Treating the symptoms as purely dysfunctional often results in further fragmentation and negative labelling, which only exacerbates the survivor's role as a dysfunctional, mental health patient with a myriad of symptoms that cannot be really understood or normalized in the context of her experience.

We are not machines: we have hearts and feelings and emotions that are connected to our bodies and our instincts. We cannot always cure our physiological symptoms without making corresponding psychological adjustments. If we ignore that connection, our bodies will inevitably remind us of our oversight.

Marion Woodman, a Jungian analyst, in her book *The Pregnant Virgin* (1985), discusses this issue at length and points out that we need to acknowledge the body's process of individuation, as well as the psyche's, in order for us to truly progress and free ourselves from the often dehumanizing rigid framework of our society.

VIII. SAMPLE ASSESSMENT QUESTIONS TO HELP ASCERTAIN TREATMENT FOCUS

As a result of the false memory backlash it is vital for the therapist to maintain a conscientious approach to the work through continual reclarification of the client's therapeutic issues and goals at each healing juncture or stage. (see Figure 2.1)

The following are examples of sample questions (by no means a complete list) that we keep in mind while assessing the focus of treatment with clients who identify sexual abuse on intake. The benefit of such assessment questions is to help ensure that the experience of the treatment process is a collaborative one that reflects the client's understanding of her own issues and not the therapist's interpretation of what they might be.

- How do you know you were (sexually) abused?
- What has happened to lead you to that conclusion?
- What have you experienced that led you to conclude you were sexually abused?
- What do you regard as abuse, sexual or otherwise?
- Do you have any specific memories of abuse?
- Have you been reading any books on the topic of sexual abuse?
- What information have you learned from these books that is significant to you?
- What impact has the reading you have done had on your understanding of your personal history?
- What is your understanding of how therapy can help you deal with these issues?

- What do you need to have happen right now in order for you to feel better?
- How will you know when these issues are being resolved?
- How would you like your life to be different?
- How will you know when the changes you seek are happening?
- How much detail of the past do you believe you need to know in order to heal?
- What is your belief about your role in the healing process?
- What is your belief about the therapist's role in the healing process?

We believe it is important that the therapist develop a solid grounding in the subject of traumatic memory and the implications of false memory from current research and literature. The therapist can then more competently and confidently develop a collection of tools and practices which she/he can apply to his/her work with survivors at the various stages of healing (refer to Chapters 3 through 7).

In our experience we have found the Ericksonian approach to be particularly useful because of its respectfulness toward the client's unique process and timing in a nonintrusive, hopeful manner.

The methods and practices described in Chapter 2 can therefore complement and enhance the previously developed skills and repertoire of the therapist.

CHAPTER 2

Tools of the Trade: Theory and Techniques to Help Equip the Therapist

The goal of this chapter is to clarify and/or introduce certain techniques and theoretical information which we use throughout the book. In so doing, our intent is to create as "user friendly" a context as possible. The authors work from an Ericksonian perspective that we have adapted in our own style over time in our extensive work with adult female survivors of sexual abuse.

Since the chapter describes a very brief overview of Ericksonian theory and techniques, we strongly encourage readers who have not experienced Ericksonian workshops and training to do so. We have found this perspective invaluable in working with survivors as we will further explain in due course. We also introduce the use of group therapy which offers many therapeutic benefits for survivors of sexual abuse.

This chapter is a reflection of the specific techniques that we have found to be extremely helpful in dealing with sexual abuse survivors and is therefore only the "tip of the iceberg"—our particular "spin" on the Ericksonian framework as it pertains to sexual abuse issues.

I. HOW IS THE ERICKSONIAN PERSPECTIVE DIFFERENT, AND WHY IS IT SO EFFECTIVE IN THE TREATMENT OF SEXUAL ABUSE?

By the time a survivor of sexual abuse enters the therapist's office, she has often experienced a lifetime of pain, characterized by shame, guilt, isolation, and a pervasive tone of learned helplessness and hopelessness from which she feels powerless to extricate herself. All too often she is caught in a web of rigid patterns that were vital to her survival heretofore but which overwhelmingly and ironically eclipse the strength and resilience that have helped her survive the abuse.

The therapist can also become trapped along with the client in that state of hopelessness and this can become a frustrating and difficult pattern to interrupt. One often finds oneself stuck in the client's cycle as the client looks to the therapist to "fix" her. Thus the theme of disempowerment is often perpetuated.

The Ericksonian approach to psychotherapy is one that encourages clients to empower themselves by accessing inner resources and abilities that may have been dormant or frozen as a result of trauma as in the case of sexual abuse.

Zeig has defined Ericksonian psychotherapy "as the technology of accessing responsiveness to therapeutic injunctions in order to elicit previously dormant resources. Social influence is used to access resources for change" (Zeig, 1990, p. 371).

In this approach, the therapist is an ally, not an expert in a one-up position to the client. We feel this is a vital difference when dealing with survivors who have been victimized into a position of powerlessness where they have often never been aware of their ability to choose different ways of relating or responding to everyday situations.

The concept of the therapist and the client as co-creating unique and tailor-made solutions to previously unresolved problems is an exciting and respectful approach to therapy.

> This position is based on two assumptions: (1) The unconscious mind tends to be benign and generally health seeking, and (2) the unconscious contains solutions to problems that can be brought into the foreground. Once the rigid sets of symptoms are disrupted, people attempt to move to more effective levels of functioning by accessing previously under utilized strengths. (Zeig, 1990, p. 372)

In our view, the role of the therapist is to assist the client to retrieve and reintegrate hidden or frozen resources in a way that works for each client, with the ultimate outcome being a more independent and empowered individual who has the tools to problem solve within, rather than looking to others or becoming dependent on the therapist.

Instead of expounding a cookie-cutter approach to sexual abuse survivors, or any other issue, the Ericksonian method takes into account each individual's uniqueness. In doing so the client receives an implicit message—that being unique is okay and that perhaps she can find unique solutions to fit her unique experience.

The idea of co-creating solutions is enhanced by the use of creative measures such as metaphor, personally relevant symbols, tasks, and ritual. The use of these tools requires that the therapist maintain an open mind as well as a mind-set that truly believes in the client's ability to make significant changes. In our experience the survivor is keenly attuned to picking up the beliefs and intent of the therapist. This is a byproduct of the coping skill of hypervigilance. Survivors are continuously testing the therapist and the healing process. The confidence and experience of the therapist to present a hopeful outcome as a distinct possibility is crucial. When the therapist and the client are open to exploring solutions elicited from clues and material that the client retrieves from within, the outcome in our experience is exciting and rewarding for both parties.

Figure 2.1 outlines the collaborative process between client and therapist as we view it. This is a continual process that involves the expression and assessment of needs and goals, the co-creation of a treatment plan that is individually tailored to meet the needs and developmental level of each client (employing specific metaphors, exercises, and rituals where appropriate), and the continual reassessment of each client's progress and process in order to ensure that the therapy is meeting her needs. By playing an active part in the assessment and reassessment process, the client can perhaps for the first time experience herself as a proactive and empowered individual who is capable of acquiring more adaptive skills, tools, and ways of being which can lead her to a healthier, brighter future.

II. CO-CREATING SOLUTIONS: RESPECTING AND HONORING THE CLIENT'S BELIEF AND PERSONAL CONTEXT

Respecting, validating, understanding, and accepting the survivor and her personal frame of reference is the most important first step in activating the healing process. One reason that the Ericksonian approach is so helpful in this process is that it acknowledges where the client is now, while both directly and indirectly sending the message that she can change. This can be facilitated in the first session by listening to her story and immediately eliciting her beliefs about why and how she is

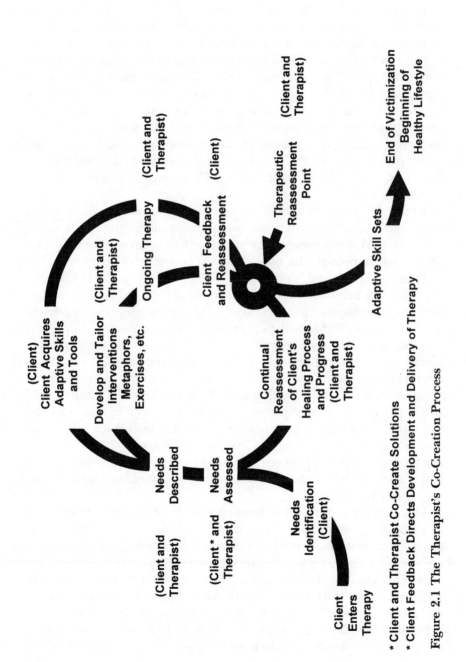

Figure 2.1 The Therapist's Co-Creation Process

* Client and Therapist Co-Create Solutions
* Client Feedback Directs Development and Delivery of Therapy

Client Enters Therapy

Needs Identification (Client)

(Client and Therapist)

(Client * and Therapist)

Needs Assessed

Needs Described

(Client) Client Acquires Adaptive Skills and Tools

Develop and Tailor Interventions Metaphors, Exercises, etc.

(Client and Therapist)

Ongoing Therapy

(Client and Therapist)

Client Feedback and Reassessment

(Client)

Continual Reassessment of Client's Healing Process and Progress (Client and Therapist)

Therapeutic Reassessment Point

(Client and Therapist)

Adaptive Skill Sets

End of Victimization Beginning of Healthy Lifestyle

currently experiencing her life, how she feels stuck, and assisting her to define some goals for herself that she and the therapist can work toward. This may sound simple; however, many survivors are so frozen in their trauma that a hopeful and different future may seem impossible.

The task for the therapist is to frame the impossible (from the client's perspective) as achievable and tangible. The therapist's own positive experience (with other survivors) and conviction that there *is* life after abuse is crucial at this time. The goals can be broken down into more manageable steps and a plan can be co-created with the client to set the stage for healing. An example of such a process can be found at the end of this section (see "Solution-Focused Treatment Planning Process: Five Key Questions" and Figure 2.2, the Co-Creative Assessment Model: The Healing Process).

We always present our belief in the process of healing from sexual abuse and invite the client to discuss and explore the possibilities. We also explain that she is the expert on herself and that together it is possible to work through the issues that are currently of concern to her and others that inevitably unfold along the way. Our belief in the healing process is just that, *our* belief based on our experience in working with others and in the approach we use. After presenting our approach, we always acknowledge to the client that each individual is unique and that the rapport and fit between client and therapist is extremely important. Only she can decide if the fit is a good one. This accomplishes two things: (1) it gives the client the power to choose to begin the healing process (choice is generally something she feels she has little of), and (2) it creates a therapeutic atmosphere of hopefulness. It is the beginning of laying a foundation of new possibilities, thereby presupposing that change can happen. Erickson and Rossi (1979) refer to this as a "yes set." "The rapport is the means by which therapist and patient secure each other's attention. Both develop a 'yes set,' or acceptance of each other" (p. 2).

This rapport is initiated in the first session. By hearing the client's story, asking questions about her experience, her likes, dislikes, and so on, the therapist can immediately uncover clues and information about the client, which can lead to a clearer understanding of how the client experiences the world and what she values. For example, the client might speak about her isolation and her desire to connect in a more positive and safe way with others. The therapist can then suggest to the survivor some ways of achieving these goals and help her understand them in the context of the abuse and the healing process. This might be done

- What will you and the client focus on, and how can you access the client's inner resources to achieve the treatment goals?

- What strategies and tools (metaphors, exercises, cognitive schemas) can you focus on as the source of your client's sustainable healing process?

<u>OUTCOME</u>

The Client

- Can be self-empowered by utilizing the adaptive skills and tools acquired in the therapeutic alliance.

    and

- Win the "victim game" and therefore be freer to reach future potential.

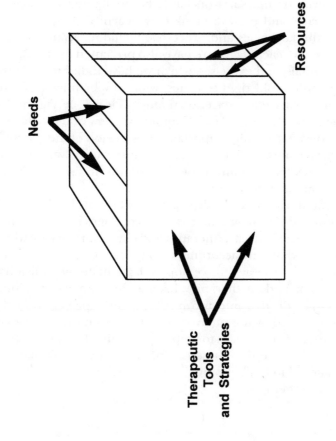

Needs

Resources

Therapeutic Tools and Strategies

Figure 2.2 The Co-Creative Assessment Model: The Healing Process

by the use of a metaphor, or a parallel story about the issue at hand as in the story of Hush in Chapter 3. That particular metaphorical story features a character who is experiencing issues similar to a survivor in the first stages seeking therapy, who learns some new tools and an alternate way of responding to fear and isolation.

Zeig points out that presenting a suggestion is not enough. Most of us know when something isn't working, we know what we *should* be doing. It is important to sequence suggestions. "Suggestions must be sequenced. Essentially this is a method of moving in small steps while accessing motivation. The therapist paces where the patient is, works to disrupt rigid mind sets, and helps to elicit therapeutic goals" (Zeig, 1990, p. 374).

The use of metaphor, anecdotes, tasks, and so forth can be employed at these various intervals to further facilitate this process. By the delineation of stages of healing from sexual abuse, we have incorporated the idea of sequencing into the healing process. Our experience as therapists who work with trauma survivors has led us to define four stages in the healing journey and then to break down each of these stages to further define the key issues and processes, including symptoms and patterns that occur at each stage. We have also presented the tools, that is, metaphors, rituals, and exercises, which we have found to assist the survivor in disrupting old rigid schemes, while respectfully honoring her own unique experience, pace, or timing. (Please see Figure 2.3, "Dynamic Co-Creative Healing Model" for an overview of these stages.) Moving at her own pace is very important. It is the job of the therapist to monitor and validate the client's pace, while introducing various techniques or exercises that can interrupt old patterns and seed new and healthy ones when the time is right.

In delineating the stages of healing presented in this book, we realize that everyone is different and that while these stages have proven, in our experience, to be valid, each therapist and client must decide which tools to employ at what time according to each client's need. We have structured this book in a way that we hope will facilitate the individuality of both the client and the therapist. Each of the chapters explaining the four stages are divided into two parts: (1) an explanation of the theoretical issues faced by the survivor at that stage, and (2) a series of metaphors, exercises, and rituals to help facilitate the therapeutic goals of each stage. We hope that these can be used as examples and be modified or tailored to fit the unique needs of each client and the personal style of each therapist.

SOLUTION-FOCUSED TREATMENT PLANNING PROCESS:
FIVE KEY QUESTIONS

The following questions can be used in treatment planning in order for the client and therapist to co-create a plan that will seed and motivate the client's change process.

1. Where does the client want to make changes? Begin by asking, "Where do you want to be 3 years from now?"
   - *Goals: hard*—better job, move, skills to be acquired or acknowledged.
     soft —how would you feel different? How will you know things are better?

2. How are you going to get there?
   - *Strategies:* —pattern interruption, resources
     —body centering, hypnosis, and so on

3. What resources will be required?
   - human
   - physical
   - financial

4. Where are the resources to come from?
   - mining of internal natural resources
   - external—support system

5. What will the resources cost? That is,
   - how will status quo be upset?
   - what will it feel like to be different?
   - what changes will I need to make?

III. METAPHOR

The use of metaphor is a valuable and creative tool for the client and the therapist. Erickson and Rossi (1979, p. 50) understand metaphor as a means of gaining access to new insight available on an unconscious level, which is then brought into consciousness by means of metaphor. This metaphor or story can facilitate a new understanding of a problem or an issue that is currently limiting the client. Because this is an indirect form of communication, it is generally less threatening to the cli-

STAGE 1 Breaking the Silence: Unmasking the Secret		STAGE 2 Becoming Visible		STAGE 3 The Reclaiming and Reintegration of Self		STAGE 4 Empowerment and Evolution of the Sexual Self	
COMMON SYMPTOMS		COMMON SYMPTOMS		COMMON SYMPTOMS		COMMON SYMPTOMS	
Psychological	Physiological	Psychological	Physiological	Psychological	Physiological	Psychological	Physiological
Isolation/Secrecy	Panic Attacks	Intense Feelings, Often Overwhelming	Panic Attacks	Less Self-Blame	Longer Periods of Stability	Free Expression of Needs	Taking Care of Body
Shame	Nausea	Gravitation from Denial to Acceptance of Reality	Nausea	More Externalization of Feelings	More Comfort	Further Reintegration of Sexuality and Self	More Comfortable in Body
Denial	Low Energy	Poor Body Image	Low Energy	Less Overwhelmed and Panicked	Few Lapses to Old Patterns, i.e., Somatic Symptoms	Better Understanding of Relationships	Connecting to Sensuality
Self-Blame/Guilt	Body Pain/Memory Genital, Back, Shoulders, Neck, Abdomen, Legs, Headaches	Beginning to Access Inner Strengths and Resources	Body Pain/Memory Genital, Back, Shoulders, Neck, Abdomen, Legs, Headaches	More Future Oriented	More Energy	Expressions of Grief, Loss, and Abandonment	More Consistent Energy
Hopelessness				More Social Contact	Increased Ability to Soothe and Relax Body and Mind	Increased Positive Future Focus	Few Down Times But Able to Soothe Self
Fear/Anger				More Control/ Less Rigid			
Dissociation/Numbing				Increased Connection to Inner Resources			
Cut Off Inner Resources				Responsibility for Abuse Placed on Offender			
Depression							

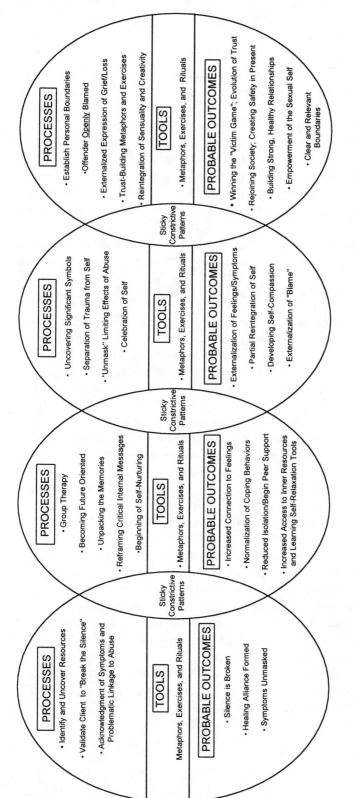

PROCESSES
· Identify and Uncover Resources
· Validate Client to "Break the Silence"
· Acknowledgment of Symptoms and Problematic Linkage to Abuse

TOOLS
· Metaphors, Exercises, and Rituals

PROBABLE OUTCOMES
· Silence is Broken
· Healing Alliance Formed
· Symptoms Unmasked

Sticky Constrictive Patterns

PROCESSES
· Group Therapy
· Becoming Future Oriented
· Unpacking the Memories
· Reframing Critical Internal Messages
· Beginning of Self-Nurturing

TOOLS
· Metaphors, Exercises, and Rituals

PROBABLE OUTCOMES
· Increased Connection to Feelings
· Normalization of Coping Behaviors
· Reduced Isolation/Begin Peer Support
· Increased Access to Inner Resources and Learning Self-Relaxation Tools

Sticky Constrictive Patterns

PROCESSES
· Uncovering Significant Symbols
· Separation of Trauma from Self
· "Unmask" Limiting Effects of Abuse
· Celebration of Self

TOOLS
· Metaphors, Exercises, and Rituals

PROBABLE OUTCOMES
· Externalization of Feelings/Symptoms
· Partial Reintegration of Self
· Developing Self-Compassion
· Externalization of "Blame"

Sticky Constrictive Patterns

PROCESSES
· Establish Personal Boundaries
· Offender Openly Blamed
· Externalized Expression of Grief/Loss
· Trust-Building Metaphors and Exercises
· Reintegration of Sensuality and Creativity

TOOLS
· Metaphors, Exercises, and Rituals

PROBABLE OUTCOMES
· Winning the "Victim Game"; Evolution of Trust
· Rejoining Society; Creating Safety in Present
· Building Strong, Healthy Relationships
· Empowerment of the Sexual Self
· Clear and Relevant Boundaries

NOTE:
Healing rings are in constant motion at varying rates.
1. Outcome timing is client specific.
2. Some "Processes" become "Outcomes."

Figure 2.3 Dynamic Co-Creative Healing Model

ent. In addition, because we all have our own stories to tell, the metaphor is a way of accessing and reframing these stories in a way that is unique to each client.

In work with survivor's, the use of a metaphorical story that may parallel the survivors own experience is a safer way of dealing with traumatic material that has often been dissociated from or stuffed down because it is too painful and overwhelming to deal with on a conscious level. The client can, therefore, vicariously experience new insight and information that may enable her to reach a new level of awareness and comfort.

There are many examples of metaphorical stories in the following chapters which have been co-created with survivors to address the various issues faced in the healing process. We have listed below some of the key components we find important to the construction of a metaphor.

1. *Understand the client's unique context.* Each survivor has her own story and set of circumstances. In order to create a relevant metaphor, it is important to elicit as much information as possible from the client. This can be done by asking general questions about hobbies, likes, dislikes, worries, belief systems, values, and so on.
2. *Identify a goal.* What is the outcome the *client* is seeking?
3. *Select a theme that is relevant to the issues and goals of therapy.* For example, isolation, control, fear, strength, or letting go of old patterns.
4. *Characters in the story.* There may be characters and they may be human or otherwise (often pets or mystical beings are significant to some clients) and they act out or parallel the experience of the client.
5. *Plot of the story.* A parallel story or plot through which a character achieves and overcomes difficulty or comes to some relevant insight or new and different experience.
6. *Utilize the client's resources and skills.* Weave through the metaphor various suggestions and ways of uncovering and reframing existing resources and strengths that may be currently eclipsed by the trauma. Introduce alternative ways of dealing with the problem. Point out new possibilities: polarities of the issue at hand, for example, isolation versus belonging; victim versus hero; feeling crazy versus feeling competent.

7. *Be aware of communication systems.* How does the client communicate with his/her environment? Is she blocked kinesthetically or visually? Is the client experiencing ongoing critical dialogue and messages internally? It is very important to balance the senses in the metaphor, that is, to use visual, auditory, kinesthetic, and olfactory descriptions and experiences. (see next section on communication systems.)

Like anything else, creating metaphors requires practice and experience. Each therapist will have his/her own style of metaphor construction. When the client's needs are blended with the therapist's ability to weave pertinent concepts and information with personally relevant material that the client presents either directly or indirectly to the therapist, the end result is an experience that has been co-created and tailored to the client's individual needs. This is a very powerful and respectful process that can unlock previously blocked or frozen resources and lead to positive change.

IV. COMMUNICATION SYSTEMS

We all have our own way of interacting with the environment which is colored by our experience, beliefs, and acculturation. We recommend that readers familiarize themselves with the work of Bandler and Grinder (see bibliography) who have developed a framework for understanding how each individual relates to, accesses, and interprets his/her environment. Neurolinguistic Programming is one approach that can help the therapist observe and understand the client's perspective and way of relating to his/her environment.

We have found this knowledge paramount in understanding the frozen patterns of the survivor and in accessing the client so that she can receive new information and possibilities for the future. When constructing metaphors it is extremely helpful to observe how the survivor sees, feels, hears, and thinks about her historical abuse experience. There are inevitable blockages in the way she relates to her environment that have often been present since the time of the trauma. By understanding these communication systems, the therapist has yet another tool to help the client solve the puzzle of problematic patterns of behavior.

V. THERAPEUTIC TRANCE: WHY AND HOW

In our work with survivors of sexual abuse we have found the use of therapeutic trance to be highly valuable for a number of reasons. Most, if not all, survivors we have encountered display a very high level of anxiety both psychologically and physiologically. This anxiety usually results in the blocking of their ability to transcend the limiting patterns of behavior that eventually lead them to the therapist. Therapeutic trance offers clients an opportunity to interrupt their problematic patterns and experience something different, which can open the door to new and more satisfying ways of understanding and relating to themselves and, in turn, to their environment.

Another result of the trauma and the high level of anxiety present in the survivor is the inability to experience comfort or relaxation. There is often a fear based on past experience that when or if she allows herself to let down her guard or relax, memories or flashbacks occur which often result in full-blown panic attacks and/or other physiological or visceral memories stemming from the abuse. As a result, many survivors never allow themselves or simply have never learned to be comfortable, in the present—to be in the here and now—or to relax in their bodies.

The first step in initiating a therapeutic trance is learning how to fix one's attention. This can be done either internally or externally. Body relaxation is one of the most common ways of achieving this. Because most survivors are very disconnected to their bodies and therefore have difficulty relaxing, this is a very useful and beneficial tool for the client as well as the therapist. By teaching the client how to focus inwardly on body sensations, such as breathing or internal imagery as in a guided imagery, not only can the client learn ways of centering herself and focusing inward in order to relax and to explore internally, she also can learn to use this as an effective tool in combatting the often overwhelming panic she may have experienced as previously being out of her control.

We have found relaxation an effective way to introduce the idea and experience of therapeutic trance. Again, the therapist must respect the client's own timing. But we have found most clients willing to learn these techniques as long as their own pace is honored.

Safety

The issue of safety is an important consideration when introducing relaxation techniques or trance. The therapist needs to continually check in with the client to let her know that if she is not feeling safe, to tell the therapist. Many survivors will not tell the therapist if they are experiencing fear or discomfort because they are used to putting others' needs ahead of their own and often aren't empowered enough to express what they really feel in case they are rejected. It is therefore very important for the therapist to watch and listen and sense cues from the client that would indicate fear or discomfort.

Often it may be very threatening for a survivor to close her eyes while doing relaxation exercises or during therapeutic trance. Again, this should be checked out by the therapist and the client must always have the option of keeping her eyes open. We have found it useful to have certain objects in the room that the client can focus on, such as stuffed animals (which many clients choose to hold onto and look at) pictures, flowers, or something the client brings with her that is often of personal significance. We would also refer the readers to Dolan's (1991) discussion of "Associational Cues for Comfort and Security," which deals effectively and creatively with this issue.

Focusing of Attention

There are many standardized approaches to doing relaxation and trance induction. However, there is no one way that always works with every client. We would again encourage readers to try a variety of different ways to learn what works best for you. It is even more important to ascertain what works best for each client. It is therefore important to glean as much information about the client as possible so that the therapist can tailor the induction or relaxation exercise to her individual needs. For example, during the first two sessions, when you're taking information, if the client tells you of tension in the neck and shoulders, you can concentrate more on those areas while doing systematic relaxation. If the client tells you she enjoys hiking or reading, elements present in these activities can be used to fixate the attention of the client for induction purposes. (There is an example of an induction and relaxation exercise on pages 37 and 38).

One of the most effective ways of focusing the client's attention is by observing and by acknowledging or commenting on what the client is experiencing while sitting in the therapist's office. For example, "As you are sitting there in that position, you can feel your back as it is supported by the chair. There is really nothing that you have to say or think about, so you can allow your mind to wander and be curious about this new experience, with your hands resting on your lap and your eyes resting on the flowers over there...."

A commentary on what the client is currently doing is very validating and can result in the client opening up to the therapist due to the acknowledgment of her current action or inaction. A "yes set" can thus be established and the client is a little less guarded and therefore more open to new possibilities.

Utilization

In the previous example, the therapist is recognizing and acknowledging the client's current experience and utilizing the behavior the client is exhibiting (i.e., looking at flowers, sitting in a chair with hands on her lap, and so on) in order to absorb her attention. By adapting the commentary or induction to what is currently happening, the client and the therapist are having an interactive encounter. For survivors, this cooperative experience helps to enhance the level of safety in the therapeutic setting by directly and indirectly letting her know that what she is currently doing is not being judged. The therapist is meeting her on common ground and both can cooperate and utilize the client's current and historical experience to solve problems and create a more hopeful future. "The utilization approach emphasizes the continual involvement of each patient's unique repertory of abilities and potentials, while the indirect forms of suggestion are the means by which the therapist facilitates these involvements" (Erickson & Rossi, 1979, pp. 14–15).

The concept of utilization is a key one to this approach. In later chapters the reader will be given examples of how the survivor's individual history, that is, her psychological and physiological reality, can be utilized to co-create solutions for overcoming her abuse. Coping mechanisms, physical symptoms, rigid patterns, and painful emotions can therefore be utilized to tailor metaphors, therapeutic exercises, and rituals which can help reassociate and restructure the client's inner experience and resources, thereby empowering her from within to make new choices about how she lives her life.

Ideomotor Signaling

Each individual experiences trance in his/her unique manner. It is therefore helpful to have a method by which the therapist can point out and assist the client to recognize certain patterns, shifts, or significant material. By *ratifying* or validating that something different has happened, that is, that the client is able to relax a bit or to uncover some significant material or reach an insight in a therapeutic trance, the client has some more concrete proof that she can experience something different and hopefully better.

One of the best ways of ratifying a trance experience is via the use of ideomotor signals. Common responses to the trance state include relaxation, eye movements, blinking, changes in respiration, swallowing, muscular and sensory changes, time distortion, heaviness in body, and slowing pulse (Erickson & Rossi, 1979). The therapist is encouraged to research and become familiar with these trance phenomena. When the therapist points out these responses to the client, he/she is validating or ratifying that there is, indeed, something happening. This can also be facilitated by requesting one or many of these ideomotor responses. For example, "If you have experienced a moment or two of relaxation in your body today, perhaps in your hands or your legs, without even realizing it, you can raise your left thumb or your right forefinger." Or, "If you have been in a trance today, you might experience your eyes blink or a sensation of heaviness in your arms."

Some individuals experience ideosensory responses more easily than others. It is important to note that because survivors experience dissociation from their bodies a great deal of the time, this process may take time to develop or may not be appropriate to use with some clients.

One of the most useful aspects of ideomotor signaling in work with survivors is how it can be employed in the exploration of significant issues or beliefs on an unconscious level. This can be an indirect way of accessing material that may be too threatening for the client to deal with on a conscious, cognitive level. For example, after the client has had some practice and experience with trance and relaxation, the therapist may ask the client to go inside and explore or identify something that is important for her to work on. "While you are sitting over there and experiencing the support of the sofa beneath you, wouldn't it be interesting to allow your unconscious mind to identify something that is of particular importance to you, now." Or, "You can continue to allow your mind to wander in that way until it selects a direction or a path that is right for you now. As you are sitting there, in that way hearing my voice from over here, you can ask your unconscious to allow your finger to lift if you are ready to work on (x) and gain a different level of understanding or experience in your body."

According to Erickson and Rossi (1979), one view of ideomotor signaling is that it is the "true voice of the unconscious" (p. 13). In our experience it is a way of honoring the client and cross-checking that the direction and timing of the therapy is right for the client. The therapist and the client can, with practice, ask questions to the unconscious which can be very helpful in directing the healing process in a personally relevant way. The variety of signals used are as individual as each client. Some clients may experience signals internally in the form of a sensation or temperature change in any part of the body. With continual feedback, the therapist can learn to identify the client's significant signals and together the survivor and therapist can determine how best to monitor and utilize these signals as resources. See Dolan (1991) for further interpretations of this technique.

Another valuable aspect of using ideomotor signaling is the amount of safety it can afford the survivor. The therapist can work out a signal such as a finger movement or a nod of the head, which can indicate to the therapist that the client is undergoing something that is frightening or uncomfortable during trance. It is always important for the therapist to observe and sense the process and state of the client while doing trancework and to intervene or interrupt the trance if the client is in distress.

Instructions such as only going as deeply and as safely as the client can comfortably go, while keeping her eyes open or closed, are important and respectful messages to impart to the client. In working with survivors this has proven to be very effective as it helps her to feel more control and choice about her ability to deal with previously overwhelming experiences. The client's traumatic history has usually resulted in the experience of becoming frozen or stuck at various times when threatening body responses or memories come up. The use of a signal can be a welcome relief and another way of breaking the isolation and enmeshment the survivor experiences when spontaneous memory occurs. This is not only a sign to the therapist about what is happening, but also it is even more relevant as a way for the survivor herself to begin to be more aware and responsible for the interruption of old, alarming reactions and patterns of behavior. Thus, the client and the therapist are cooperating and co-facilitating change. Through the use of ideomotor signals the client can explore the unconscious, ratify and validate changes and responses that do occur and may not otherwise be acknowledged, and introduce more safety into the healing process while giving more control and awareness over previously frightening or overwhelming patterns or responses.

Sample Induction and Relaxation Exercise

It is always helpful to begin any metaphorical story, imagery, or meditation with a brief relaxation induction, which most clients find soothing and enjoyable. The following is one such example:

As you are sitting there in that position, listening to my voice and looking at me, it might be interesting to pay attention to your breath as it enters your body, at your own pace and rhythm, filling up your lungs, and when you exhale, noticing how it feels, releasing tension in all those tight places. Just listening to the sound of that breath coming in and going out. That's right. And as you continue to breathe, you can feel free to make any adjustments anytime you like. There is no right or wrong way to do that or to be here. Nothing you have to do or say. You can leave your eyes open and focus on that spot or any place you choose, or you may want to close your eyes now or later on, if they become heavy, or your eyelids begin to flutter, it doesn't really matter. It's nice to know you can just simply be there in any way that you like. Paying attention to the rhythm of your own breath inside or the sounds around you outside. The sound of my voice or sounds outside the room or simply drifting and not paying attention to anything in particular.

I don't know where in your body you might feel some comfort or what a comfortable sensation or sound might be for you. Maybe you experience a pleasant sensation of support as your back rests against the chair, or as your hands lie there quietly, in that way. Nothing you have to do or think about. I don't know when you might have experienced that before. Maybe while going for a walk outside in nature. Smelling the fresh air, the scent of flowers or an ocean breeze. Hearing the sound of your feet crunching along a path or through some woods, listening to a favorite piece of music or losing yourself in a good book or at the movies. (*pause*) Feeling the warmth of the sun on your face or back, or the cozy feeling of snuggling up in a blanket by a fire or holding a favorite pet. (*pause*) Just allowing yourself to experience a bit of tranquility, whatever that is for you.

Feeling free to adjust anytime you need to, and maybe your breathing may become slower or deeper. And you might begin to notice some of the tension or tightness leaving your neck or shoulders as you rest there supported by that chair. And will that finger or thumb move ever so slightly as your body is experiencing being there in that position with a little more comfort? And will your body automatically take an easy breath, deeper, as your unconscious mind does what it needs to do, adjusting in any way that is right for you now?

You may experience some interesting images, thoughts, or feelings— just allow that to develop any way you can. It might be interesting to imagine a favorite color or perhaps a light emanating from your core, reaching out, spreading to other areas in your body, your chest, and abdomen, your neck, back, arms, legs, and feet. Circulating through- out your veins and arteries, permeating every cell, every organ of your body.... That's right, a different sensation that can develop even more. A comforting sound like that of your own breath, that familiar sound of you. Just allowing your body and mind to float in any direction at all.

Just as your breath continues to come and go, your unconscious mind can do whatever it needs to do, discovering, uncovering some different ways of being and feeling and responding. With each breath you take in, you can become aware of that comfort spreading through- out your body, developing in your own way. You can experience those relaxing sensations in various parts of your body. On the left side or the right side, in your upper body or your lower body, and why not allow those comfortable feelings to develop even further? And you really don't have to give up those comfortable feelings when you come back to the room, just as you don't have to consciously listen to my words, because your unconscious mind can hear whatever it needs to and find whatever meaning from this experience that is relevant now, or later, even though you may not be aware of that meaning until an- other time. Tomorrow, or next week, or the next time you enter this room. It doesn't really matter what you remember when you come back to the present, but it's nice to know that you can experience some- thing more comforting and relaxing. That drowsy feeling similar to when you are about to fall asleep. So why not take a moment of clock time and allow your mind to continue to drift wherever it wants to. (*pause*) And when you are ready now or a moment from now, you can take some easy breaths and give yourself a message of self-appreciation for all you have experienced and survived. (*pause*) Gradually reori- ent back to the room, remembering as much as you need to for now and letting go of anything you need to. That's right. Opening your eyes or looking around the room, stretching—just doing whatever comes naturally.

Debriefing of Relaxation or Trance Experience: Practical and Ethical Considerations

It is important to allow the client to interpret any trance experience her own way. Some clients may report that they experienced nothing, others may be unsure of exactly what they felt or noticed, and many will have immediate associations or insights that they wish to share with the therapist.

The therapist who finds it necessary to control, comment on the contents or try to make interpretations for the client, will only inhibit the survivor's own individual process of self-discovery. Many clients feel more comfortable being explained by an "expert" rather than allowing their own inner process to unfold. If the client wants further explanation or feedback from a particular relaxation or trance experience, we recommend that the therapist encourages the client to further explore her own understanding of the event rather than providing an explanation or interpretation for the client.

It may be helpful to make a statement such as "Your conscious mind probably has many questions about your experience; you can learn to understand and respect your own unique way of doing things." Or, "You may not yet know the significance of that experience, but your unconscious understands more about you than you may presently realize and you can continue to review those images, feelings, memories, and thoughts that are significant to you until you learn or realize what your experience means to *you*." In using fairly open-ended statements or questions, the therapist is both validating the client's unique process and empowering her to draw her own conclusions. It is also important to remember that relaxation, imagery, and trance experiences, like most things, require familiarity and practice before they can be effectively utilized as therapeutic tools.

We would also recommend that the client be advised to take some time to reorient after relaxation exercises, guided imagery, or metaphor experiences. It is natural for anyone to feel a bit disoriented, extremely relaxed or "spacy" after such an experience. It is important for the therapist to carefully assess each client in this area, as virtually all survivors dissociate and experience that dissociation in varying degrees. We would not recommend these techniques as appropriate for anyone who dissociates or fragments for long periods of time, perhaps in the form of blackouts. Referral and consultation with medical doctors and psychiatrists should be utilized in such extreme cases.

VI. GROUP THERAPY

It is our opinion that group therapy is one of the most cogent routes to breaking the isolation and secrecy resulting from sexual abuse. Many clients, however, are intimidated by the thought of group therapy. In Chapter 4, we discuss the therapeutic benefits of the group and how it fits into the healing journey. Throughout this book most, if not all, of the metaphors, exercises, and rituals can be used with individuals as well as in a group setting.

The following are some important practical and ethical considerations that are of particular importance when working with survivors of sexual abuse.

Screening and Assessment

It is always important to do an assessment interview with each potential group member. The goal of both client and therapist should be to have the most positive and healthy experience in therapy as possible. During an assessment interview each party has the opportunity to understand the intent and structure of the group and to decide if the fit is right.

We have designed a series of questions that, in our opinion, help us to determine suitability. This is not a perfect process; even with careful screening, occasionally an individual who may present well in the assessment can later have difficulty in the group. It is then up to the facilitator to intervene and decide on the most effective course of action at that time.

Some key points to consider are:

- How is the client generally functioning on a daily basis, that is, is she currently suicidal or depressed, active or inactive, and so on?
- What resources is she able to utilize to comfort herself in difficult times? The group itself will help her utilize tools to manage critical times, but if she is too fragile or if she is experienc-

ing serious and frequent suicidal ideation, other appropriate interventions are necessary before she is ready to participate in a group experience.

- It is important to find out what other psychosocial stressors are present in her life. If there are other critical events happening while the group is in progress, the potential positive experience of the group may be eclipsed by those other factors.
- Drug and alcohol use must be assessed. In our experience, occasional lapses and recreational use are common; however, a consistent dependency would be likely to interfere with therapy, and needs to be addressed appropriately.

The following questions are examples of screening questions we use during an assessment interview.

SAMPLE ASSESSMENT QUESTIONS

1. Have you ever attended counseling regarding sexual abuse issues? What was that like for you?
2. Have you ever had any group experience? If so, what was that experience like for you? Do you have any fears or concerns about the group process?
3. What is your support system like? (i.e., Who can you talk to? Friends, family members, other individual therapists?)
4. Can you tell me a little bit about your life right now (i.e., work, relationship, children, etc.)?
5. What do you do when you feel overwhelmed? How do you know when you start to feel that way? What are your cues and how do they start?
6. Have you had any thoughts of suicide recently? If so, can you tell me about that?
7. Do you have any concrete memories of the abuse?
8. Can you tell me a bit about the abuse?
9. How do you feel about talking about the abuse? What do you think it will be like to hear others' stories?
10. Does anyone else know you were sexually abused?
11. Do you have any drug or alcohol problems?
12. Do you take any medication or have any medical problems that could interfere with your participation in this group?

13. What are your goals in coming to the group?
14. Explain the structure of the group.
    Talk about commitment to the group.
    Do you foresee anything coming up that might interfere with your regular attendance?
15. Do you have any questions to ask me?

Group Size and Structure

After many years of running survivor groups, we have found the optimum size of a group to be eight members. Although we realize in these times of limited funding and tight budgets that a group of eight is not as cost-effective as a larger group, this size affords a level of safety and individual time per member that is necessary to process information, therapeutic exercises, and discussion in a dynamic yet secure environment.

We have designed two levels of groups with a duration of 13 sessions each. Participants always request even longer time frames, but with a Phase I and Phase II format, there seems to be a good balance of safety and didactic, experiential components. The goal and main focus of the Phase I group is to introduce the survivor to the group experience as a way of breaking the isolation and secrecy that surround the abuse while in a positive and open atmosphere of peer support. The first four sessions are spent on building an atmosphere of safety and trust in which the survivor can begin to explore the complex, multifaceted nature of her abuse. Throughout the 13 weeks of the Phase I group, the facilitators introduce such topics as safety, relaxation techniques, debriefing of an abusive experience, physical, emotional and behavioral effects of sexual abuse, coping skills, grief and loss, recognition and expression of feelings, the offender relationship, body image, and self-esteem. Throughout the book we will present examples of various exercises, metaphorical stories, meditations, and rituals that are utilized throughout the group process to facilitate the healing journey. We use a variety of mediums in order to access as wide a range of sensory and cognitive processes as possible.

The Phase II group is a continuation of the topics and issues presented in Phase I. However, on entering this next phase of therapy the survivor now has some practical tools as well as a more concrete understanding of her abuse experience. Thus, the second phase of group therapy offers her the opportunity to explore in greater depth how her experience has impacted her and what she can now do to rebuild her life and plan for the future. More time is spent in discussion of relationship issues, setting clear boundaries, reexamining values, and building a strong foundation for the future. Phase II groups tend to be filled with lively and intense discussion among participants and we as facilitators begin to step back in order to allow the group to do more problem solving and initiation of discussion that is relevant to their current needs.

We have found that having a focus on skill and resource building, as a result of a cumulative curriculum, has an outcome of more independence and increased self-management, which leads to more reliance on "self" and therefore less dependence on the therapist.

Closed Versus Open Format

It is our opinion that a closed group format—with a set number of eight participants who participate in the group for its duration—is most beneficial. Due to the high level of anxiety and the nature of the abuse experience, most women are concerned with issues of confidentiality and safety, which are difficult to control in an open-ended group. It is vital to create as secure an environment as possible and in our opinion this can only be achieved by a closed group.

We have found that having a defined structure with a specific curriculum that consists of a topic for each session and complementary experiential exercises, tasks, and discussion to be very effective. Survivors are often confused, fearful, and unfocused upon entering therapy and a consistent structure helps to alleviate some of that anxiety. We also have found it important to include an additional structuring of each session, such as check-in time for each member, homework review, key topic, break, discussion, sharing of exercise and task results, and check-out. A predictable format reduces anxiety and helps to create a supportive therapeutic environment.

Group Rules

Group rules such as confidentiality, regular attendance, respectful listening, and so on should be determined with group input during the first session. It is helpful to brainstorm (on chart paper) these group rules in the context of creating an atmosphere of safety and comfort. One way of doing this is to ask each member to think about and to discuss what she needs in order to achieve such an environment. The facilitator can suggest any key guidelines that the group may be un-aware of and have the list typed and distributed to members for the second session.

Group Leaders

Due to the intense content of survivor groups we think it prudent to have two group leaders. We realize this is not always possible or cost-effective; however, it is not only practical but it also serves as a good example of cooperation and communication to the participants. Two viewpoints are always more beneficial, and when issues crop up in the process of the group, it is advantageous to have another therapist to consult and strategize with.

The issue of male versus female group leaders also deserves mention here. Although we clearly acknowledge that many male therapists do excellent work with female survivors, we have found that virtually all female survivors, when given a choice, choose a female therapist, par-ticularly in the first stages of healing from sexual trauma. Many women will not have the confidence or feel they have the right to request a female therapist. We have had many cases where women were too in-timidated to express their discomfort and inhibition on this issue. We therefore are of the opinion that particularly in a Phase I group, female facilitators are preferable. Although we have not conducted groups with male/female co-facilitators—there is limited literature on sexual abuse groups concerning this issue—we have based this opinion on our own experience of feedback from the many women we have worked with over the past 10 years.

Simultaneous Individual Therapy

For most women commencing sexual abuse work, it is advisable to have an individual therapist the client can check-in with during the course of the group. Due to the intense emotional content and vicari-ous expressing of trauma that is generally present in the group environ-ment, having a support system in place is vital. We have found, however, that it is often advisable to decrease the frequency of individual work while the group is underway so as to encourage the survivor to proactively utilize the group to problem solve and process personal issues. We therefore suggest that a therapist be present as back-up if critical issues arise due to content and topics that require additional processing, which can therefore complement the healing process underway in the group curriculum.

The intent of this chapter is to present a brief overview of many of the key techniques and theories of the Ericksonian solution-focused framework from which we work. It is our goal that this condensed module will help to provide the foundation and context with which the therapist can build on and creatively enhance his or her own repertoire of skills. The presentaion of this material is also significant in order to fully utilize the information and practices of Part II of this book, "The Healing Stages of Sexual Abuse" and the many metaphors, exercises, and rituals presented herein.

PART II

THE HEALING STAGES OF SEXUAL ABUSE

CHAPTER 3

Stage One: Breaking the Silence and Unmasking the Secret

To illustrate the essence of the first stage of healing we identify several key achievements, acknowledgments, and awarenesses that create the focal points of recovery for the survivor. In addition, we also trace the concurrent steps that the healer takes to assist the survivor as she negotiates her way through this challenging first stage.

Within the healing process, it is key for the therapist to have a working knowledge of the stages of childhood development, so that he/she can assist the survivor in catching up on old learning gaps that were missed during the time of the initial trauma.

Remember, it is essential that each step the survivor takes towards her own recovery needs to be validated and honored by the therapist, so that she can develop an appreciation of her courage to move forward, even though the future may be fraught with uncertainty. This is the therapist's opportunity to co-create with the survivor an environment where future possibilities and solutions become a reality.

In this chapter we trace the substages the survivor passes through in order to successfully negotiate the first stage:

I. Prevalent Psychological and Physiological Symptoms
II. Isolation
III. Denial/Ambivalence/Fear
IV. The Power of the Secret
V. Blaming Self/Magical Thinking
VI. Reclaiming My Voice and My Herstory

Following our discussion of these substages, we will present Metaphors, Exercises, and Rituals which will help the client reinforce and anchor the healing tasks which challenge her at this juncture.

I. PREVALENT PSYCHOLOGICAL AND PHYSIOLOGICAL SYMPTOMS

The survivor's clinical presentation in this first stage of the healing process indicates a tendency toward isolation from others, so that the secret of her sexual abuse may be more easily concealed. The need to isolate and remain secretive is borne out of feelings of shame, anger, and depression about being a victim of sexual abuse and having to deny that *it* is there and out of a sense of guilt and self-blame, as the survivor feels she is somehow responsible for her sexual victimization. The survivor-client often presents with a sense of hopelessness about having any control over her present and future state of mind, and she may express a great deal of fear around the possibility of retaliation from her offender(s) if she discloses her secret. The therapist may be aware that when the survivor is discussing her feelings she dissociates from them by presenting with flat affect, for she has had to become numb to her feelings in order to survive. As a result, the survivor of sexual abuse is cut off from her own inner resources and abilities: she is powerless to alter her present dysfunctional behavior in any way.

From a physiological perspective, the survivor of sexual abuse will often describe experiencing panic attacks in situations that may trigger unconscious, fragmented memories of the original abusive experience, which are sometimes accompanied by nausea. The survivor often presents as physically lethargic and often identifies parts of her body where she is experiencing physical pain—for example, the genital area, back, shoulders, neck, abdomen, legs, head—which may be indicative of a body memory of the abuse.

II. ISOLATION

In the initial stage of recovery from sexual abuse, the survivor emerges from a place of isolation. Up until this time, she has been merely existing—her daily routine often constricted to a basic level of subsistence. She cannot dare to dream of future possibilities or even consider that her life could be better. She is coming from a place where the thought of anything more than just basic survival would place her at risk for further pain and abuse. In order to survive, she must remain hyper-vigilant of who or what may be standing behind her, on the side of her, or in front of her and be aware of whatever entity may be lurking in the shadows waiting for the opportunity to take away what little she has that she can call her own.

> Julia, a 28-year-old survivor of childhood sexual abuse, spent a great deal of time in her bedroom as a teenager, refusing to attend school because she was terrified to leave her room in case she encountered her abuser in the house, her older brother. After she ran away from home, Julia eventually was able to afford a place of her own, where she continued to isolate herself socially, fearing that if she allowed herself to meet other people, they might hurt her in some way. It seemed, for Julia, at the time, that it was safer to avoid the company of others, so she constricted her existence in order to survive.

The initial connection that the survivor makes to her own sense of isolation is when she comes to think that she is the only one who this has happened to, and therefore, she feels weird and different from others. At this stage, the survivor often identifies the sexual abuse as "something wrong with me" and "something bad happened to me because I'm bad." This first awareness of past childhood trauma can create an overwhelming feeling of being trapped by the abuse, and as the survivor connects with her feelings of being different, she creates a self-imposed exile, which may temporarily block her belief that she deserves support and assistance from healthy others. It is at this point that her personal challenge becomes one of suspending her own self-disbelief for long enough to give herself permission to consider the merits of therapy. The therapist, at this time, may be the survivor's only link to her real self—where the healer's office becomes an abuse-free, honoring, and respecting sanctuary that she can enter into, where she can begin to view her sense of "not okayness" as a natural response to her past abuse, freeing her to begin to make distinctions between her own self and her perpetrator's values and beliefs. O'Hanlon and Martin (1992) discuss the importance of the therapist's own beliefs about survivors as key to the healing process:

> What we are oriented to in solution-oriented hypnosis, however, is determining what strengths and abilities they have. What resources do they have? Instead of finding out what function their problems serve or why they are messed up, we are looking for what capabilities

they have and stimulating those resources and abilities to help them in the healing process. (p. 143)

As the intervening therapist, you provide the link that assists the survivor in taking the risk of receiving help and support through therapy, even though she may not be fully convinced that she is entitled to it at this point. In providing this link, you are often encouraging the client to take her first steps toward trusting another—albeit a healer but, nevertheless, still a stranger. If the survivor can overcome the natural fears that would surface as a result of taking this leap into therapy, she is initiating for herself perhaps the first healthy alliance to an adult in her life so far. Therefore, the building of the therapeutic bond over time is key to the survivor's recovery, as within this environment she has the opportunity to enjoy a corrective healthy attachment experience with the therapist. She then has the opportunity to grieve what she didn't get from her original caretakers and eventually go on to becoming receptive to present and future possibilities around developing healthy attachments to healthy others. The story "The Discovery," found in the "Metaphors, Exercises, and Rituals" portion of this chapter, provides the survivor with the message that she is not alone, but rather in the company of hundreds of others whose courage and strength allowed them to survive childhood trauma and bravely forge ahead into adulthood.

III. DENIAL/AMBIVALENCE/FEAR

The survivor's experience of uncertainty over whether or not she should disclose the secret surfaces as a sense of denial, fear, and ambivalence—"Maybe it didn't really happen," "Maybe I'm just imagining it," and "Yet I know there is something wrong and I need to deal with it." When she is able to, in part, move past the sense of self-blame, once she discloses the secret, it begins to lose its power over her.

Sarah, an 18-year-old survivor, was initially terrified to disclose the secret of her father's ongoing sexual abuse of her from a young age, even though he had died of a heart attack a few years before she came into therapy. She felt that his ghost would return to haunt her if she revealed his abusive behavior. Following her father's death, Sarah would tell everyone that she had a wonderful father who had been loving and kind, for she needed to hold onto the belief that she had only imagined the abuse and that, in fact, her childhood had been a happy one. It was on her 18th birthday that Sarah went into an almost catatonic-like state, and she was willing to, with the support of therapy, take some time out to understand her body's need to react in the way it did.

The survivor often remains in this stage until she is willing to risk looking at what it is that is creating that wave of nausea and/or heavy feeling in her stomach or chest. Or, perhaps there is nothing wrong and she is only imagining it—a crazy-making belief that she can only overcome when she gives herself permission to recognize that there is most definitely something unresolved within. Often the internalized voice of the perpetrator is much louder than her own, threatening her as he did when she was a child, that if she releases the secret she will be punished, surfacing an internal tug of war with denial, ambivalence, and fear of retribution. In her book, *Trauma and Recovery*, Herman (1992) illustrates the challenges facing the victim when she risks questioning the perpetrator's words:

> In order to escape accountability for his crimes, the perpetrator does everything in his power to promote forgetting. Secrecy and silence are the perpetrator's first line of defense. If secrecy fails, the perpetrator attacks the credibility of his victim. (p. 8)

When she connects with the secret, she often identifies with splintered fragments of memory that do not initially fit together logically into a whole, clear, visual, auditory, and kinesthetic picture. These seemingly unrelated pieces of memory can create ambivalent feelings regarding whether or not it is worth remembering. Often, a wish to temporarily deny the abuse at this time can occur, with fear taking over and tightening its grip. It is the therapist's role at this point to assist the survivor in gradually reintegrating the splintered fragments so that she can reclaim the lost parts of herself. However, it is imperative that the healer has a clear understanding of the impact of traumatic events on the traumatized person. Herman (1992) describes the survivor's reaction:

> Traumatic reactions occur when action is of no avail. When neither resistance nor escape is possible, the human system of self-defense becomes overwhelmed and disorganized. Each component of the ordinary response to danger, having lost its utility, tends to persist in an altered and exaggerated stage long after the actual danger is over. Traumatic events produce profound and lasting changes in physi-

ological arousal, emotion, cognition, and memory. Moreover, traumatic events may sever those normally integrated functions from one another. (p. 34)

The story of "Victoria" and her doll, Peggy, in the last section of this chapter on "Metaphors, Exercises, and Rituals," provides a hopeful message to survivors regarding the possibility of self-reintegration. As you will become aware in this particular metaphor, Victoria experiences her abuse through the misadventures of her doll, Peggy, which provides a sufficient enough distance from the survivor so that she can begin to give herself permission to remember at a pace that is comfortable and relatively safe.

IV. THE POWER OF THE SECRET

Once the survivor enters into a therapeutic alliance with the healer, the stage is set for self-disclosure of her burdensome secret. Consider, however, that this secret has been up until now an essential part of her being, and she may hesitate to let go of it. The secret has been her cover, and in releasing it she may risk exposing huge, gaping wounds. At this point the survivor may ask herself, "What is it that I'm holding onto, carrying around with me?" "It feels like a secret," which at the time appears more powerful than the survivor herself. There may be, at this point, a sense of what the secret may contain, and she may feel torn between maintaining its power over her by not telling, versus making it okay for herself to disclose the secret even though she may not fully believe or even remember what is locked inside. Often the thought and fear of what may be concealed in the secret can be more terrifying than its actual contents. For one client, overcoming her fear of the unknown by acknowledging to herself that she was carrying a powerful secret meant that she could rest more peacefully at night. The "Little Shadow," located in the "Metaphors, Exercises, and Rituals" portion of this chapter, is a simple story that can be imparted to the survivor at this healing juncture.

At this point, the survivor must weigh the advantages and potential drawbacks to disclosing the secret. In telling the secret, she risks opening old wounds, which then initially connect her back to her vulnerable self, a necessary step toward her eventual healing. Conversely, in maintaining the secret, she may be choosing to be eternally enshrouded in darkness and despair. It is our experience that each survivor's disclosure is unique and that sometimes the secret consists of knowing just that—that there is a secret, without an awareness of its contents, leaving her with a sense that all is not right—that she is carrying some unidentified burden. Sometimes when traumatic memory surfaces, it is described by the survivor in physicalities—a feeling of nausea, a lump in the throat, butterflies in the stomach, or sometimes a fist arising from the chest. Conversely, like a dormant volcano suddenly awakening from a long sleep and spewing forth its lava, some survivors will quickly disclose all the details of the abuse that they remember in the first session, breath a sigh of relief, and then wait for the therapist to respond. Thus, the degree of readiness to disclose varies, and as a result, it is essential for the healer to co-create with the survivor an opportunity for her to set her own recovery pace. Herman (1992) further confirms this process: "The traumatized person may experience intense emotion but without clear memory of the event, or may remember everything in detail but without emotion" (p. 34).

Once the survivor takes that initial leap of faith in letting go of the secret, it is the therapist's responsibility to remain sensitive to the potential gaps that the disclosure exposes, so that they can be addressed, worked through, and ultimately healed. Dolan (1991) suggests a "symbol for the present" that the survivor can use prior to disclosing the details of the abuse to her therapist:

> Ideally the client should be asked, before she begins the narrative of her victimization, to identify something in the room, a "symbol for the present" (Dolan, 1989), that can be used to remind her of the here and now. Clients often choose a personal item such as their purse, a picture of their kids or partner or other significant person, a ring or other piece of jewelry. Others simply focus on some object in the office that reminds them of the present. (p. 27)

In emerging from the shadows of the secret, the survivor can now, in a small but significant way, begin to loosen the grip the abuse has had on her and begin to speak the truths that have been locked inside her body for so long. The therapist can assist the survivor in developing and strengthening her own voice, so that she can accept that she was abused and become aware of the possibility that the fear of disclosure she is experiencing may in part be the fear she experienced as a child. The key is to assist the survivor in initially creating enough distance between herself and the abuse until she is personally ready to begin to initiate the steps toward reintegrating those parts of herself that were lost as a result of the trauma, going at her own pace, so that each reintegrated piece of memory can ultimately assume a healthy permanency.

V. BLAMING SELF/MAGICAL THINKING

The power of the secret over the child is so profound that it is almost like a magical spell. As previously mentioned, it is important for the therapist to keep in mind the stages of normal childhood development while working with survivors. In early and middle childhood, the phenomenon of "magical thinking" is instrumental in the cognitive and emotional development of the child. She lives between the worlds of magic and reality and does not yet fully understand that one world is separate from the other. The child's sense of reality at this time is not yet mature enough to evaluate and make distinctions between what is fact and what is fiction. In most cases, the offender has projected the blame and the responsibility for the abuse onto the child. When this is added to the fact that it is normal for children to try to make sense of their experiences, we can better understand the dilemma of the abused child.

In a safe environment children learn to understand and relate to their world through play. However, the natural spontaneity and delight in play and exploration are not safe for a child who has been sexually abused. Blaming herself for the abuse is a natural conclusion, a way of coping with what she does not yet understand. It therefore makes sense that survivors of childhood sexual abuse often describe themselves as being "evil," as though they deliberately brought on the abuse. This is further complicated by the blaming tactics of the offender. The sense of being "evil" or "possessed" often occurs during the sexual abuse when the survivor goes through the process of incorporating the offender into herself. Thus, the development of a sense of autonomy (a developmentally normal phase at this stage of life) is sabotaged and she becomes unable to make distinctions between self and other. It is usually not safe for her to exercise any measure of autonomy within this oppressive relationship. The result is that she has to "shut down" for her own preservation.

Elaine, a 42-year-old incest survivor, described her childhood experience as constantly battling against her "evil nature." Elaine was raised in an environment where religion played a dominant role. She interpreted her feelings of shame, guilt, and confusion about the abuse in the context of her own evilness. Her father and brother, who were the perpetrators, used their religion as a tactic to maintain Elaine's silence. It wasn't until she reached her 30s, and began to struggle with her beliefs and values about the religion she was raised with, that she realized her experience and her own spirituality as well as most other aspects of her life had been clouded by the abuse she suffered in her childhood. She was then able to realize that she was not evil, but an innocent child without the means or the power to stop the abuse. The evil was not from within herself but a symptom of the abuse she suffered at the hands of her father and brother. This was an important realization for Elaine, which helped her view her past from a different and healthier perspective. This was the first step for Elaine in releasing and separating herself from the blame and responsibility for the abuse.

Many survivors describe their experience in the world as being "frozen" or "stuck." The normal spontaneity and delight in play and exploration is not safe. Feelings, thoughts, and reactions are guarded and restricted. Life becomes very tentative and one dimensional.

Elaine revealed the following in therapy:

"I don't ever remember just having fun. I was always concerned about what everyone else thought of me. I didn't feel that I deserved to have fun. I thought everyone could tell I was sexually abused—I kept my distance from everybody and everything."

The survivor takes a huge leap in faith when making the decision to enter into the healing process. It is extremely important for the therapist to acknowledge and honor the client at this very vulnerable crossroad. More specifically, the survivor needs to know she is not alone and that others have come before her to the therapist's office to seek refuge and healing.

We have found it helpful to utilize the natural phenomenon of magical thinking to help the survivor break the spell of the secret by the use of a ritual we call "The Healing Cape" found at the end of this chapter. This cape is a special piece of cloth that the survivor can surround herself in (if she chooses) to remind her of her own personal power and ability to nurture herself and successfully contain often overwhelming feelings and memories. We emphasize to her that many other survivors have worn this cape before her and that it can be a symbol of her own internal resources, power, wisdom, and strength which she too can now draw from.

It is important at this time for the therapist to seed hope and success in the survivor. This exercise is another small step in breaking the silence and isolation. It can also assist the survivor to acknowledge and appreciate that there are many positive qualities within her yet to be uncovered and that others before her have been successful in doing so. It is important to let her know that she can reveal her true self in this protected environment, as others before her have.

VI. RECLAIMING MY VOICE AND MY HERSTORY

Once the survivor acknowledges her secret, she begins the process of reclaiming her voice and her herstory. She is now starting to accept that she was in fact sexually abused. We think it is important to note that this realization is one that wanes and intensifies throughout the first two stages of the healing process. It seems to be a constant struggle to accept the reality of the abuse. Just as the survivor often describes herself as vacillating between belief and disbelief around the existence of the abuse, she now begins to fear the visibility that comes with reclaiming her voice and breaking the silence. By speaking about the abuse she must come face to face with many of the realities that have been cloaked in the silence. There is often an overwhelming terror that if she begins to remember and feel more, she will "lose it" or "go crazy." One client described her terror as feeling so totally overwhelmed that she "would slip into the darkness forever."

Since the survivor has been isolated for so long, the idea of unmasking the secret is often associated with panic or trepidation. She becomes aware that being noticed may mean that she is once again vulnerable to attack or abandonment. This issue will be dealt with in more detail in Chapter 4. However, it is important to recognize that the beginning awareness of this visibility can be extremely anxiety-provoking, but it offers the therapist an opportunity to introduce the idea to the client that she can overcome this debilitating apprehension.

Rossi (Erickson & Rossi, 1979, pp. 61–63) discusses the importance of utilizing emergency situations which are times of increased suggestibility. The nature of the traumatic experience is an altered trance-like state. Therefore, why not utilize these opportunities to introduce some new, more adaptive, and comforting learnings?

In situations such as this, the patient experiences a tremendously urgent need to have something done. Recognition of this need, and a readiness to utilize it by doing something in direct relationship to the origin of the need, constitutes a most effective type of suggestion in securing the patient's full cooperation for adequate measures. (p. 63)

At this stage of therapy, relaxation techniques and metaphorical story telling can help survivors experience some comfort and sense of hope for the future. The story of "Hush," found near the end of the chapter, was co-created with a client at this critical stage of healing.

This particular client, Elisabeth, was beginning to experience flashbacks. These flashbacks would result in panic attacks and a sense of overwhelming doom. She was afraid that if she allowed herself to fully accept what had happened in her childhood, she would cease to exist. Elisabeth was extremely isolated, had trouble keeping employment, and was very much cut off from the outside world. She was terrified of being noticed and always wore black, baggy clothes in order to draw as little attention to herself as possible. After several sessions of light trancework (mainly focusing on relaxation), she was able to enjoy the story of "Hush" who was experiencing many of the same symptoms. This story had a calming effect on Elisabeth and at her request we taped the trancework and metaphor for her to use at home whenever she began to experience these old feelings of doom.

The survivor gradually begins to understand the effects the abuse has on her present experience. She becomes able to emerge from the numbing, frozen existence which has inhibited her experience up until now. Many women describe this time as "coming out of a fog." There are now other options available. One client said she had felt like "an impostor in her own life." She can now become more present in the present.

An exercise for helping the survivor to entertain a stronger sense of self and perspective is to suggest drawing a series of past, present, and future self-portraits. One client, Holly, drew her past self as a small figure in the center of the page with many people immediately surrounding her. Holly explained that she was dependent upon the others in her past to direct and control her. Holly's present depiction of self was of a larger, more dominant figure with fewer people controlling her. She described feeling connected to herself in a more cognizant way with an inner voice that she could begin to listen to and trust. Relying less on external feedback to shape her self-image afforded Holly the opportunity to develop a more centered and grounded sense of her "self" in the present.

At this point in the exercise, more specific detail of Holly's past sexual abuse was disclosed spontaneously as she was able to gain a safe enough distance from, and perspective on, the past. This young woman's future picture of self depicted a strong, well-muscled figure with a clearer delineation between herself and the others around her than in the previous two drawings of the past and the present. She recounted an image of her projected future self who could bring forth her own inner strength and creativity. Therefore, by creating a shifting image of herself in the present and future, and by acknowledging where she came from in the past, this client could begin to rewrite her own personal history of recovery. Holly was beginning to reclaim and recognize the power she had been giving away to others all of her life.

Setting the stage for new learning by way of reiterating past learning can assist the survivor in retrieving and identifying inner resources and skills that can spark the process of reclaiming parts of the self left behind at the scene of the abuse. Erickson often used "early-learning-set" inductions as a way of reinforcing the client's ability to acquire and practice new information. This can be achieved by reminding the survivor (as we reminded Victoria in the story at the end of the chapter) of her ability to learn her ABCs, recalling the success of finally being able to read and write her ABCs, or to remember her excitement the first time she was able to walk across an entire room without any assistance. Such reminders of the survivor's ability to learn new skills can help her to entertain new possibilities and therefore presuppose that new learning and understanding is possible now and in the future.

Creating an environment of safety and comfort both at home and in the therapist's office can further enrich the healing process. Tackling the many issues, emotions, and memories along the road to recovery is a formidable undertaking. It is important to remember that up until the point of embarking on a healing journey, most survivors had been existing in a world with little joy, spontaneity, or nurturing. We encourage the survivor to construct an environment in her own home where she can experience a sense of containment: a healing sanctuary where she can begin to experience her own daily routine, which may consist of journal writing, reading, or meditation. We recommend that she choose an established time each day in a place where she is the most comfortable or the least uncomfortable, as Dolan (1991) would say, and that she make this a special time for herself and for healing.

The therapist may also suggest that the client bring to the therapist's office some kind of transitional object that symbolizes comfort and is special to her, such as a favorite cushion, cherished doll, stuffed toy, or blanket. This can help to provide a sense of continuity and structure to help ease the sense of chaos that sometimes surfaces when pieces of memory begin to return. Some women like to bring this object with them to each session and others prefer to leave it at the therapist's office.

We also encourage the survivor to honor herself each week by doing something nurturing and/or fun. This helps to keep her grounded in the present and introduces the notion that it is healthy and important for her to express and fulfill her own needs. Most survivors have a difficult time accepting that they have the right to feel good and have some enjoyment especially while they are dealing with these often overwhelming issues (see Celebration Exercise at the end of the next section).

METAPHORS, EXERCISES, AND RITUALS

"THE DISCOVERY"

As this story may be one of the first you impart to the survivor, it will be important for you to refer to Chapter 2, "Tools of the Trade," in order to take some time to explain the process of trance and relaxation to your client. It is possible that at this first stage of her journey the survivor may not wish to do trancework, and it is, of course, important to respect her wishes. However, when and if she is ready, the survivor of sexual abuse will derive much benefit from this and the other metaphors, exercises, and rituals presented in this book.

This metaphorical story communicates to the survivor, who is just beginning to emerge from the shadows of her past sexual abuse, that she is, in fact, not alone in her experience.

Through the image of washed-up broken shells, the story also imparts to the survivor her sense that she is broken as a result of feeling responsible for having been abused—feeling that there is something wrong with her. Therefore, the message is that once the survivor comes forward and begins to acknowledge her abuse, she will gradually realize that it was not her fault, and that many others, like all the people Savannah discovers on the beach with the same interest of collecting shells, share her history of sexual abuse. When ready, she can look forward to the opportunity of receiving a great deal of support both in individual therapy and, later on, in becoming a member of a group of survivors of sexual abuse.

You CAN TAKE SOME TIME, now, to find a comfortable place…making any adjustments you need to make in any part of your body to experience that sense of comfort…. And as you take some nice deep breaths in you can take in even more comfort…and, on each exhale, let go of anything that you choose…as you listen to a story about a friend of mine named Savannah….

I recall a particular beach holiday that a friend of mine, Savannah, took a while back. Her favorite activity while she was away was to take time out of every day to search for shells washed up by the ocean onto the smooth, white, sandy shore. Each time Savannah looked for shells on the beach, she would return to her room disappointed, for the waves washed up only the broken remains of shells, and not the whole forms that she searched for. Until, one day, Savannah met a wise, old beach-comber who told her that the best time to search for shells was very early in the morning when the tide was out, and there were many choices to make.

So, early the next morning, Savannah awoke with a renewed sense of purpose…hastily returning to the beach to look for the shells that the wise beachcomber suggested she would find. Much to her surprise, when she reached the shore, there were many people walking on the smooth, white sand collecting shells! Feeling the crisp coolness of the morning air touching her cheeks, and the warmth of the sun on her back, she too joined the crowd and began to discover what others before her had experienced…the early morning presence of hundreds of shells on the beach! For the first time Savannah was not alone, realizing that many others shared her new discovery!

Each shell was unique in its shape, form, texture, and color, and each beachcomber appeared to value different qualities in the shells… choosing the ones that they experienced as most appealing to them personally, tossing back others that did not suit them, only to be picked up by other beachcombers who considered them to be of value. Savannah found herself now able to appreciate the choices she had made, and even though the shells she valued were different from other beach-combers' shells, she realized that they all shared the special feelings of excitement and joy of discovery…. She was not alone!

And, isn't it nice to know that when ready, you too can discover that you are not alone.... There are many others who share a similar struggle, and that there is something about being together in your struggle, that can begin to feel empowering and healing ....

You can take some time, now, all the time that you want...two minutes of clock time, to return to the room...bringing with you as much as you choose...letting go of what doesn't belong....

⌘   ⌘   ⌘

"HUSH—PART ONE"

Hush was written with a particular client in mind to address many of the physiological and psychological issues and symptoms the survivor faced when she began to break the silence and face her trauma.

ONCE UPON A TIME there was a tiny lynx named "Hush." Hush lived with her Aunt Kit in the mountains of British Columbia. Now Kit wasn't really Hush's aunt, but she had found Hush all alone in a meadow one day when she was hunting for food, and being the sort of mountain lion she was, she adopted Hush and brought her back to the den where her own cubs lived.

Kit was a very famous medicine lion in the mountains. It was said that she could heal wounds, make flowers bloom, and even make animals invisible! The mountain lions in Kit's community were suspicious and not very accepting of outsiders. Kit was concerned about Hush's safety and so she thought it best to make Hush invisible until she could convince the other lions to accept Hush or until Hush could be united with other lynx.

Hush found it very difficult to get used to living among Kit's family; since she had been isolated, alone, and fending for herself for so long, she felt as though she didn't belong anywhere and being invisible complicated matters even more. Sometimes she wasn't sure she existed at all. Hush would sit for hours in the darkest corner of the den (the only spot she felt relatively comfortable in); she would watch the lion cubs play with each other, laughing and learning the lessons of how to be grown-up lions.

Kit tried to coax Hush out of her corner, but even though part of her wanted to come out and play with the others, she didn't feel she deserved to be having fun like they were. She thought she was bad because she was different—deep down inside she knew there was something very wrong with her and that deep, dark secret kept her frozen in her dark corner. She was afraid to draw any sort of attention to herself; if someone noticed her, they might discover her secret and make fun of her or even worse—make her go out into the mountains all by herself, where she would surely fall prey to the lions or wolves.

One winter night when everyone was asleep, a pack of wolves raided Kit's den in search of food. One of the wolves heard there was a small lynx hiding out nearby and there was a rumor that Kit knew the lynx's whereabouts. Hush was terrified, and even though she was still invisible, she was sure they would find her and gobble her up. Kit threatened to put a spell on the wolves if they did not leave her den and was successful in scaring them off.

This episode convinced Hush even more that she was evil and brought bad luck to herself and everyone around her. Kit assured Hush that those wolves were the evil ones, not her, and that she should not allow them or anyone else to keep her isolated from the rest of the world. "There is so much out there to see and experience, Hush; it may seem overwhelming at first, but I can help you learn what you need to know in order to live out there. It's really not as difficult as it seems. Isn't there anything you can think of that you would like to experience or do?"

Hush thought about that for a long time—she wasn't used to thinking about what she might like to do in the future. She was so consumed with getting through the terror and emptiness of each day, she hardly had the energy to hope for something different.

That night Kit gave Hush some magic dreaming tea before she went to bed, and Hush had an amazing dream about travelling to the top of the Lions (two mountain peaks that were shaped like lions), where she saw for the first time that there was a whole world beyond her own small den. Hush saw the sparkling water of the ocean beyond and smelt the salt air breeze as it swooshed by her, ruffling her fur. She could hear the many new sounds of the city in the far distance. Hush woke up the next morning with a sense of excitement and curiosity that she hadn't experienced before. She was still nervous and fearful of what was out there, but a part of her that she was unfamiliar with seemed to be willing to venture outside for the first time.

Hush asked Kit if she could make her visible again so she could learn how to exist in the outside world. Kit was worried about reversing the spell because Hush was still very tentative and didn't really have a sense of who she was. One has to believe that one has the right to exist in order to become visible again.

Kit mixed up a potion and Hush drank it down with great anticipation. After a few hours, parts of Hush's body became partially visible but she had an almost ghostlike appearance, and one had to really concentrate on seeing her to tell if she was there or not. So Kit mixed up another batch of her potion. This time Hush's body was there, but her head was still not visible. Hush felt very strange. She could see her paws and torso but she didn't feel as though they were part of her.

Kit had an idea—what if they designed a mask for her to wear until they were able to help make her whole again? "What would you like your mask to look like?" asked Kit.

Hush thought hard about how she felt on the inside versus the image she would like to project on the outside. She felt ashamed and weak and worthless, but how would that look? What would it feel like to look that way? Kit suggested that Hush think about how she would *like* to look and feel. "Imagine how you would look if you were feeling more confident and comfortable: What sort of expression would you have on your face and how would you hold your head? What expression would you have in your eyes?" With Kit's guidance and encouragement a mask was finally created. For the first time Hush was able to experience visibility. It was frightening at first—the others in the den began to notice her and treat her as though she did exist. Hush felt very vulnerable. It took a few weeks of wearing the mask for Hush to begin to feel that she was attached to the rest of her body. It was very strange when she saw her reflection in the nearby pond for the first time. She couldn't believe that she looked like a real lynx—she was even beginning to appreciate some of the unique and distinct markings on her fur.

As the season passed from winter to spring, Kit decided it was once again time for Hush to try her visible potion. This time it worked! Hush's body was whole. She could feel and see herself from the tips of her tasseled ears to the pads of her paws.

The cubs admired her tasseled ears and beautiful big clear eyes. Hush was gradually able to look at herself in the pond without feeling embarrassed or ashamed. Kit knew it was time for Hush to venture out into the world where she could live freely among other lynx and simply be Hush.

Hush learned and practiced all the skills that Kit said lynx needed to survive out there in the real world. By the fall, Hush realized that she had always had the skills and strength inside that she needed to survive or she wouldn't have made it this far in her life. She just needed to trust herself more. Kit said that would just take time, persistence, and that most of all, she had to keep believing that she could make it out there. When she felt scared and vulnerable inside, Hush would remember what it was like to wear her mask, and soon she was able to be more comfortable with herself and think about how it would be to reach the peak of that mountain and really experience what was on the other side. She was ready. She was finally ready to be Hush.

⌘   ⌘   ⌘

"VICTORIA"

Victoria is a metaphorical story written for survivors who are in the early stages of coming to terms with their abuse. It is written in a nondirect manner so as to allow the client to vicariously experience the realization of the abuse via Peggy, a treasured doll. The intent is that with enough distance and a pervasive attitude of hope and belief in a more happy and healthy future, the survivor, in the early stage of acknowledging her experience, will receive a message that it is okay to allow herself to remember and to heal at a pace that is right for her.

I'M WONDERING AS YOU ARE SITTING THERE, if you can imagine what it would be like to be in trance? Do you remember a time when you felt very relaxed? Perhaps it was like reading a good book, when you were completely absorbed and all of the worries of your conscious mind were temporarily distracted—you just enjoyed that good book, that's right.

And as you are sitting there listening to the sound of my voice outside, you can also hear the sound of your own breath inside, that's right, paying attention to your breath as you feel the comfortable support of the cushions beneath you. It's nice to know that you are supported by those soft pillows. Everyone likes to feel supported. And that you can simply be there, anyway that is comfortable for you...while your conscious mind can listen to this story about a childhood friend of mine named Vickie.

Vickie was a very shy little girl in a family where her two older brothers bullied her and constantly told her she was dumb and ugly and criticized just about everything she did.

Vickie's father and mother were divorced and she hadn't seen her dad for a long, long, time. Her mother had to work all the time it seemed. So Vickie was very lonely a lot of the time. Sometimes she would go into the basement beside the furnace where she made a cozy nest for herself and she would take her most prized possessions, her favorite blanket and the beautiful ABC book that her grandmother had given her for her birthday. Now Vickie was only 5 years old and she didn't know how to read yet, but she loved to look at the letters of the alphabet and, besides, Grandma, who gave her the book, was her favorite person in the whole world! So she felt good whenever she had her book nearby.

Grandma would visit her whenever she could, and on these visits, she taught Vickie her ABCs. At first Vickie thought she would never be able to tell one letter from another... "a", "c", and "e" looked almost the same to her and so did the "b" and "d." But Vickie practiced and practiced and soon she could tell each letter of the alphabet from all the rest. Soon she could even print her own name, and how wonderful it was when she could read her own name for the first time. Grandma said she was *very clever.* After a while she could read whole sentences and eventually she could read a whole story, and it seemed easier every time. Soon she didn't have to concentrate so very hard; it seemed almost natural.

On one of Grandma's visits she brought Vickie a very special doll. She said that she was so proud of Vickie, and she knew that Vickie was old enough to take care of and appreciate this very special doll. This was an antique doll with a china head and a very beautiful painted face and real hair! Vickie loved and treasured her doll more than anything. She took her everywhere and slept and ate with her, too. Vickie named her Peggy.

Vickie's brothers knew how important Peggy was to Vickie, and they often played cruel games on her by stealing Peggy when Vickie was asleep and hiding her for days at a time. One day when Vickie was playing with Peggy in the backyard by the tool shed, her brothers snuck up behind her and scared Vickie. An overwhelming feeling of terror and nausea took hold of Vickie; she knew she had to protect herself and get away from her brothers, but she didn't think she could. She was shaking all over and she tried to scream: nothing came out of her mouth but sobs as she gasped for air. She started to run away from her brothers but they soon caught up to her and grabbed her by her skirt, causing her to lose her balance and fall down a small hill by some bushes. Vickie bumped her head and was not completely conscious as she lay on the ground. Out of the corner of her eye she thought she noticed that Peggy's head had cracked open and one of her legs was missing.

Vickie didn't remember how she got back inside the house. She felt numb all over, kind of like part of her was in a dream. Later that night, she realized that Peggy was missing. Vickie searched high and low for her. The next day she tried so hard to remember all the details of what had happened, but she couldn't remember what had happened to Peggy or exactly where she might be. Vickie felt so hurt and ashamed that she had let harm come to Peggy. And even though she didn't remember exactly what happened to Peggy, she had a sick feeling inside her that Peggy was damaged and it was all her fault. After all, Grandma had trusted her and now she had betrayed her trust. Grandma would be so ashamed of her if she found out. She would probably think she was very bad and evil for allowing Peggy to be lost and probably ruined forever.

Vickie's brothers teased and taunted her about Peggy's loss, and they told her if she dared to tell what happened to Mother or Grandma, they would tell Grandma that Vickie was very careless and purposely threw Peggy away.

Vickie was beside herself with fear and she couldn't concentrate on anything anymore—not even her ABCs. And every time she fell asleep, she had horrible nightmares and woke up terrified. Then Vickie's worst nightmare was about to come true…Grandma was coming tomorrow for supper!

That night Vickie went to bed and it took her a long, long time to finally fall asleep. She was exhausted. She began to dream about Grandma—at first it was just like it always was when they were together: Vickie felt safe and happy when she was with Grandma; they would cuddle and talk and laugh. But then Vickie started to get that sick feeling in her stomach and she remembered about Peggy and that Grandma was going to find out. Vickie was terrified and felt like she was going to be sick to her stomach. Then she heard her Grandma's voice telling her how clever and good she was, just like the way she learned her ABCs so quickly, and how she could do anything she wanted to if she put her mind to it (*pause*).

Vickie woke up at that point of the dream. It was very early in the morning and the sun was just rising. Vickie quickly got dressed and ran outside, determined to find Peggy even though part of her was so scared to find her mutilated and perhaps beyond repair! She kept listening in her mind to those positive words of her Grandma: "Victoria, you are very clever and you *can* do whatever you put your mind to." She remembered that she had been near the tool shed when her brothers had frightened her—so that's where she began her search. She began to feel frightened and weak at the knees; she had a fleeting memory of something but then she lost it again. The harder she tried to remember, the less she could remember and the more frustrated and angry with herself she became. She sat down for a while until the nausea stopped and then she kept repeating over and over that she could do it—even though part of her was very afraid that her Grandma might be very disappointed and ashamed of her. She knew she had to find Peggy.

As she approached the hill by the bushes, an overwhelming sense of fear and nausea took over her body. She became frozen in a dreamlike state, but in her mind she heard Grandma's voice again: "You can do it, you can do it, Victoria." Grandma was the only person who called her by her full name, Victoria. Just then out of the corner of her eye, she saw Peggy lying in the bushes. All of a sudden it all came back to her—she began to sob as she grabbed Peggy and ran for her favorite spot by the furnace. She didn't remember how long she sat there holding Peggy tightly and crying until she had no more tears.

Victoria started to get very angry as she really looked at Peggy for the first time and saw all the damage that was done. Half of her head was missing and so was one of her legs. Victoria went outside to search for the missing pieces. She found them and wrapped them safely in her favorite doll blanket. She waited all day for Grandma to come. Part of her was paralyzed with fear, but there was another part growing inside her that was so angry she knew she had to tell Grandma what really happened—even if her brothers did threaten her, she had to tell her story.

Grandma finally arrived. Victoria didn't run to her immediately like she normally did to give her a big hug. Grandma knew something was wrong. It took her a long time to convince Victoria that she would believe anything that Victoria told her because she knew what a wonderful brave child Victoria was because Victoria had always been truthful with her before.

Finally Victoria was able to tell Grandma the whole story from beginning to end and to show her Peggy. Much to Victoria's surprise and delight Grandma assured her that she was not to blame for what happened. Wow, she did understand. Grandma placed the blame where it belonged with her two brothers. Grandma also reminded Victoria of how brave she was to tell her about what happened to Peggy and said once again that Victoria was a very special person—one whom a Grandmother could be very proud of.

Grandma took Peggy to an old friend of hers whose hobby was healing broken dollies. It seemed like it took forever for Peggy to come home again. But when she did, she looked almost like she had before. Grandma said that there were some scars left from her fall, but thanks to Victoria, all of the pieces had been secured and put back together again. Grandma's friend had healed Peggy so well that she looked and felt even stronger than she was before and that made Peggy even more special to Victoria.

Victoria still thinks and dreams occasionally about Peggy's ordeal, but now that she is a grown woman with different choices and perspectives, she understands why it was such a traumatic time for her. She also realizes how that experience helped her to be stronger and to stand up for herself. Even though Victoria still has some difficult times in her life, especially when dealing with her brothers, Peggy helps to remind her of all the positive choices she has since made in her life. Every time Victoria looks at Peggy (who has a special place of honor in Victoria's house), she thinks about her Grandma: All those good feelings come flooding over her, and she is able to put the ordeal with her brothers in the corner of her mind so she can feel those good feelings and remind herself of how far she has come and of all the unique accomplishments and abilities she has inside of her.

And you can give yourself a message of self-appreciation for all of the unique resources and skills that you possess. Opening up and nurturing yourself with each breath you take in—taking in even more comfort and letting go of whatever you need to let go of on every exhale—that's right. Your unconscious mind integrating that new information in whatever way you need to heal and experience comfort—even more comfort…(*pause*) and when you are ready you can reorient back to the room, bringing with you whatever you need to, to increase your level of comfort and tranquillity.

With a deep sense of self-appreciation and comfort.

⌘   ⌘   ⌘

"THE LITTLE SHADOW"

This is a short metaphorical story designed to communicate to the survivor that the secret of her sexual abuse continues to overshadow the rest of her identity, until she gives herself permission to talk about it. Once it begins to dawn on the survivor that she was not responsible for the abuse and, accordingly, discloses her secret, its power over her diminishes considerably, and even though the experience of her abuse will remain a part of her identity, it will occupy considerably less space in her life than before. This metaphor helps to set the stage for the future when the space that was previously occupied by the sexual abuse now becomes available, so that the survivor can begin to fill her person with other healthier life experiences and skills.

YOU CAN TAKE SOME TIME, now, to just focus...focusing on the sound of my voice outside and the sounds of your own voice inside.... Taking in some nice deep breaths...and, then blowing them out...that's right...feeling the support of the cushions beneath you...and isn't it nice to know that support is there for you whenever you want it.... Taking some time, now, to listen to the story of the little shadow....

This is the story of a little shadow who had a secret. Every day the shadow hid the secret, it grew bigger and bigger, until finally the secret outshadowed the shadow, and she could no longer tell the difference between herself and the secret. After spending many hours eclipsed by the secret, the shadow grew lonely and tired of being in the dark; so when she felt ready, she stepped out into the bright sunshine with the other little shadows and, like magic, the big secret began to melt (as it could only thrive in dark, gloomy, isolated places), until the little shadow began to feel lighter and lighter, and freer, and more able to feel herself again—joining in with the other little shadows—merrily skipping and jumping in the warmth and brightness of the summer sunshine.

And now you, too, can make the choice to take your place in the sun...gradually emerging from the shadows, to reveal your own truths, when ready. Isn't it nice to discover that you are not alone...and as you start letting go of what does not belong to you, you can begin to feel lighter and lighter, giving yourself permission to bask in the sunshine...

⌘   ⌘   ⌘

THE HEALING CAPE RITUAL
(METAPHORICAL MEDITATION)

This particular ritual assists in empowering the survivor to transform history into herstory via the symbol of the healing cape. If the survivor chooses, she can don the healing cape during this and other metaphorical meditations while the therapist describes the cape as a symbol of the support and energy of the other survivors who have worn it before her, seeding a relinking with community to help overcome her sense of isolation.

AS YOU SURROUND YOUR BODY with this special healing cape, it's comforting to know that many others before you have worn this cape on their journey of self-discovery and empowerment. As you sit there in that comfortable position, it's nice to know that you *can* draw from your own inner strength as well as those who have come here before you, and you can experience the support and energy of those other women as well as your own vitality and courage even more.

Your unconscious mind has all of the knowledge and strength to guide and support you in this new adventure. I don't know how or when you will begin to notice that different experience of support and comfort. It might be today, tomorrow, or next week and your unconscious mind can utilize this experience in any way that it wishes to. There are so many possibilities and you can look forward to discovering so many new ways of feeling, hearing, and seeing comfort and support. Just as you can feel the warmth and containment of that Cape, it's nice to know you can also nurture and comfort yourself with each breath you take into your body. And wouldn't it be interesting to give your nurturing breath a color or sound of comfort. Taking a few easy breaths, experiencing that breath as it travels throughout your body, comfortably, loosening up some of those tight places, listening to the sound of your breath inside and paying attention to the rhythm of your breathing, allowing yourself to enjoy that breath comfortably.

I don't know what color or sound you might choose, it doesn't really matter but it *is* important to remember that you can experience some new ways of being and those choices are as unique and remarkable as you are. And you can take a few moments to experience that even more...as you begin on your new path of self-discovery...remembering that you have all the strength, resources, and abilities you need to help you now and in the future. That's right...and remembering as you feel the Cape around you that you also have the support of all those who have come before you.

⌘ ⌘ ⌘

SELF-PORTRAIT EXERCISE

The goal of this exercise is to assist the survivor in reclaiming her "self." Most survivors come into therapy with very little sense of self. Their identity has been eclipsed by the silence and secrecy surrounding the abuse. This exercise gives the client an opportunity to explore herself in the past and the present and also sets the stage for a future self which can be defined by her according to how she would like to be in a future that she can determine for herself.

Note: With some clients it may be helpful to initiate this task with a short relaxation exercise or guided imagery to assist significant internal images. It should also be noted that many clients worry about their artistic ability. We therefore encourage the client to draw anything that is representative of them at that time—it could be a scribble, a series of shapes or colors...any representation or symbol is okay. There is no right or wrong way to do this exercise. You can give the client the following instructions:

Step 1: Draw a portrait of yourself in the past.
Step 2: Draw a portrait or representation that best describes yourself in the present.
Step 3: Draw a portrait of or representation of how you would like to be in the future.

⌘   ⌘   ⌘

CELEBRATION EXERCISE

This exercise can be introduced in Stage One and can be continued throughout the therapeutic process to remind the survivor that she is a unique and valued individual. It is a way of helping her to acknowledge the strength and courage that brought her to this point in her healing and it can serve as a reminder on an ongoing basis to appreciate and nurture herself.

Suggest to your client at the end of each session that she take a moment and think about one way she can honor or nurture herself during the next week. It could be going for a walk, treating herself to a movie, manicure, or hot bubble bath. Anything that is significant to her.

It is helpful to then ask her to write it down on a small piece of paper that can be carried with her throughout the week as a concrete reminder of the commitment she has made to herself. It is also helpful if the therapist writes a short message of affirmation on the same piece of paper to remind her that she does deserve to nurture herself in this way.

CHAPTER 4

Stage Two: Becoming Visible

Once the secret has been unmasked and the survivor has begun to talk about her experience and break out of isolation, she must face the often disquieting experience of becoming visible. At this stage of the healing process, the survivor is usually beginning to experience feelings and behavior that have been present all along but are now manifest in new and unpredictable ways.

At this stage it is vital for the therapist to validate and honor the survivor's experience while at the same time gently introducing change by presenting some new ways of viewing and experiencing her symptoms and coping strategies, which can lead to a more flexible and less limiting frame of mind. As we pointed out in Chapter 3, it is important for the therapist to utilize the opportunities that the client presents to co-create future possibilities and solutions.

We have identified several key substages the survivor must traverse in order to continue to advance along the path to a more positive future:

    I. Prevalent Psychological and Physiological Symptoms
    II. The Healing Is in the Telling: Joining a Survivor's Group
    III. Minimizing the Abuse Experience
    IV. Realizing That It Is Okay to Feel: Some Common Coping Skills
    V. Vocalizing the Experience

Following our discussion of these substages, we will present Metaphors, Exercises, and Rituals, which will help the client reinforce and anchor the healing tasks which challenge her at this juncture.

I. PREVALENT PSYCHOLOGICAL AND
PHYSIOLOGICAL SYMPTOMS

Although every survivor is unique, we have identified some common responses that clients display at this point in the healing process. In our experience, most survivors experience a range of emotional and physical disturbances including intense panic; fear; anxiety; depression; sleep disturbances; flashbacks; suicidal gestures; self-medicating or numbing in the form of substance abuse or food intake; and feeling detached and different. There is often denial and ambivalence that re-occurs at various points. Usually there are also a variety of somatic complaints that accompany the emotional responses such as pressure in the chest; shortness of breath; choking feelings; nausea; pain in the lower abdomen; various muscle aches; cold sweats; constipation; and diarrhea. In addition, there is often a fluctuation of energy level depending on the intensity of the above symptoms and their duration.

As always it is important to note that each case is unique and that each survivor may manifest symptoms that are specific to her individual experience. Many of the aforementioned symptoms have no doubt been present on some level since the abuse began. Most of the anxiety or panic responses have probably been present since the first traumatic episode occurred. We know that the body and mind undergo sudden and complex changes in reaction to danger. Most of us are familiar with the "fight or flight" response, which has been a vital survival mechanism since the dawn of man. This response is controlled by the hypothalamus, which controls such automatic reactions as increased heart rate; muscle tension in preparation for action; increase of perspiration, saliva, and hormone production; escalation of breathing rate; and cessation of digestion so that blood can be diverted to the heart and brain.

In *Trauma and Recovery*, Herman (1992) says: "Traumatic symptoms have a tendency to become disconnected from their source and take on a life of their own" (p. 34). It is therefore little wonder that survivors experience such a range of psychological and physiological symptoms. We have found that these symptoms often escalate as the survivor begins the process of connecting these reactions to the traumatic event. This will be dealt with in more detail later in the chapter. Table 4.1 lists the effects of abuse as compiled by survivors in a Phase I group. Al-

TABLE 4.1
Effects of Abuse Listed by Survivors

- No trust
- Suspicion
- Reaction to anger
- Low self-esteem
- Taking things personally
- Isolation
- Negative self-image/talk
- Poor boundaries
- Ambivalence
- Lack of affection
- Distancing
- Lack of intimacy
- Dissociation
- Self-destructive
- Compulsive thoughts
- Obsessive
- Insecure
- Overly responsible
- Controlling
- Sexuality issues
- Expression of sexuality
- Invalidating personal gains
- Self-sabotage
- Being mute
- Inability to stand up for yourself
- Too accommodating
- Rationalizing
- Minimizing
- Judgment
- Self-conscious with body image
- Anger
- Drug use
- Numbing out by watching TV, reading
- Sexual addiction
- Negative, unhealthy relationships
- Difficulty forming any relationship
- Unassertive
- Self-hatred, no ego
- Isolation
- No healthy idea of sexuality
- Sex triggers flashbacks about abuse
- Projecting feelings onto others
- Fear of commitment
- Shame
- Guilt
- Insomnia
- Feeling of being evil
- Can't relax, feel safe
- Depression
- Secrecy
- Silence
- Overprotective of children
- Fear of rejection
- *Chronic illness*:
  - TMJ
  - Stomach problems
  - Neck problems
  - Gynecological problems
  - Difficulty focusing on work
- *Lack of intimacy with*:
  - Children
  - Partner
- Lack of healthy ways of being affectionate
- Sleep disturbance, nightmares
- No concept of what is healthy
- No positive role modelling for parenting
- Can't distinguish healthy vs. unhealthy touch
- Eating disorders
- Nail biting
- Promiscuity
- Vulnerability to repeated victimization
- No boundaries
- No knowledge of personal rights
- Extremes (tendency to react to events in an extreme manner, many experiences are interpreted as all-or-nothing situations)
- Inability to identify and express feelings

though we find it necessary to list all of these reactions, it is important to note that not all of the responses are negative ones.

II. THE HEALING IS IN THE TELLING: JOINING A SURVIVOR'S GROUP

"To recognize one's invisibility is to finally be on the path to visibility."
—*Mitsuye Yamanda*

At this stage the survivor begins to experience tremendous relief as the burden of the secret is lifted. The most powerful realization at this time can be that the client begins to see a glimmer of hope for her future. In seeking out therapy she has found an ally in healing and can begin to establish more social contact as she negotiates her way through the formidable and courageous journey ahead.

Stephen Gilligan (1993) explains incest and sexual abuse as negative rituals, which break with the community and society as a whole. The survivor is therefore forced into identification with the traumatic event: "I am the traumatic event" and "I am the victim." This identification with the trauma results in isolation from the community, the family, and, most importantly, the SELF. As we discussed in Chapter 1, life becomes very one dimensional and constricted. This was an amazing revelation to us which resulted in one of those "Aha" moments during which our positive experience in doing group therapy with survivors made perfect sense. The group process is like a positive ritual. As Gilligan points out, rituals are important events in our culture that can shift or transform one's identity or status, as in the case of marriage, graduation, bar mitzvah, or confirmation. We view group therapy as a positive ritualistic event that can reframe or alter the identity of the survivor once again. The group is in itself a marker that changes those who participate in it just by experiencing it. Therefore, the group experience can become an initiation back into the mainstream of society—a very powerful tool for the therapist and the client.

Survivors in Stage Two feel a tremendous release from the solitude they have experienced prior to disclosing the abuse. In our opinion, this is an ideal time to assess clients for attending a survivor's group. As a rule, most clients participate in up to six months of individual therapy before feeling ready to enter a group. The choice to enter must be left to the individual client. Such choices are of paramount importance to survivors, as they have had no choice in the context of the abuse and the oppressive relationship with the offender.

Some clients go into group therapy after only a few individual sessions. Quite often women who have had experience in 12-step programs find this transition an easier one than others. During individual counseling we set the stage for entering the group process by discussing the benefits and describing the topics covered. We also let clients read some of the final group evaluations (with the permission of the survivors who wrote them) so that they can understand firsthand the benefits of the group process. It has been our experience that most women are willing to give it a try. We believe that such groups, when facilitated in a caring and future-focused way, which addresses all of the key components and stages of healing, can considerably speed up the healing process. Many women come into therapy expecting the recovery to be years in length. By providing two or three phases of survivor groups, it is possible to significantly shorten the recovery process.

By telling one's personal story in the presence of other witnesses who have also experienced abuse, the survivor can further accept the reality and diminish the shame associated with her experience. As she tells her own story and listens to others' stories, it becomes evident that she is no longer alone. As Gilligan (1993) points out, "Healing rituals provide recovery from trauma and reincorporation of the dissociated person into the social-psychological community" (p. 239).

Cindy, a 26-year-old client, had been abused by several different family members from the age of 4 or 5 until she left home at age 15. Cindy had been in therapy for approximately two months when the subject of group therapy was introduced. She was initially alarmed by the idea but was agreeable to exploring the topic.

In a subsequent session, she related a dream she had had. Cindy told of speaking to her mother who had died when she was 7 years old. In the dream Cindy's mother told her that she was not responsible for her mother's death (her father repeatedly told her she was responsible for her mother's death). After this dream was discussed in the next therapy session, Cindy was able to disclose a fear that she had been harboring most of her life; she felt that part of her was evil and she lived in terror of her evil nature being exposed. Cindy also felt that she might "infect" other members of the group if she joined it.

In the next session, hypnosis was used to help Cindy imagine what it would be like to be accepted by others in a group setting. She was asked to picture herself being accepted by the other members. She was led through an imagery in which she listened to them welcoming her and she was then encouraged to ask her unconscious mind what words she needed to hear in order to be accepted. On reorienting back to the present, Cindy was able to tell us that she needed to be accepted for who she was even though she still felt she was not a very lovable person.

Cindy joined a survivor group a month later and was able to relay this story in the first session. She was overwhelmed by the support and validation she received during that group and it proved to be a definite turning point in her recovery.

We have found it most beneficial to initiate each opening session of a survivor group with a group induction. This can set the stage for new learning as well as ease many of the fears associated with this new experience. An example of such an induction can be found at the end of this chapter. This can quickly help to facilitate group cohesion, as the members immediately experience something collectively and discuss their response or lack of response. In his book, *Therapeutic Trances*, Gilligan (1987) observes the advantages of group induction: "...the many different experiences reported by group participants expands a person's viewpoint about how trances can be developed and beneficially utilized. More generally, such reports demonstrate dramatically that people think and respond in many different ways, all of which can be valid" (p. 334).

Some therapists may not feel comfortable using formal hypnosis to further group work. It is often just as effective to tell an anecdote or to relay an experience that parallels the group topic in some way .

It is important for the therapist, as a facilitator, to be flexible and open to the fact that some members may not care to partake in some of the exercises. We always give clients a choice to participate in any of the planned group tasks. In our opinion, the client picks up valuable information just by being present in the room—by being privy to the discussion of others' experiences that takes place during any given activity. Experience has shown us that most members eventually participate in group exercises, albeit with trepidation, but when given a choice, they usually include themselves in the activities. Each group takes on its own culture; some are easier to facilitate than others, but the support of peers that is offered in the group context cannot be duplicated elsewhere.

The experience of testing out new ways of relating to others in a safe environment is an experience that most survivors have been deprived of since childhood. This results in arrested social development. The group process can therefore help the survivor catch up developmentally on stages that were missed in childhood.

> Karen, a 30-year-old survivor of incest, who presented in a very shy and self-effacing manner, disclosed to the group her recurring nightmare in which her mouth had been sewn shut by her father. Even though she repeatedly tried to take out the stitches, the threads were indestructible. After some discussion, the facilitator asked Karen what it would be like for her to read out loud a poem she had written about her experience as a survivor. Karen blushed but agreed to read her poem to the group. Karen was clearly moved by the very positive support and feedback she received. The following week Karen reported to the group that she had had the dream again, but this time she was able to dislodge the threads from her mouth and cry out for help. During stressful periods, Karen sometimes still has her recurring dream; however, the new ending has persisted. She has also come to realize that the dream is her own signal that indicates that there are some underlying issues that need to be expressed or verbalized. The group has proven to be a place where Karen can feel safe airing these concerns in an environment that is accepting and encouraging.

We are continually awed by the dynamic environment that is created when women who have never had the experience of speaking out about their background, fears, emotional life, and dreams are able to come together as peers and help each other through the healing process.

At the end of one of our survivor groups, a participant said it more eloquently than we ever could: "We have made peace with the ghosts that have been haunting our lives, we have attained peace within ourselves, and we have opened the doors to the future."

III. MINIMIZING THE ABUSE EXPERIENCE

The survivor's own minimization of the sexual abuse experience is one of the most persistent effects of abuse and one which continues to surface throughout the first three stages of recovery. As the reality of the abuse solidifies, it can become extremely overwhelming. There is often a struggle with the self to accept the abuse as reality or to minimize it and blame the self for not stopping it or for allowing it to happen in the first place.

This minimization of experience is closely related to the tactics of the offender and the views that unfortunately are still prevalent in our society (i.e., the victim is somehow responsible for the abuse or has "asked for it").

The offender generally has projected blame for the abuse onto the victim and uses statements such as "She liked it" and "She was being very seductive." Perpetrators also make statements such as "I was very gentle—it didn't hurt her" or "We had a very special, caring relationship" or "I only fondled her a few times—it was pretty harmless stuff."

Most survivors retain these messages from early childhood. They live on in internal dialogues or as auditory loops that replay over and over again in the survivor's mind. Once this negative self-talk is identified, the therapist can help the survivor counteract these persistent thoughts and replace them with more accurate and self-supporting messages.

Jennifer, a 28-year-old woman who had been abused by multiple offenders, came in for therapy after switching therapists several times. She spoke of hearing voices during sporadic periods of dissociation and had been on medication that she discontinued due to the many side effects she experienced. When Jennifer was asked about when the voices were heard, she reported that it always happened at night and only when she was alone in her apartment. In taking some background information about the voices, the therapist established that they said things such as, "You are dirty and evil and only good for one thing" and "You don't deserve to be alive" and "You are always luring me into your room." These voices were eventually connected to statements made by Jennifer's first offender when she was very young. She also reported that the abuse had always taken place at night after her mother left for work.

The therapist guided Jennifer into an hypnotic trance and via the use of ideomotor finger signals elicited answers to co-created questions such as, "Can you take some time to consider when and how you first became aware of those messages?" "Are you aware of anyone in your past who has made statements like those you just described?" Jennifer was then asked if her unconscious mind was ready and willing to try some exercises to exorcise the voices from her once and for all. Jennifer was given an exercise and agreed to do it whenever she was alone in her apartment or whenever she began to hear the voices. Please see the exercise and accompanying ritual at the end of this chapter entitled "An Exercise for Reframing Critical Voices or Messages."

After several months of practicing positive self-talk, as well as using some relaxation exercises, guided imagery, and metaphorical stories concerning self-image, Jennifer ceased to hear the voices and felt ready to enter one of our groups where she continued to progress and experience a new sense of freedom.

Hearing others' stories in a group setting can sometimes result in a comparison of a survivor's own experience as being "not as bad" as someone else's. This can often bring to the surface those critical messages once again as the client struggles to believe she was not responsible for the abuse. This is an excellent opportunity for the therapist to help her reframe, via metaphor, those negative minimizing statements and therefore put them into perspective.

Elisabeth, the 42-year-old client who was mentioned in Chapter 3, was struggling with the reality of her quickly returning memory (cognitive and visceral) and was having a very difficult time socially. Although she didn't want to be alone, she found it equally hard to be around others. When the topic of joining a group came up, Elisabeth was torn. Although she longed to speak about the abuse to someone other than her therapist, she felt that she might be "taking up the space of someone who needed the group more than I do." Since the metaphorical stories we had been collaborating on had worked so well with Elisabeth previously, the story of "Hush" was once again utilized to encompass many of the emerging fears, feelings, and coping skills that Elisabeth was facing. As before, Elisabeth found this story to be helpful, and since it was taped she could listen to it whenever the need arose. Please refer to the end of the chapter for "Hush—Part Two."

IV. REALIZING THAT IT IS OKAY TO FEEL: SOME COMMON COPING SKILLS

The positive outcome of minimization is that although the details of sexual abuse may be different for each survivor, overall, the residual feelings and effects each person is left with are quite similar. At this juncture, the group members can begin to connect more meaningfully with one another, with each member reinforcing the other, so that the need to minimize one's own experience of abuse becomes an historical stage that the survivor passes through and necessarily rests at for a while; when she is ready, she can then move forward into encountering and connecting with her feelings in the present, allowing her to move, eventually, in a future-oriented direction.

In the present, the survivor often faces the struggle to find effective methods of coping with the feelings that are desperately trying to find some means, some outlet, for expression. Again, the survivor may dip back into the past to search for historical methods of coping with her often overwhelming feelings. The work here is for the therapist to help the client normalize such coping mechanisms as dissociation, flashbacks, nightmares, anxiety attacks, hypervigilance, numbing, and self-mutilation by making it clear that these mechanisms are and were necessary methods of dealing with the abuse, which allowed the client to survive. Then the therapist and client can seek to reframe them. *A word of caution here:* it is critical that we as therapists honor whatever coping mechanisms the client has employed in order to survive, until she is fully aware of what they are, how she has used them in the past and present, and what she can replace them with—a practice that the writers utilize throughout the healing process, that is, assisting the survivor, when ready, to connect with more viable alternatives.

Dissociation

Dissociation is a coping mechanism that can assist the survivor in stepping outside her body, sometimes for hours at a time, to become a distant observer of her emerging feelings and experiences. The therapist here has a wonderful opportunity to reframe the dissociation, as Lankton (1979) describes in his work with a female survivor of childhood trauma: "The dissociations allowed her to make more adequate use of the information and wisdom of her early family life without the danger of being overwhelmed by the intense feelings and misinformation that the memories contained" (p. 11). It is key for the therapist to assist the survivor in creating a comfortable distance from her feelings, particularly when she is encountering them for the first time.

One such client, Daphne, a 48-year-old woman who had been sexually abused by her father, brother, and uncle as a child and had been diagnosed with chronic depression by her previous therapist, connected with a sense of her own readiness to express her feelings for the first time in her life, following many years of dissociating them, which resulted in several serious suicide attempts. Once she felt ready to express herself, she was not quite sure what sort of outlet she would employ to externalize her feelings.

Several months later, Daphne walked energetically into the therapist's office, proudly describing the methods she had utilized to unleash her emotions. As her apartment had badly needed painting, she purchased three buckets of paint: one color was fire-engine red, the color of her anger; the second, midnight blue, the color of her despair; and the third, canary yellow, the color of her shame. She then described how she took hold of each of the buckets of paint, throwing them, smearing them, and splashing them against the apartment walls, connecting with her energy and the sheer exhilaration of just being able to let go of the angry, despairing, and shameful feelings she had stuffed down and internalized for so long. Later on in the course of her therapy, when she felt ready, Daphne was able to repaint her walls with the colors of hope, self-acceptance, and self-respect. This process allowed Daphne to make a significant shift in her healing work, where she was able to begin to retrieve the lost memories that she had previously been too terrified to recall.

Flashbacks

Flashbacks are fragments of memory that can return to the survivor at any time and usually do not contain a complete visual, kinesthetic, and auditory picture. These memory flashes are often experienced as quite frightening and disconcerting, particularly for the client who has recalled little of her past trauma up until this point. We assist the survivor in imagining each flashback as a missing piece to a very large jigsaw puzzle; over time, when she is ready to remember, each piece will eventually float up from the unconscious mind to surface in the conscious mind, so that ultimately a full picture/memory can be pieced together. Please note that it is not always necessary for the survivor to remember every single detail of her abuse in order to heal. She will remember the parts of the trauma that are key to her healing process, and you as her therapist need to provide her with this important reassurance.

Nightmares

Another coping mechanism employed by the survivor are nightmares, that is, dreams that the unconscious mind often provides as a clue to the upcoming emergence of new memories or as a response to past trauma. In order to cope with these newly emerging memories, a method we have found useful is to encourage the client to draw her nightmare, superimposing any creature, object, person, or part of herself to assist her in transforming the feared outcome.

Jillian, a 25-year-old survivor of ongoing sexual abuse by multiple offenders, had a recurrent dream that she was being pursued by creatures with masks covering their faces, holding sharp knives, who were
about to murder her as she fell to the floor—unable to run any further. With the support of the healer, Jillian was able to superimpose,
with colored pencils on paper, her adult self protecting the cowering
child from the murderous knives of the hooded creatures, thereby,
providing her with an opportunity to change the outcome of the nightmare. In empowering herself on paper, Jillian was able to overcome
her fears around disclosing the secret, freeing her to begin to connect with the emerging memories. In addition, once she was able to
bring her adult self into the picture, her nightmare transformed into
a dream that included the adult self, who could begin to make herself
available to protect the fearful child.

Anxiety/Panic Attacks

Anxiety/panic attacks often occur when a traumatic memory may be
surfacing from the unconscious mind. Once the memory makes its way
into the conscious mind, the survivor may desperately try to dissociate
it—stuffing it back down so that she can avoid remembering, resulting
in feelings of panic and anxiety that can gravely impact on her life—
causing her to sometimes quit her job and avoid her friends—unable
to leave the confines of her home, causing further isolation from the
outside world.

The therapist can assist the client in getting her life back into perspective, by learning to cope with the panic attacks in such a way that
she can overcome the feeling that her anxiety is controlling her. A very
simple method of accomplishing this is to encourage the client to
breathe deeply when she first encounters the feelings of panic and anxiety, so that she can feel okay about allowing the memory to emerge,
breathing through it, and then letting go of it, until she is personally
ready to deal with whatever she previously attempted to dissociate from.
For a more detailed account of relaxation techniques, refer to Chapter
2 of this book.

Hypervigilance

Another coping skill that the survivor may have employed to deal
with her emerging feelings is hypervigilance, that is, the constant watch-

fulness and anticipation of potential warning signals in her environment, alerting her to the possibility of future abusive episodes. Here, the therapist has an opportunity to assist the survivor in transforming the skill that it took to be hypervigilant to anticipate self-abilities that can function as useful tools for future planning. In addition, from a career perspective, the survivor can begin to develop and transform hypervigilance into such highly valued skills, for example, as predicting and anticipating future outcomes in business.

Numbing

Numbing behavior is a coping strategy that often begins in adolescence with the use of food, drugs, and/or alcohol to anesthetize the intense emotional pain of dealing with and remembering the sexual abuse. While in the process of numbing, the survivor often becomes frozen in the trauma, where she is temporarily trapped. Once she replaces her addictive behavior with healthier coping methods, however, she can then permit herself to consciously control the painful memories by distancing and dissociation. When the survivor is able to overcome these addictions, she can then, with the assistance of the therapist, be encouraged to call on her innate abilities to control/numb the pain for a while, until she is truly ready to cope with the feelings connected to the surfacing memories.

Self-Mutilation

Self-mutilation, a coping skill sometimes utilized by sexual abuse survivors, initially may be perceived—particularly by less experienced therapists—as a suicide attempt. However, often we find that a self-induced cut, slash, and/or burn on the arm, leg, or other part(s) of the body is an attempt to survive and express the pain. These painful feelings are often so dissociated from the survivor that she struggles to make the intangible tangible—with self-mutilation she can actually see her pain, maybe even dares to feel it for the first time in her life. As a result, each scar comes to symbolize one more abuse memory she survived, for every scar represents what we view as a badge of courage.

A 42-year-old client, Sheila, began cutting and burning small sections of her arms when she began to retrieve the lost parts of her memory regarding her stepfather's ongoing sexually abusive behavior that began early on in her childhood. During the process of her recovery, Sheila reached a stage where she was becoming increasingly aware of her need to cover up her arms with long-sleeved clothing.

This awareness became particularly poignant when she traveled on vacation by herself to the Caribbean and went into crisis during the time she was there, connecting with the realization that she was too ashamed to wear a bathing suit and risk revealing her scars in public. Sheila ultimately decided to return home early—her self-mutilating behavior had become more intensified and more aggressive than before.

During a therapy session soon after her return, she connected with feelings of being out of control. The metaphorical healing story "Alisa's Badge of Courage" and subsequent ritual found at the end of this chapter assisted in transforming Sheila's out-of-control feelings to a sense of pride over surviving the abuse. This particular metaphorical story and subsequent ritual (to assist in anchoring the leanings and transformations from the metaphor) was co-created by Sheila and her therapist in order to make it as personally relevant as possible. Following a number of weeks of listening to the story (that had been taped by the therapist during one of Sheila's sessions), and incorporating the ritual into a daily part of her routine, Sheila's self-mutilating behavior gradually began to subside, and the feelings that she had always felt extremely fearful about expressing began to slowly surface. This process assisted Sheila in reintegrating and retrieving the lost feelings in a way that was respectful of the pace she personally needed to set for herself, in order to replace the self-mutilating behavior with new healthy coping mechanisms.

V. VOCALIZING THE EXPERIENCE

In speaking openly about the abuse, the client may begin to identify and to externalize her feelings, resulting in a newly found ability to unpack and unstuff them after being out of her awareness for so long. As clearly evidenced in the previous case example, it is empowering for survivors to co-create metaphors, rituals, and exercises with the therapist, which can then be personally tailored to suit individual needs.

Debbie, a 30-year-old single parent who had been sexually abused by her father, and who was in the process of reestablishing a more positive relationship with her mother, co-created in conjunction with her therapist, the metaphorical story, "Clara's New Suitcase" and its subsequent exercise found at the end of this chapter. The significance of the suitcase metaphor was that the client had recently received a gift of a set of luggage from her mother, so this was a key transitional point in her recovery process.

In Stage Two of the healing process it is vital to assist the client in maintaining a future focus, rather than becoming stuck in the trauma of the surfacing feelings. Creating future memories is another important task now, as a way of instilling hope and planting the seed and therefore reminding the survivor that she has the ability to make a profound difference in her own life. Helping the client visualize the self in the future, where she can consider where she would like to be, and then send herself a postcard from that place, is an exercise that can greatly benefit the survivor at this stage (see "Checking in with the Future Self" exercise in the Metaphors, Exercises, and Rituals section of this chapter).

The resourcefulness of the survivor and her unconscious to co-create meaningful metaphors with the healer, when given the support and opportunity in therapy to do so, is amazing. The writers are continually astounded by the ability of the human psyche to heal and regenerate, if the seed of hope is planted appropriately.

METAPHORS, EXERCISES, AND RITUALS

GROUP INDUCTION METAPHOR

The purpose of this induction is to introduce the members of the group to the experience of community, choice, and freedom to explore and to speak about their experience in a way that is nonjudgmental and supportive. Since they may never have had any freedom to make decisions or choices for themselves, it is important to lay the groundwork for the possibilities of life without the constrictions they have heretofore experienced.

The by-product of this type of activity is that it immediately gives each

*member a common experience to draw from and to discuss with one another—
a metaphor for things to come. This can also be adapted for use with individual clients at the beginning of therapy or to begin to acquaint a client with
the idea of being in a group.*

A S WE BEGIN THE FIRST SESSION of our journey together, I'm
wondering what it would be like for you to just sit back for a
moment, feeling free to adjust any way you need to, and to take some
nice easy breaths as deeply as you can. Allow yourself to be in tune with
the natural rhythm of your own breathing, listening to the sounds inside as you breathe as deeply and as comfortably as possible. Wouldn't
it be interesting to think back to the last time you felt even a little bit
relaxed? It could have been while reading a book or watching a movie
or perhaps sitting on the beach feeling the warmth of the sun or hearing the sound of the water soothe your senses.

Just take a few moments and enjoy the possibilities that are now available to you as you enter into this experience together. If you don't feel
like participating, you can simply be here, doing whatever it is you are
doing in any way you like. Just as you can pay attention to the rhythm of
your own breathing, it is important for you to also pay attention to your
own timing and pace while participating in this group. Just as there is
no right or wrong way to go into a trance, there is no right or wrong way
to enter into your own healing process. Only you can know what is
valuable for you to integrate into your unique experience.

Your unconscious mind knows more about you than you may realize,
and whatever way you choose to participate, it is important to remember that you now have the freedom to say and express things that you
may not have said or felt before. You may even express or say things
that you do not yet understand or fully believe. But it is important to
remember that this is a place to explore, play, experience, remember,
or forget—a place to witness the past, present, and future together in
an environment of safety, understanding, and support without judgments
or criticism. This is a place to uncover all of the strength and resources
which you have been utilizing all of your life and to appreciate all of the
amazing courage and coping skills you possess. Your unconscious mind
can help you discover some new ways of utilizing those skills in a different way that is more satisfying and comfortable for you now.

We invite and encourage you to gather together and wander and
wonder through the next few months, collecting some new thoughts,
skills, ideas, and memories that can be employed in countless ways to
apply to your life now and in the future in any way you choose.... That's

right, even more creatively…even more uniquely…with a deep sense of self-appreciation and wonder for all that you are. Take a moment of clock time, all the time you need, and once again be in touch with your own breathing, and when you are ready, gradually reorient back to the room, perhaps ready to greet and witness the other women in the room in a way that is comforting and connecting to you.

⌘   ⌘   ⌘

EXERCISE FOR REFRAMING CRITICAL VOICES OR MESSAGES

As we discussed earlier in this chapter, the replaying of critical statements and messages over and over in a survivor's mind is often one of the most difficult patterns to interrupt. This ongoing internal dialogue is often a lasting effect of the offender's minimizing statements, combined with the child's attempt to rationalize and take on blame for the abuse as a means of making sense of her reality. Many survivors have also endured physical and emotional abuse which further complicates the cycle of self-blame. These internal dialogues or tapes serve to maintain the silence and isolation by constantly playing on in her mind and interfering with her ability to seek out positive relationships with others, which could help her to gain confidence and independence.

The purpose of this exercise and its accompanying ritual is to help reframe and externalize these judgmental and negative thoughts so that the survivor can begin to reframe her self-image and to decrease the anxiety and stress that these critical thoughts help to perpetuate both psychologically and physiologically.

1. The first step in this reframing process is to identify the recurring problematic messages. This can be done by asking the client to identify and record her most intrusive and disturbing critical thoughts and blaming statements. Some common examples are the following:

- "If anyone really knew how bad I am inside, they wouldn't like me."
- "If I weren't such an evil person, none of this would be happening to me."
- "I can't imagine what it would be like to feel different; I can't remember when I ever felt good."

It is often helpful to access these messages while the client is in a light trance. The therapist can ask the client what critical messages she is hearing. The therapist can then further verify that these are troublesome messages, which the survivor would like to be free from by checking with the unconscious via ideomotor signalling (see explanation in Chapter 2), and see if she is ready to replace these old negative messages with some new more positive and forgiving ones.

Respecting the client's timing is very important at this point. It often takes time for the client to be ready to let go of this old dialogue. This is why we recommend the validating experience of asking the unconscious mind if these old patterns are ready to be altered. With practice, the use of ideomotor signalling can be a useful tool throughout the healing process. Its employment can serve as an inner guide for the client so that she can begin to depend on and utilize herself more and more, with the end result being a stronger sense of "self" and trust in her own decision-making capabilities and processes.

2. Once the problematic messages are identified, the client and the therapist need to co-create some alternative, gentler, more constructive messages. It is very important that the survivor have some clearly identified alternate messages with which to replace the old ones before trying to banish the former. We always point out to the client that although these old messages have been stressful and hurtful, they have been part of a familiar pattern of self-communication and it is vital for her to be ready to let go of these old voices. But it is also equally important for her to hold onto them until some new messages are ready to take their place. This reframing process can also begin to help her experience having some choice and control over her life.

The client and the therapist together can brainstorm some possible alternate messages. One helpful technique at this stage is for the therapist to ask the client to think of someone she highly regards—this could be an aunt, teacher, grandparent, pet, or some imagined benevolent person. Ask (during trance or just in conversation) the survivor to imagine overhearing a conversation during which that person speaks in a complimentary way about her. What sorts of things would she like to hear that person say?

3. The therapist can then take some of these new statements and with the client co-create a letter of appreciation to the survivor, encompassing some of these new messages and attitudes.

4. The therapist can then assist the survivor in making a tape of this letter of appreciation to be listened to as frequently as possible—especially when the client is experiencing critical voices or internal dialogue during the many difficult periods of transition along the road to recovery.

Some clients prefer the therapist to read the self-appreciation letter on tape, and although we honor this request, we also encourage the survivor to eventually record this message in her own voice so that her own positive messages can gradually overcome the old critical voices (which usually originated from the voices of offenders and critical parents or caretakers).

⌘   ⌘   ⌘

REFRAMING RITUAL FOR RECLAIMING THE INNER VOICE

The following is a ritual the survivor can perform regularly to help establish and practice new coping strategies with regard to more positive self-talk, thereby reinforcing a kinder more accepting inner voice. We recommend that this first be carried out in the presence of the therapist who can act initially as a coach and a witness to this new ritual.

S T A R—is a helpful way to remember and practice the new ways of counteracting old inner voices and reframing them with the new, alternative messages that have been co-created with the therapist.

S—*Sense the feelings of anxiety* that accompany and are often a clue that negative self-talk is occurring, and pause for a moment, taking a deep breath.

T—*Think about the old messages playing out* in your mind, examine the feelings, images, and critical statements such as "I am no good," "I can't do anything right," "I'll never be able to...."

A—*Alter self-talk* by replacing the old messages with those new ones that have been co-created in the previous exercise for reframing critical voices or messages. For example, when I hear those old messages I can tell myself _____ instead.

R—*Reframe and Relax.* When I tell myself [fill in new messages], I can take a deep breath and hear and feel [fill in those new messages and images], noticing where in my body I experience the tension of those old ways and releasing that tension on every exhale. I can breathe in and nurture my body with a different sense of appreciation for my strength and [name positive qualities] that I possess to help me reach my goals for the future.

⌘　　⌘　　⌘

"HUSH—PART TWO"

As previously stated, the story of Hush was co-created with a particular client in mind. However, it encompasses many of the key issues and characteristics of the emotions that many survivors face at this stage of the healing process. It is always helpful to begin any metaphorical story with a brief relaxation induction, which most clients find soothing and enjoyable.
This or any of the metaphors and exercises can be modified to suit the individual needs of the client. For example, we have substituted other animals, locations, and specifically troublesome coping mechanisms to help make each metaphor as personally relevant as possible.

HUSH HAD BEEN VERY BUSY preparing for her journey to the other side of the mountains where Kit told her there was a whole community of lynx. She and Kit had had many long talks about what it would be like to travel on her own through the mountains and the forest to that other place. When she was finally ready to depart, Kit gave her a special going away gift, a backpack filled with some very important tools and resources that she could utilize along the way. Kit also gave Hush a map that she had carefully and lovingly made herself. On the map was the name and address of another medicine lion who was a friend of Kit's and who would help and encourage Hush on her journey.

Well, the time had come and Hush and the cubs exchanged tearful goodbyes. Kit handed the backpack to Hush and told her that she would think of her at sundown each day and that as long as she could keep a tight grip on her bag of resources, she knew Hush would make it to her destination. With one final hug, Hush was off. She was so petrified that she could barely put one paw in front of the other.

Hush's first night alone was the most terrifying of all. She had a flashback of that time when the wolves had raided Kit's den, and it flooded her with a variety of feelings she hadn't experienced for a few months.

She was nauseous and paralyzed and even though she was exhausted she couldn't sleep; everything she was afraid of kept going around and around in her mind. Gradually, that old numb feeling began to take hold and it was as though she was watching herself from a distance.

Hush tried to remember what her Aunt Kit used to tell her when she felt like that before—it was something about taking slow, deep breaths and feeling the earth under her paws. As she was remembering to take those deep breaths, she gradually felt her tremulous heart slow down and soon she wasn't feeling quite as foggy. She then remembered that she was holding on for dear life to her precious backpack. She opened it up and began to sort through its contents. The first item she came across was her cherished mask. That mask had helped her through some arduous times, so Hush put on her mask once more to help her connect with the courage and resourcefulness that Kit kept telling her was down there somewhere inside of her just waiting to be set free. Hush's mask was beautifully crafted from the wood of an arbutus tree. It had a dauntless expression that was also very wise and benevolent, with a touch of mischief and humor. It was beautifully painted with all of Hush's favorite colors. It immediately helped her feel more safe and soon she was able to fall into a much needed deep sleep.

The next morning Hush woke ready to once again continue her journey. She studied Kit's map (no easy task) and it took her deep into the forest where she came to a crossroads that did not seem to be on the map. A sense of panic overcame Hush as she told herself how stupid and worthless she was. She couldn't even read a map correctly. Once again it seemed she had caused her own demise with all of those old critical messages that were going around in her mind: "I don't deserve to reach my destination." That old badness inside of her was finally coming out—she knew it would happen sooner or later. She had managed to fool Kit for a while, but the real Hush was this evil and pitiful lost creature.

Hush began to panic and for a fleeting moment she considered giving up. She was so tired of what seemed like an endless journey she had been on for as long as she could remember. When was she ever going to feel better? Why was every day consumed with this futile struggle to feel and to be different? She just wanted to scream, but try as she did, nothing would come out. She couldn't even do that right. Every sound and movement around her seemed exaggerated and startled and unnerved her. Hush sat down on the forest floor in a frozen state that must have lasted for quite some time.

The sun was about to set when a beautiful butterfly landed on Hush's backpack. Even that soft fluttering motion jolted Hush. But the butterfly just sat there calmly as though she was deliberately trying to catch Hush's attention. Hush watched the butterfly for quite some time. It was as though she was trying to communicate something to Hush. It was almost sunset and for a moment Hush thought she heard the butterfly speak to her. It was her Aunt Kit's voice telling her to trust herself and her ability to get where she needed to go. There was help available: she just needed to keep in touch with what was inside so she could make it on the outside. Hush reached for her backpack and the first item she touched was once again her mask. She put it on, while the butterfly looked on, and she decided to wear her mask all night for protection. The gentle butterfly also stayed with her that night and just before she fell asleep, she once again thought she heard her aunt's voice reassuring her that she would find her way the next morning: "Try again" were the last words she heard before falling asleep.

Sure enough, the sun came up the next morning and Hush had made it through another night. Her first image that bright morning was of the butterfly who had kept her company all night. She seemed to be fluttering back and forth in a particular direction as though she was trying to guide Hush out of the forest. So Hush followed her and eventually came to a path that led her out of the woods. What a relief. For the first time since she left Kit's, Hush was able to enjoy her surroundings. She breathed in the fresh air and enjoyed the soft breeze as it ruffled her fur. There was a scent of autumn in the air and she noticed some of the bright leaves beginning to change color. As she came to a clearing, she was once again able to recognize some of the markers that were on her map; ahead in the distance, her keen ears detected the small community in the foothills where Kit's friend, Eidolon the medicine lion, lived. The butterfly circled around Hush as if to say farewell and then drifted away, carried by the fresh breeze up into the foothills.

Part of Hush was very excited with the prospect of meeting her aunt's friend, but she still had that old foreboding that she might not be accepted and indeed, that she was not worthy of acceptance. Hush climbed the final hill on top of which was the tiny community headed by Eidolon. At first she hung back and just observed the small village; her heart was beating too quickly and she remembered to take some slow comfortable breaths to help center herself. Just then a very wise looking old lioness walked up to her and introduced herself as Eidolon. "You must be Hush," she said. "We have been waiting for you; welcome."

She led Hush to her cozy, warm den and introduced her to three others who were also passing through this place on their way to the other side of the mountain. There was another lynx named Crystal, a small mountain lion named Raye, and an ocelot named Dot. At first they were too shy to introduce themselves, but the elder mountain lion began by introducing Hush and by asking each of the others to reciprocate by saying a little bit about themselves. Raye was the first to break the silence and told of how she had lived in many foster homes since the death of her mother, and she spoke of all of the sadness and cruel treatment that she had lived with until she ran away and was taken in by Eidolon. Raye said she found it very hard to trust anyone and she wasn't even sure if Eidolon's den was a safe place for her to be, but she had nowhere else to go, so she was still weighing her options. Crystal, like Hush, had been left to fend for herself at a very young age. She had been blamed by her relatives for the demise of her family and had wandered around the mountains surviving the best she could. She was easy prey for other animals who took advantage of her innocence and vulnerability. Dot was a bit older than the others and had a difficult time looking directly at anyone else when she spoke; she had a very tiny voice and told of being the runt of the litter and how she was always picked on both physically and emotionally until she too had to run away. Apparently, Eidolon the medicine lion had quite a reputation in the mountains for taking in and helping those who were lost and needed some guidance and support to begin a new life.

It was Hush's turn to speak, but try as she did, the words would not come. Eidolon reassured Hush that it was quite natural for her to be nervous about sharing her story with the others, but when she felt ready, it would be received without judgment. This was a great relief to Hush, who felt quite overwhelmed by the events of the last few days. Each of the others also reassured Hush to take her time, and she thanked them and withdrew to her corner of the den where she could unpack her things and settle in for the night.

That night Hush had a nightmare of being chased again by wolves and awoke to the soothing voice of the medicine lion who told her that she would eventually feel safer and better able to verbalize and sort through all of the confusing feelings she had buried deep within. "You needn't feel ashamed or guilty about your past life or of all of those feelings and secrets you are holding onto so tightly; there are others too who have experienced many of the same circumstances and we can all help one another to reach a clearer understanding of that turmoil within." This was a huge relief to Hush; even though she was still doubtful, she promised herself she would give it a try. After all, she'd thought she would never be able to become fully visible—but she had with persistence and the help and belief of Kit.

The next day marked the beginning of a whole new way of life for Hush. She began the day by warily saying good morning to the others and watching carefully for their response. Dot, Raye, and Crystal all said good morning back to her and invited her to join them as they went down to the pond for some fresh drinking water. During the next few weeks as the group became better acquainted, Hush began to realize that even when she told the others about her experience, she was still accepted by them, and even though some of their stories were different, they all shared many common feelings and needs. For the first time in her life, Hush was beginning to feel that she belonged somewhere and that there were others that she could tell her secrets to who truly understood and still accepted her. For the first time, she had friends.

(To be continued)

And you can take a few moments to integrate this information in any way that fits for you (*pause*).

It's nice to know that you can begin to be aware of your own inner voice that can help guide you in a direction that is relevant for you.

And you can appreciate even more the skills, resources, and strengths that you possess, which can help you be more in tune with your inner self even more comfortably and even more naturally now and in the days and weeks to come.

⌘   ⌘   ⌘

"ALISA'S BADGE OF COURAGE"

The following metaphorical story can be used to assist the survivor in containing the often overwhelming feelings that arise when abuse memories begin to resurface or surface, perhaps for the first time. The message to the survivor here is that she can make a collection of her feelings and hold them in a small container, and that when she is ready to be in a certain feeling, that she can open the wooden/glass/cardboard box and allow herself to be in the feeling for however long a period of time she chooses.

The key message to the survivor is that when she connects with certain

feelings, it is her choice as to the amount of time she allows herself to experi-
ence that feeling or those particular feelings and, when ready, she can place
the feeling(s) back into the box and contain it, until such time that she is
ready to connect with that feeling or those feelings again. Although the fol-
lowing metaphor was designed for a survivor who was self-mutilating, this
story can be used with survivors in general who are at the stage of their heal-
ing where they are initially connecting with the kinesthetic/feeling part of the
abuse memory.

I'M WONDERING AS YOU ARE SITTING THERE, if you
can imagine what it would be like to be in trance? Do you recall a
time in which you could see yourself embroidering a design that you
had created completely by yourself? And that when you were in the process of creating that design you were completely absorbed, and all of
the worries of your conscious mind were temporarily distracted and
you could just enjoy seeing the results of your efforts that you created
on the cloth? That's right.

And as you are sitting there listening to the sound of my voice outside, you can also hear the sound of your own breath inside, that's right,
becoming aware of your breath as you feel the comfortable support of
the cushions beneath you. It's nice to know that you are supported by
those soft pillows. Everyone likes to feel supported. And that you can
simply be there any way that is comfortable for you [*presupposing comfort*], while your conscious mind can listen to this story about a young
girl called Alisa.

Alisa was a quiet young girl who spent a great deal of time on her own
playing and imagining herself as a fairy princess being rescued by a
handsome prince, and at other times, as a fire-breathing dragon successfully fighting the enemy, and sometimes she even imagined herself
as a wise owl, knowing everything that there was to know, so she could
help others who needed her counsel and advice.

Alisa lived with her mother and stepfather in a small house overlook-
ing the forest. Often Alisa's stepfather, who had married her mother
after her father died, would discipline Alisa with a stick if she expressed
her feelings strongly, often leaving bruises and sometimes welts on her
arms and legs that would take some time to heal. Whether she felt
happy, sad, or angry feelings, Alisa learned after a while to keep her
feelings locked deep inside herself where no one, sometimes not even
herself, could find them.

Now, it just so happened that Alisa's 10th birthday was drawing near,
and like every year since her father died, there was no talk or plan to

celebrate her day of birth by either her mother or stepfather. On the day of her birthday, Alisa awoke to the sound of a knock on the front door, and when she opened the door, she found a beautifully wrapped gift on the porch step addressed to her! Alisa eagerly unwrapped the gift, finding inside a beautiful little wooden box that contained many colors of embroidery thread and embroidery needles. Alisa was filled with joy as she read the note attached to the gift from an elderly woman called Belinda who lived close by, with whom Alisa visited on fairly regular occasions on her way home from school. The note contained an invitation from Belinda offering embroidery lessons to Alisa if she was interested. Alisa felt happy and excited at the opportunity to learn embroidery, for she had always admired the beautifully handstitched cushions and quilts that Belinda had proudly displayed in her home. Now, thought Alisa, she too could create beautiful patterns and pictures out of the rainbow of colors of thread that her neighbor had given her.

The very next day after school, Alisa called on Belinda, thanking her for the beautiful birthday gift and expressing her interest in learning how to create the exquisite stitches she had seen on display in Belinda's home. It just so happened that Belinda had some free time right then and there to begin to help Alisa create her own patterns and pictures. And so each day after school was over, Alisa spent a few hours with Belinda learning such stitches as the running, cross, and blanket stitch. It meant so much to Alisa to hear Belinda's encouraging words saying to her, "You can do it Alisa, just be patient and learn at your own pace, and when you are ready, in time, you too will be able to create beautiful embroidery designs of your own."

Alisa soaked up Belinda's supportive, loving words like a sponge, and just before she went to sleep at night, her thoughts would be filled with Belinda's kind voice, lulling her into a deep, restful sleep, that's right. After some time, Alisa began to connect with her own embroidery style, and so each time she removed the piece of cloth (that she happened to be working on at the time) from its small wooden box, she would select a color and stitch that would match and express the particular mood that she was experiencing at the time. Sometimes her stitches would be large bold ones in red, hothouse pink, and in a brilliant orange hue, and she would splash them dramatically with her embroidery needle on the cloth canvas. On other days, Alisa's stitches were finer and covered a smaller, more confined section of the cloth, where she would usually choose blue, green, or purple-toned thread to match her mood at the time.

Alisa would set a goal for herself as to how much of the design she would work on each day, and when she completed that portion, she would carefully fold the cloth so that it fit inside the small wooden box—placing that container in a drawer that was close by—until she was ready to resume her embroidery the following day.

Once Alisa safely contained the embroidery cloth in the wooden box, she could rest her eyes and just listen to the birds outside, that's right—feeling the warmth of her favorite quilt as it covered her body with a sense of security and love.

Following many days of embroidering, Alisa began to notice that each run of stitches began to take on a form, which over time emerged into a larger pattern—a complete picture.

Now, it just so happened that Alisa had a very special teddy bear called "Sunny," which she loved very much and would keep close to her at all times. That's what she would do, she decided, she would make a big straw hat for Sunny and sew the beautiful embroidery picture she had stitched all by herself to the crown of Sunny's hat as a constant reminder of what she had accomplished. Alisa decided to call her creation her badge of courage—that even though she felt uncared for by her mother and stepfather, now she felt able to begin to give herself permission to value herself. Alisa felt proud and appreciative of the time she had taken to create her own design—for each stitch had contributed to the creation of this special badge that represented an expression of all the different parts of herself.

As Alisa admired her handiwork, she could now see more clearly than ever before that each color and each stitch that went into creating her badge of courage expressed and honored all the parts of herself in an integrated, clear, whole, distinct way. How wonderful it was, she thought, that she had been the composer of this remarkable creation from its very beginnings to its completion. This process rewarded Alisa with a deep sense of satisfaction and self-appreciation—unencumbered feelings that she allowed herself to freely experience for the first time.

Now, I'm not sure what that badge of courage looked like to Alisa or how it might emerge as a whole and complete picture to you. You may have a sense of what your badge of courage looks like for you right now—the colors, shapes, and forms that you may be seeing in part or perhaps fully and completely. Sometime in the next day or few days, I'm not sure when, you can connect with an image that will provide you with an opportunity to create your own badge of courage. And when you have completed the process, you can display your handiwork somewhere, where both you and others can admire it, and you can feel proud of the time you have taken to express yourself in a way that is your very own unique style.

⌘   ⌘   ⌘

BADGE OF COURAGE RITUAL

It is essential, now, to follow up the "Badge of Courage" story with a ritual that will anchor and solidify the new skill that the survivor has now acquired—that is, having the ability to express and then contain her feelings at a pace that she has established for herself.

The following ritual is an opportunity to put into practice this newly acquired skill on a daily basis outside of the therapist's office, so that the client can begin to overcome her sense of helplessness and begin to integrate healthy methods of self-care.

Both the metaphorical story and ritual work well with clients who enjoy sewing, embroidery, crocheting, knitting, needlepoint, and/or painting. It is possible that even though your client may be talented in one or a number of the above-mentioned areas, she may not have ever given herself an opportunity to tap into these skills. Here is where you, as her therapist, can encourage the client to explore potential ways of expressing herself so that she can access, perhaps for the first time since the abuse, the kinesthetic, auditory, and visual sensory systems that may have been blocked out or shut down as a result of past childhood trauma.

Suggest to your client that she choose a certain time each day to begin the process of creating her own badge of courage. Encourage her to find a cardboard/glass/wooden box with a lid on it so that each day when she has completed a portion of her badge, she can open the lid of the box and contain the piece of cloth, putting it away in a safe place where she can find it when she is ready to continue with the process.

It is important that once she has completed that particular portion of the cloth for that day and contained it in its box, she rest her eyes— allowing herself to just listen to the different sounds surrounding her, feeling the warmth of her favorite quilt or blanket covering her body with a sense of security and love. This completion of the ritual allows the client to tap into her auditory and kinesthetic sensory systems, after focusing visually for some time on her badge of courage.

Once your client has created her own unique badge of courage, you can suggest to her that, when ready, she can choose a location that is special to her, where she can proudly display her handiwork—a place where both she and others can admire and value her creation.

We have experienced this whole process to be most beneficial in assisting the client to overcome the sense of shame that has developed over time and caused her to stuff down her feelings and, perhaps, as Sheila did, to resort to self-destructive behaviors to get the feelings out. We have found that this process ultimately transforms the shameful feelings for the client into self-acceptance and pride.

⌘　　　⌘　　　⌘

"CLARA'S NEW SUITCASE"

As was mentioned previously in this chapter, this particular metaphorical story was co-written with a client who had been in the process of reestablishing a more healthy, equal relationship with her mother. One of the highlights of this part of the client's healing work was when she received a set of new luggage from her mother. This event became a significant turning point in her healing, as she was now able to pack with her on her life's journey what she chose, and to let go of the heavy burden of guilt and shame that had been weighing her down and interfering with her progress ever since she could remember.

Although this was specifically tailored to a particular client's healing needs, we use this story, with alterations to certain details, to address the healing work of many clients.

YOU CAN TAKE SOME TIME, now, to focus on your breathing…making any adjustments you need to in any part of your body to experience that sense of comfort…with each inhale, taking in more comfort…and with each exhale…letting go of what you choose…as you listen to a story about a young woman named Clara….

I recall a story about a friend of mine named Clara, who planned to go away on a long holiday following her 35th birthday. During the days of preparation prior to her journey, she ventured into the attic of her home, where she searched for a suitcase to use on her travels. After looking for some time, Clara finally found an old, dusty trunk that she pulled down from the shelf so she could take a closer look at it. But when she went to unlock the trunk, it stuck fast, for there was no key to unlock it with.

She searched and searched for the key all over the attic to no avail—

until she noticed a loose floorboard under her right foot. Clara carefully dislodged the floorboard and, much to her amazement, she discovered a shimmering gold chain with an astounding number of keys attached to it! Surely, she thought, one of these keys must fit the lock of the dusty old trunk—so Clara began to try each key in the trunk's lock. Some of the keys almost fit, but were either too short or too long or didn't have the right markings on them to actually turn the lock. After some time, Clara began to feel a sense of hopelessness about ever finding the right key to open the lock—until, finally, the very last key on the golden chain fit perfectly!

Clara turned the key and opened up the trunk to discover that it contained many layers of memorabilia—clothing, old photographs, and possessions from many years ago, back to her school days and childhood. As she examined the contents of the trunk, Clara began to find herself so utterly entranced by the memories, that she almost forgot her reason for visiting the attic in the first place!

As she lifted each layer of memorabilia out of the trunk, Clara began to associate certain memories with each piece of clothing or item that she examined. Here was a very special dress given to her by a beloved aunt for her fifth birthday, which she would wear whenever she could, and a photograph of her favorite dog, Kippy—oh how she had loved that dog! And here was her favorite blanket that she would cover herself with whenever she felt cold and in need of the warmth and comfort it provided. The next layers revealed some old toys that Clara used to play with—one in particular, a teddy bear called Happy, looked up at Clara with his bright, shining eyes, and she began to connect fairly strongly with a sense of pain and despair for the child who had treasured and loved that teddy bear so completely.

All of a sudden, the sounds of a certain song she used to sing came back to her, and as she held Happy in her arms, she began to hum the tune very softly at first, and then Clara's voice gradually became louder and stronger as she not only connected with the pain and sadness of lost memories, but also with the sheer joy of just expressing herself, which came back to her for the first time, for she had not been allowed by her family to use her strong, confident voice. The buried feelings that she had kept locked away inside of her—hidden and invisible for such a long time—were finally finding their way to the surface of Clara's memory.

"What an incredible achievement," Clara thought, "for I can voice the unspeakable for the first time in my life!" It was at that very moment that Clara felt a huge burden lift from her shoulders, freeing her to breathe more easily and more deeply than before. She began to allow herself to feel in ways that she had never felt before—she felt whole and fulfilled.

Clara felt empowered as she repacked the old trunk—holding onto the items that she highly valued and wanted to take back with her and discarding the items from the trunk that she no longer needed. For the first time in her life she felt she could make her own personal choices, unencumbered by the pressures or expectations of others.

As she was closing the trunk and placing it back on the attic shelf, Clara heard the sound of the front doorbell ringing, so she hurriedly climbed down the old staircase and opened the door. Standing there was a delivery person holding a huge cardboard box. Clara quickly signed for the parcel and began to unpack the box, and, much to her surprise, it was a beautiful set of new luggage from her mother! Now, she, Clara, could personally choose the items that she would pack into her suitcase.

In preparation for her journey, Clara packed into her new suitcase as much as she needed, but not too much to create an extra burden. She had suddenly realized that the new suitcase symbolized what she chose to carry with her, now and into the future.

And now, you can, like Clara, take some time to consider the extra baggage you may be carrying at this moment...giving yourself permission, when ready, to let go of anything that feels like it may be somebody else's.... I'm not sure whose.... letting go...now, can allow more room for what you would like to pack on your journey...your very own choice.... And isn't it nice to know that you, now, have that choice, and those choices to make?

⌘   ⌘   ⌘

UNPACKING THE MEMORIES EXERCISE

In order for this exercise to best fit the needs of your client, you may need to alter some of the instructions so that it holds a special significance and relevance to her healing process. Please note that it is extremely empowering to involve your clients actively in the stages of their recovery, so that they can continue to tap into their inner strengths and wisdom between sessions and throughout their lives.

Suggest that the client take some time between this session and her next therapy session to choose a memory/story/message that she has carried with her for some time—inviting her, when ready, to unpack the story/memory/message, letting go of the parts that no longer fit for her now, in the present. Then, suggest she rewrite and add in new parts that more fully express and represent her as she is now. You may also want to encourage your client to keep the memory/story/message close by, so that whenever she chooses, she can continue to omit or change parts of the story/memory/message to truly represent each part of her newly emerging self over time.

⌘ ⌘ ⌘

CHECKING IN WITH THE FUTURE SELF EXERCISE

Throughout the healing process, it is the therapist's role to assist the survivor in moving on when she has completed her work at any particular stage, allowing her to maintain a future focus and not to become stuck in the trauma of the surfacing feelings. Creating future memories, discussed in Chapter 2, is another important task at this phase—as a way of instilling hope and planting the seed to remind the survivor that her life can be different.

During the therapy session, you can invite the client to visualize herself in the future—suggesting to her that she can, if she chooses, imagine herself somewhere she would like to be—and then have her future self send a postcard from that place to her present self. To provide an example of this process, one of our clients sent a postcard to herself from Long Beach on Vancouver Island, a place that she had always wanted to visit. She wrote:

Dear Lisa,
Well, as you can tell from the postcard, I have finally arrived at the beach! I never thought the day would come when I could really take a holiday like this, and actually enjoy myself without feeling guilty. I'm going to spend the whole day on the beach relaxing and doing whatever I please!

Love, Lisa.

CHAPTER 5

Stage Three: The Reclaiming and Reintegrating of Self

Once the survivor has come forward with the disclosure of the secret, the opportunity to retrieve and to reclaim the parts of herself that may have been left behind during the time of the abuse emerges. The client necessarily needs to break with both the traumatic and the more positive childhood memories in order to survive the abuse, bravely bringing herself to the place where she is in her present life. Now the survivor's focus, with the therapist's assistance, is to initiate the process of reintegration of the true parts of the self. Often, up until she reaches this stage of readiness, the survivor may have unconsciously been carrying remnants of the offender—experiencing those particular remnants as belonging to her, which can, in turn, create a distorted self-image.

Stage Three flows from Stage Two, "Becoming Visible," in that the emerging self of the survivor has the opportunity to make distinctions between herself and the offender(s), so that she can uncover and reintegrate the child she once was. Stage Three provides the opportunity for the survivor to initiate the letting go of any remaining parts of the offender in order to reunite with the lost parts of herself. Once this process has begun, the survivor is freed to pass through the following substages in order to truly regain, or perhaps to develop for the first time, a sense of her genuine self with the key parts of self retrieved and intact:

I. Prevalent Psychological and Physiological Symptoms
II. Struggling to Gain Approval and to Feel Loved
III. Recognizing One's Own Power to Contain Feelings and Not Be Overwhelmed by Them

IV. Loving Self: Developing Compassion for the Child
V. Reclaiming the Positive Memories as Well as the More
   Painful Ones
VI. Celebrating the Child

Following our discussion of these substages, we will present Metaphors, Exercises, and Rituals to help the client reinforce and anchor the healing tasks that challenge her at this juncture.

I. PREVALENT PSYCHOLOGICAL AND PHYSIOLOGICAL SYMPTOMS

Although the physiological and psychological symptoms from Stage Two may often persist into Stage Three—especially initially—the survivor at this point has developed a deeper appreciation of her pain and is therefore more able to externalize her symptoms through the conscious recognition of the messages she is sending to herself. An additional indication that the client has shifted from Stage Two to Stage Three is her newly found courage and willingness to take the risk of connecting more consciously to the abused child, which she can gradually confront directly instead of, for example, choosing to withdraw or experience her feelings as symptoms in her body. This conscious awareness often connects her to feelings of shame, guilt, anger, and betrayal that are, at least initially, directed toward the abused child parts of the self.

The focus here is to be able to acknowledge these feelings and at the same time to work through the sense of being "crazy" (as discussed in Chapter 3 pertaining to Stage One) for having these feelings in the first place. In addition, the dissociation that was more prevalent through Stages One and Two becomes less necessary in Stage Three, when the survivor courageously risks bringing her feelings about the child she once was into conscious awareness. Therefore, an indication that the survivor has reached the resolution of Stage Three is when she has provided herself with enough of a sense of safety (with the assistance of her therapist) to connect with the traumatized child without having to retraumatize herself.

At this juncture, in order to assist the survivor in making this part of her recovery tangible and meaningful, the concept of the inner self (also known as the inner child) can be introduced. As a result, the client has the opportunity to complete the following steps:

1. Acknowledging mixed feelings towards the child parts of the self;
2. Separating the child from the abuse and the abuser;
3. Accepting the child parts of the self with conditions (i.e., "Even though I will acknowledge your presence some of the time, I will continue to feel betrayed by you for not being able to protect me from the abuse"); and
4. Accepting all parts of the self unconditionally (i.e., embracing and loving the self with both the painful and the more positive memories intact).

Stage Three, therefore, marks a significant turning point for the survivor, as now she can retrieve and reintegrate the lost parts of herself. Having developed a healthier relationship with self, she can now emerge as a whole person, ready to move into the sphere of relating to self and others with a greater awareness of her own genuine identity. This process assists the survivor in replacing the up-until-now internalized distortions of the offender to a place far outside of herself, so that she has room within to welcome back and honor the child who survived the abuse—taking the time to develop an awareness of and an empathy towards the child separate from the abuse.

II. STRUGGLING TO GAIN APPROVAL AND TO FEEL LOVED

In this substage of Stage Three, the survivor struggles to feel whole by seeking approval from others to feel loved. At this point, she will sometimes manifest promiscuous behavior, which continues to trigger the belief that this is the only way she can be loved and that she is "less than," surfacing feelings of guilt and shame. In objectifying her relationships with others, the survivor may gain a sense of control, albeit false, that in some way she can initiate sexual contact before she becomes someone else's victim. Unfortunately, these attempts at gaining control back over her life eventually become empty victories, as her behavior tends to reinforce her sense of never being "good enough" and feeling "dirty and contaminated"—all the old messages left over from the offender(s) and often from her family.

Out of the connection she makes with these old, ingrained messages, the survivor becomes aware of her relationships in the past and also in the present, recognizing that within these so-called "intimate" affiliations, she may have desperately tried to gain approval to feel loved; this was and is sometimes thought to be achieved through connecting with a needy "other" that requires caretaking, with the rationale being, "If I take care of you, will you love me?"—messages that once resonated from the perpetrator(s) and nonoffending caregiver(s). Up until now the survivor is usually dissociated from the affective impact of past sexual abuse, where relationship intimacy is often only tolerated if she can fulfill the caretaker role, connecting with abusive partners who are often also coming from unresolved, traumatic pasts, where, once again, she becomes the victim of another's pain and anger. The survivor at this point may not be aware of or feel she deserves alternative healthier possibilities/choices in relationships. However, following a number of unfulfilling, failed relationships of the above-described nature, she may begin to recognize, possibly for the first time, how profound the pain is, pain that she has attempted to internalize in order to just struggle through her daily existence.

The experience of self as a failure, as a result of unsuccessful relationships with others, may be the impetus that brings her into the therapist's office. At this point, a necessary skill that the therapist can utilize is to gradually, at the client's pace, assist her in recognizing that there is no "quick-fix" solution, and that taking a sabbatical from potentially dysfunctional relationships to tap into her own needs and feelings may be necessary. In her book, *Getting Through the Day: Strategies for Adults Hurt As Children,* Napier (1993) emphasizes the importance of encouraging the survivor to go at her own pace:

> A theme that comes up often in therapy with survivors of childhood abuse is the slower you go, the faster you get there. There is a great deal of wisdom in this simple statement. Because abuse creates feelings of being overwhelmed, it's not unusual for survivors to move into high gear and overwhelm themselves as part of their recovery process. While it's understandable that you want to be free of the pain and struggle that may characterize your present life, going slowly will allow you to learn how it feels to respect your needs for safety. You'll have a chance to experience mastery, to go through a natural process of absorbing new information at your own pace, a pace you can manage. (p. 22)

The survivor at this point may begin to get in touch with powerful new feelings about herself that may have been dissociated up until now— including connecting with the child she once was with mixed feelings—

some of which may include love, hate, acceptance, rejection, guilt, anger, self-betrayal, and shame.

III. RECOGNIZING ONE'S OWN POWER TO CONTAIN FEELINGS AND NOT BE OVERWHELMED BY THEM

The survivor's recognition that she has the power to contain her own feelings and not get overwhelmed by them allows her to connect with her own childhood hurts and the accompanying feelings, including betrayal, anger, guilt, and shame. Putting a name to these previously unspoken sentiments towards the child frees the survivor to develop an awareness of how self and others may have blamed the child for the abuse.

> Chelsea, a 20-year-old survivor, had been told by her parents that she was a "bad child" throughout her childhood. As a result, Chelsea believed that she was "dumb" and "bad," and her behavior, that is, drug and alcohol abuse, reflected that label. In the process of therapy, she was encouraged to bring in some old scrapbooks and photograph albums from her childhood, which revealed excellent kindergarten report cards! As Chelsea had not read these report cards in detail prior to the session, she was shocked to realize that she had been internalizing false beliefs about herself, and here was proof that she had potential and ability. This new information ultimately freed Chelsea to develop a markedly different sense of herself separate from the old labels and messages, which became patently apparent through her behavior when she made the decision to pursue a college career.

Within the context of sexual abuse, betrayal is often thought of as the survivor's sense that she was in some way responsible for the abuse, and prerecorded internalized messages from the offender such as "she enjoyed it," "she asked for it," and "she's just a slut anyway" become the survivor's messages to herself. In fact, up until now, the intimidating stance of the abuser may still be maintaining its hold on her, and blaming the offender could create the possibility of retaliation from him. Even if the offender is dead, the survivor may fantasize that his ghost will return to destroy her, or even worse, she might break up the family that has remained together because she has continued to blame herself for the abuse.

Even though 32-year-old Angie was enraged that her mother chose to stay with her stepfather after she disclosed his sexual victimization of her, she continued to stuff the feelings, denying herself the right to feel betrayed by her mother. Instead, Angie had felt it safer, at the time, to assume responsibility for the abuse and label herself as the family's betrayer.

Often a sense of betrayal may also surface alongside anger, which became apparent in Angie's situation. Anger is a feeling that the survivor may have turned inward onto self, creating feelings of depression and oppression, which can result in rage directed toward the child parts of the self that were unable to say no to the offender or protect herself from him.

The subject of anger is one that comes up at various stages in the healing process. It is often one of the most difficult effects of the abuse to deal with. Once the survivor is in touch with her anger, learning how to cope with it and allowing its expression is often a formidable task, but one that will be a powerful, healthy, and much-deserved release.

We have found it very empowering for the survivor to openly discuss this topic within the group process as it affords her the opportunity to communicate to her peers the many ways she experiences and expresses her anger and to realize she is not alone.

The following are some key points and sample questions we use to address the topic of anger and to brainstorm with clients around this issue to help survivors generate new and healthy strategies for identifying and dealing with anger and other feelings that often accompany or lead up to an anger response. These questions can be addressed to the group or the individual client.

ANGER QUESTIONS

- How do you know when you are feeling anger?
- What are your internal cues? That is, what are you feeling and experiencing in your body and your mind?
- Do you show different feelings to different people?
- Is it easier to be mad, sad, happy...around certain people?
- Is it always necessary to resolve every situation of anger?
- How would it be to just acknowledge that you *are* angry and that it is appropriate to the situation?

- Are you angry and critical with yourself as a result of your abuse?
- How would you like to respond when you're feeling angry?
- What would you like to say to yourself when you're feeling angry?
- Taking some time, ask yourself what it would be like to let go of the anger that has built up over the years in your body. What would it be like to take a full deep breath, knowing that you can let go of the anger?

When dealing with this topic we find it helpful to remind clients of their increasing ability to soothe themselves by utilizing relaxation techniques, such as being in touch with their bodies, breathing and allowing themselves to feel and be with their anger rather than stuffing it down until it is released in some other often self-defeating way. There are many exercises, metaphors, and rituals throughout the book which address anger as well as the many other accompanying emotions as they surface and are worked through in the healing stages.

Guilt also contributes to the survivor's sense of responsibility for the occurrence of the abuse; there may be such abusive self-talk as, "If only I had not been so provocative," or "If only I had not been so sexually aggressive" (as one family court judge described a 3-year-old female who had been sexually abused by a middle-aged male), she would not have been targeted or victimized.

Even though shame is often paired with guilt, it is distinct from guilt in that it is the primary way that the survivor experiences herself in the world. As a result, shame is a feeling the survivor may have the most difficulty letting go of, particularly if during the sexual abuse her body responded physically with pleasurable feelings. As a child, she was not yet developmentally mature enough to understand the body's natural response to sexual stimulation; she may have begun to associate her own sexual feelings with a deep sense of self-shame throughout adolescence into young adulthood and beyond.

Stage Three is a distinctly hopeful phase of recovery, in that the survivor begins to recognize that the betrayal, anger, guilt, and shame she has carried and directed onto herself may in fact not belong to her. Often these feelings can be externalized once the survivor is actually able to recognize and to honor the inner strength that it took to survive and that shame, anger, betrayal, and guilt are the weapons used by the offender so that he can deny his responsibility for the abuse.

At 18 years of age Tara was referred to therapy as a result of an ongoing depression she had been experiencing for the past year. Following 6 months of weekly sessions, Tara disclosed that she had been molested by her mother's boyfriend at 7 years of age. At the time of the abuse, Tara had informed her mother of the boyfriend's behavior; however, Tara's mother minimized the seriousness of the messages her daughter was giving her. Upon initial disclosure to the therapist, Tara expressed a feeling of acceptance and okayness with her mother's disbelief of her as a child. However, following one year in therapy, when Tara began to recognize the impact the abuse had had on her life, she was able to connect with her anger towards her mother. In recognizing the outward direction of her anger, Tara's depression lifted, and gradually she also began to connect with feelings of betrayal by her mother.

Please note that often the externalization of the types of feelings that Tara experienced are further directed outside of self toward the offenders. This will be explored in Chapter 4.

Jackie, a 35-year-old single parent who had been struggling to accept the child parts of herself, acknowledged a sense of self-betrayal as a result of the child's lack of ability to protect her from the abuse. These feelings of betrayal toward self created a strong barrier for Jackie, in that as an adult she felt fearful of the sense that she was not able to protect herself. This fear was manifested through an inability to sleep in the dark, at which time she feared losing control of her surrounding environment. In acknowledging the sense of self-betrayal, anger, and even the hatred she felt toward the child (within the safety of the therapist's office), other feelings that had been lurking underneath her rage began to emerge.

The therapist's acceptance of the client's mixed feelings towards the abused child assists the client in overcoming her initial tendency to feel only the extreme emotions, such as love or hate, towards the self that survived the trauma.

If the child experienced physical sensations of pleasure during the sexual abuse, the adult part may interpret sexual arousal as body betrayal, and because her body responded to the abuse, she is guilty of encouraging and even initiating the abuse, which in turn surfaces a sense of guilt and shame turned inward onto self.

Karen, a 20-year-old survivor, had a history of relationships with men with whom she would initiate sex fairly early in the relationship, resulting in the quick dissolution of the partnership. As these types of relationships were the only ones she had experienced, her understanding of the concept of intimacy was limited; she had not given herself the time or the opportunity to establish an intimate relationship with herself. Through the course of therapy, Karen began to recognize that the short-term sexually oriented relationships she had been involved in continued to provide her with guilt and shaming messages toward herself of being "dirty," "provocative," "a slut," and this continued to promote her self-hatred.

With this realization, Karen was able to recall responding to her cousin's sexual molestation physically, which she had felt made her partially responsible for the abuse. In bringing this awareness into her conscious mind, she was able to, as an adult, gradually shed the self-blame and redefine her own self-image, which, in turn, freed her to develop a sense of self-respect. This new sense of self-respect gave Karen permission to avoid potential relationships with men that would reinforce the old tapes, and instead she made the decision to take a sabbatical from sexual relationships with others in order to focus on developing a more intimate connection with herself.

A word of caution for the therapist here: even though betrayal, anger, guilt, and shame are negative feelings initially held by the survivor toward herself, it is important to be respectful of them as necessary coping skills that allowed her to survive the abuse and reach adulthood. Only when she is ready and able to actually name what she can replace these feelings with is it appropriate for the therapist to assist the survivor in initiating the process of challenging and transforming these and other feelings. Please refer to the metaphorical story "Alice Sheds Her Shell" and the subsequent anchoring ritual found at the end of this chapter; these will help to prepare the client for the possibility of change and transformation.

In the following substages described in this chapter, we will focus on methods of assisting the survivor to further challenge and transform the feelings described in the initial substages of Stage Three.

IV. LOVING SELF: DEVELOPING COMPASSION FOR THE CHILD

The pivotal task at this stage of the healing process is the separation of and externalization of the abuse from the self. When the survivor is able to develop compassion for the child she was while undergoing the abuse, she can then begin to connect (perhaps for the first time) with positive feelings and ultimately with love for herself. She can now more safely understand and perhaps feel her pain and anger for the first time. Our goal as therapists at this crucial point is to help facilitate the connection of the feelings associated with the abuse in a way that allows their expression without becoming overwhelmed with fear and panic. When this is successfully achieved, the client can begin to reintegrate and to reclaim the lost parts of herself and be more open to admiring her ability to survive and ultimately to being able to let go of the responsibility of the abuse that doesn't belong to her. She can finally begin to make peace with the child.

When she has been able to successfully reconnect with the feelings and experience of her childhood, she is usually able to reclaim some happier, more positive memories also. It is generally a pleasant surprise to reconnect with some of these other memories, which have been buried along with the more painful and negative ones, and this can further assist the survivor to develop an awareness of the child as separate from the abuse.

> Debbie, a 30-year-old survivor of incest who had been in therapy for about 5 months, went through the process of externalization in a particularly unique way. She had a dream in which her body had an acrid odor that was, she believed, contaminating her immediate environment (both internally and externally). On awakening from this dream, she took a bath and repeatedly scrubbed her body with strong soap. After drying herself, she immediately threw away the towels and face cloth she had just used. This olfactory memory triggered some additional memories that had been out of her conscious awareness since she was a child of 9 or 10. She expressed interest in using hypnosis to explore and to recall a safe place that she had discovered in the woodsy area of a park near her family home.
>
> During the trance she recounted in detail a sanctuary she created for herself using twigs, bushes, and rocks, which acted as a natural boundary and enabled her to experience feelings of tranquillity, peace, and self-containment. The therapist helped her realize that this was a positive coping skill and encouraged her to appreciate what a resourceful and creative act this was. She had chosen this sanctuary as her real home and shelter from harm. Through this newly retrieved memory, Debbie was thus able to connect with the strength of the child that helped her to survive the abuse.

Shortly following our session, Debbie accompanied a trusted friend to a "white sale" at a local department store where she purchased a new set of towels and other accessories for her bathroom. On returning home and treating herself to a long bath, Debbie experienced a visceral flashback, during which she once again became aware of the acrid bodily smell she had previously experienced in her dream. At first, she considered throwing away her towels once more, but the thought of parting with her new purchases angered her. She would later recount in therapy that it was as though the adult part of herself jumped out of the bathtub and exclaimed "No! These are my towels and I'm going to keep them." This was a significant shift as almost everything she had valued as a child had been taken away from her. Now in the present, Debbie the adult was able to reclaim what was rightfully hers. Therefore, in retrieving this piece of memory, triggered by the dream and flashback, we were able to work through and externalize some key aspects and effects of the abuse and for the first time acknowledge and embrace the strength that had enabled her to overcome her trauma.

At this point in her therapy, via trance, Debbie was now free to reclaim more positive memories of her childhood. One important memory was of waving goodbye to her mother on her way to school one day and recalling and sensing a meaningful connection between them through eye contact. This was particularly significant to Debbie as she had just resumed contact with her mother after a number of years.

In order to reclaim and to reintegrate eclipsed parts of the self, the survivor must face many heretofore overwhelming and often "crazy-making" feelings and coping strategies that hamper her ability to develop compassion for the child she was at the time of the abuse. One of the most helpful ways of achieving this end is a three-step exercise that employs a series of paper dolls.

The first doll represents the survivor as she recalls herself at the time of the abuse. The survivor is led through a guided imagery in which she is asked to recall what she was like during the time the abuse was going on. It is important for the therapist to elicit as much sensory information as possible (i.e., to include visual, auditory, and kinesthetic information while leading the client through this process. There is a detailed description of this process at the end of this chapter). It is also important for the therapist to use the third person while doing the imagery as it helps the client distance from the threatening material. After she reorients back to the room, the survivor is given a blank paper doll, of approximately 24 inches in length, and various art supplies, such as wool for hair, construction paper to make clothes out of, markers and so on, from which she can construct a representation of her abused self.

The second doll is completed in a subsequent session after a guided imagery in which the survivor is asked once again to recall herself at the time of the abuse, but this time she is asked to try and notice something about her that she can like or appreciate. Again, on reorienting, the client is asked to make another doll, noting something about her that she perhaps hadn't noticed before.

The third doll is created following a guided imagery that focuses on the survivor imagining herself as she would like to be. Again, the therapist walks her through what it can be like, how she can look, think, and feel differently. The survivor then constructs a doll that represents herself as she would like to be.

This exercise can be used with individuals or with groups. We have found it to be most beneficial in a group setting, as it enables the survivor to express many of her own feelings, such as anger, shame, and guilt, while also hearing others talk about their reactions and experiences while being supported and validated. The construction of the dolls as they progress from victimization to self-actualization serves as a powerful metaphor for future possibilities. The survivor can begin to entertain the idea of a different more complete self.

In addition, the act of making the dolls innocuously regresses the adult survivor to a playful state which often triggers some positive memories. This mood can be utilized to gently explore her childhood with the intention of reminding her of skills and abilities that may have been forgotten or disregarded. Most women enjoy this process and it is often an exercise filled with laughter as well as the more intense emotions of anger, shame, and grief. It is a powerful experience to be able to connect with many long-buried emotions while being surrounded by one's peers. It affords the survivor the opportunity to externalize and to gain a new perspective on these previously overwhelming emotions.

This task also helps the survivor to practice staying present while dealing with difficult topics. The busywork of the dolls can keep her from dissociating while connecting with herself at the age the abuse took place. She can begin to express intense feelings such as anger or sadness while staying present and speaking about it to the other women (or the therapist if in an individual counseling session) who become witnesses of her experience. This exercise can often be the beginning of experiencing control and containment while connecting with strong emotions, and this is often the start of learning new and healthier outlets for the expression of her affect.

Karen, the 30-year-old incest survivor mentioned in Chapter 4, was having difficulty coping with many of the feelings of anger and abandonment she was experiencing at this stage of her healing process. Her old dream of her mouth being sewn shut was recurring with more frequency. Karen felt a great deal of anger that she was expressing at times that seemed inopportune to her, which jeopardized her ability to relate to friends and co-workers. At work she would have an overwhelming wish to run away when asked to do something that was expected in the context of her job.

While constructing the first doll in a group session, Karen was able to reconnect with part of herself as a child who wanted to "crawl into a hole and die." She was able to disclose to the group that she hated herself because of all the dignity and self-respect she had to compromise to earn love and any sense of importance or belonging. Karen had not been able to put words to the feelings that had been buried for so long. She hadn't been able to develop compassion for herself and to begin to identify the needs of the child that were not met.

The doll is symbolic for the child I was as a young girl and who still exists, frozen by trauma, in my subconscious mind. I can feel what she feels. I feel such love and empathy towards me/ her. I hope she can see it in my face and trust me enough to come over to get a big hug. I hope she'll know I can listen to her and not mind but understand her tears. I know her as I know myself because she once was me and still is me. By helping her to heal, that part of me heals. I know she wants a hug, wants to be listened to, believed, understood, acknowledged, and loved with respect.

Karen was able to accept support from the other women in the group when her feelings were too intense for her to bear alone.

Somebody listens.... I have something to say, I must, you listened. What I think and say matters. You didn't judge or criticize or advise, you just listened. I exist. I matter to you. Somebody hears me. My words reached somebody's mind and heart.

Karen

The support and friendship offered at the group level is sometimes the survivor's first positive experience of relating to others that is not tied to her sexuality. It is a new and different sort of relationship, both with others in the group and with herself.

V. RECLAIMING THE POSITIVE MEMORIES AS WELL AS THE MORE PAINFUL ONES

One of the by-products of beginning to integrate and connect the feelings of the child at the time of the abuse with the survivor in the present is making a new connection to some of the positive memories one had as a child. So many survivors come into therapy with huge blocks of their childhood out of awareness. As parts of the puzzle of their past begin to fit together and the survivor realizes that she can feel the feelings without slipping into a void forever, she no longer has to avoid all memories for fear of remembering the trauma. In our experience, this is also the beginning of the end of responding to situations or circumstances in black and white, all or nothing terms.

The extreme reactions begin to become more balanced. The survivor doesn't have to isolate herself from all relationships in order to protect herself; she can begin to introduce some new elements into her life. She no longer has to try and control her environment with the same rigidity as before. She can let down her guard a bit and explore some new possibilities.

The survivor can now begin to develop a new sense of appreciation for herself. There is a different type of internal dialogue with the self beginning to emerge. At this time the second part of the doll exercise is helpful for encouraging this process. By appreciating and understanding the coping mechanisms and strength of herself at the time of the abuse, she can begin to more easily and creatively access her resources, thereby enabling her to develop an awareness of herself as separate from the abuse.

Another helpful exercise at this time is one of creating a mask that represents the previously unclaimed fears and feelings connected to the abuse and deals with them openly without the need to continue to "mask" these emotions. This offers the survivor another opportunity to experience the pain of the child in an indirect way, enabling her to let go of it through its outward expression (see the end of this chapter for details of this exercise).

Repetition of newly acquired skills and awareness is very important while the client is integrating, relearning, and assimilating the various previously fragmented parts of herself. Just as children need and seek out repetition while learning new developmental tasks, so does the survivor. The Mask Exercise therefore repeats the objectives of the Doll Exercise in a slightly different way. The client generally enjoys the opportunity to practice these new ways of being and we encourage her to continue this exploration on her own outside the group, but only as much as she feels she can safely do alone.

At this stage, while accessing the emotions of the child at the time of the abuse, it is important not to anchor the client into that frozen, helpless child state. One way of guarding against this pitfall is through the use of the third person while using guided imagery or hypnotic induction. When the therapist speaks of "she, her, or the child," the client is able to remain one step removed from the memories. Some survivors like to give the child a name other than her own given name. This may help her establish a safer, more indirect relationship while still allowing her to become more familiar and accepting of herself at the time of the trauma.

At the beginning of any induction or imagery we always give the client permission to leave her eyes open if she wishes or to only remember as much as she is ready to remember or notice about the child. We go over ways of managing anxiety attacks or panicky feelings. Reminders of being in touch with her breathing and surroundings are given throughout each session and eventually these anxiety-management techniques become second nature—tools to carry with her in the present and into the future (please see Chapter 2 for more details). Therefore, the client is better able to handle or control alarming feelings and body memory on her own.

All of these techniques allow the survivor to gain safer access to memory in general. Group sessions are often very lively at this point, with members talking about the favorite games, TV shows, music, and other pleasures they enjoyed as children.

During this substage, Abby, a 27-year-old survivor and mother to a 5-year-old, was able to access memories of playing jacks with friends in her neighborhood. This was a great source of pleasure for her. She was able to find her original set of jacks among some stored belongings. Abby was then able to teach her son how to play. This was a game they could share together and she found it helped her to bond with her son in a new more relaxed way. Abby would carry her jacks with her in a small sack, which she would hold and look at when she felt the need.

VI. CELEBRATING THE CHILD

We can see from the previous example that the survivor is now beginning to access her playfulness. Some women who have been abused from a very early age may have never really experienced a child's sense of spontaneity or playful abandon. Learning to play and be playful is an opportunity for the adult to connect with the joyous parts of childhood. It is also a chance to catch up developmentally on this critical phase of normal child development.

As previously mentioned, towards the end of Stage Three, many women choose to change their names. This often occurs as the survivor goes through the process of reclaiming the child part of the self. This is often a significant symbolic act for the survivor.

Judy, a 36-year-old, very quiet and reserved incest survivor, told the group of how she always hated her name. She never felt comfortable with her given name and every time she heard her name spoken by any male friend or co-worker, she heard it in the voice of the offender. She also remembers her mother calling her Judith whenever she was "in trouble" in her childhood. Toward the end of the group, she decided to change her name to Heather, which was the name she had given to her favorite childhood doll.

One of the facilitators suggested to her that she might like to celebrate this name change in some special way during group. She chose to have a rebirthing party outside of the group, where she invited only those friends and family who were supportive of her and whose company she enjoyed. Her best friend read a tribute to her new-found self, which Judy had written for the occasion, after which Judy formally introduced herself to the gathering as Heather.

We have included some examples of transformation rituals at the end of this chapter.

We often invite the adult survivor via trance to take time to be with the child through playing a game of catch. The adult initiates the game, throwing the ball to the child while remaining close enough to each other to actually catch the ball (boundaries intact) and gradually moving a little closer as the game progresses. Assisting the survivor at her own pace through a series of play activities with the child can help to facilitate the adult self to be more available to the child in a nurturing and playful way. This can be a powerful opportunity to reclaim and reintegrate the self. "The Reunion" and the accompanying exercise at the end of this chapter are examples of anchoring the concepts of reintegration and reclaiming of fragmented parts of the "self" and offer ways the survivor can gradually become reacquainted and more comfortable with those lost pieces of her past.

We encourage the survivor to celebrate and honor the child who survived the abuse as much as possible. The third step of the doll exercise is helpful at this point as it encourages the client to explore her newly emerging and integrated self as she would like to become in the future. The third doll is always an amazing contrast to the first one and thus the survivor is able to appreciate her progress and movement from past to present to future. By celebrating and honoring via the use of rituals and special events significant to the survivor, she is able to mark the often profound changes she has experienced. This helps these events to become even more tangible and valid. It also allows the survivor to begin some new traditions and personally meaningful customs and practices that fit with the new choices and direction in her life.

METAPHORS, EXERCISES, AND RITUALS

"THE REUNION"

The following metaphorical story provides the survivor with an opportunity to solidify the newly forged link to the child part of self. Up until this point in her healing, it may have been far too threatening and unsafe to reconnect with the child part of herself that was sexually abused; however, she may be more ready now than ever before to take that risk.

As the story unfolds, we find Candida, the child, and Leana, the adult, gradually getting to know one another in a way that transcends Candida's abusive relationship with her family, reuniting her with Leana, the adult that she has grown to trust and love over the course of the story.

N OW, YOU CAN TAKE SOME TIME, with each breath, to just focus comfortably on the messages of hope you have been able to give to yourself recently. That's right, just allowing that strong voice of yours to permeate your body and your mind—noticing how those new messages allow you to connect with more and more comfort—until you feel the support of the cushions underneath your body and behind your head.

Try to imagine small distinct snowflakes quietly falling from the sky, surrounding you with soft and cleansing snow that transforms to water and evaporates on your skin—giving you that cooling, refreshing sensation on your face. And now you can bring those sensations back inside to the warmth of this room—taking time to experience whatever it is you may be experiencing right now—taking in further and further comfort as your conscious mind listens to the story about a little girl called Candida—freeing your unconscious mind to wander....

Now, Candida was an honest child who lived in a home where people shouted a lot at one another and kept secrets from each other. This made Candida feel very sad and alone, except for her beloved cat, Trudy, who was the only family member that she could truly trust. Candida would spend a great deal of time with Trudy, confiding her feelings, and every time she spoke to, stroked, or fed her most beloved cat, she would always feel much better, a sense of calm blowing like a soft breeze across her face—that's right, taking in more and more comfort.

Now, it just so happened that Candida had a good nose for sniffing out tension in her family, as conflict had a certain stale smell about it that she abhorred. And when Candida smelt that smell, she would take Trudy and run outside, taking in deep breaths of the fresh, clean scent of the pine (as the house was surrounded by evergreen trees) feeling the perfectly shaped cones that dropped from the trees onto the forest floor under her feet. There just so happened to be a tree house deep in the forest that Candida and Trudy had discovered on one of their travels through the woods, and it was a favorite sanctuary of theirs, where they would play house, and Candida would prepare make-believe tea and biscuits for herself and her Trudy—enjoying their private tea party.

It was on one particular day when Candida and Trudy had escaped an especially tense situation at home that they spent many hours in the tree house until they felt the coast was clear and the fighting had died down so they could return home. But, as they drew closer and closer to the house, Candida could hear her mother arguing with her father:

"We cannot afford to give Candida a birthday gift this year—it's different for Liza, our oldest, and Caine, being the only boy, for they hold special positions in our family and deserve special gifts on their birthdays—let's rather spend our money on the tobacco you seem to always be running out of."

Candida overheard her mother's words, and she began to weep, blaming herself for being the dumb, unwanted, not good-enough child between her two brilliant, deserving siblings. In fact, she felt she didn't even deserve to be a part of the family. "Maybe," Candida thought, "if I run away and never come back, I can relieve my parents of the burden of having to care for me, and they will be forever grateful to me for the rest of their lives. Maybe, by running away they will finally love me." And, having made that decision, Candida cried from the depths of her soul so loud, that she could hear her father's footsteps walking towards the front door, and just in the nick of time, she grabbed Trudy and ran back through the forest to her special tree house where no one could find her.

She spent many days and nights there, with the sound of her mother's voice in her head. As she held Trudy close to her heart, Candida thought about the possibility of returning home, because she was starving, cold, and tired, but when she thought about what her mother might say, all she could hear was: "How dare you, you stupid little tramp? Why didn't you just stay lost so we wouldn't have to be bothered with you any more?"

Just as she was beginning to feel very much alone in the world, Trudy's gentle purring distracted her from her thoughts, and she found herself staring into some very bright lights, as she held her hands up to her face to protect her eyes from the glare. Walking toward the light, she saw the outline of many dark figures almost dancing towards her. Just then Trudy began to shiver in her arms, and so Candida held her little cat closer as she connected with her fear. She wondered who this group of people were, and what they wanted from her.

After some time, Candida mustered up a strength that came from deep inside as she introduced herself and Trudy, explaining that they were hungry and didn't have anywhere to go. And, just at that moment, she began to weep, realizing that apart from her cat, she was now all alone in the world. Just then, a beautiful young woman with big black eyes and long shining black hair, wearing huge earrings, approached Candida with a blanket: "Here, my child", she said softly, "is a blanket that you can wrap around to keep you warm and protect you from the cold." As Candida took the warm, soft covering from the young woman with the kind, smiling eyes, there was something about her that she felt vaguely familiar with and comforted by—but she was not quite sure why or how.

Another older woman came forward and spoke to Candida, explaining, "We are a band of gypsies who roam from forest to forest, in search of places to put up our tents and our caravans, so we can stay for a while until it is time to move on and find a new home." This was all very strange to Candida, who had lived in the same home all her life and had never had the opportunity to visit and travel to other places, except to the forest surrounding her house.

No longer feeling fear, Candida, feeling quite helpful and important, directed the gypsies to a clearing located in the heart of the forest, with a running creek nearby, where they began to set up their tents and caravans for the night. The leader of the gypsies thanked Candida for being so helpful in finding them a place to stay. The gypsy's acknowledgment of Candida's helpfulness was confusing, for it did not fit with the messages she had received constantly from her family about being a burden and useless—"Could they be wrong?" She wasn't sure.

Just then, the beautiful young female gypsy that Candida had first encountered approached her and offered her food and shelter for the night. At first Candida was not sure if she should accept—after all, she had only just met these people—what if they tried to harm her in some way? The young woman, noticing Candida's hesitation, tried to reassure her: "I understand that we have just met, and you don't know me; my name is Leana, and for a very long time now, I have been searching for a little girl just like you—someone I knew once but lost a long time ago. Now, I don't know if you're the child I've been looking for, but you and your cat seem very tired and sad, and it seems as if you are in need of some support, but I would understand if you say no and walk away." Just then Candida felt exhausted and hungry, explaining to Leana that she would stay the night only if Trudy could accompany her, which Leana consented to almost immediately.

After sharing the evening meal with Leana, Candida was given a room of her own with a small bed on which she lay, holding her dear Trudy close to her heart as she fell into a deep, comfortable sleep until the morning, when she awoke to the brightness of the sun and the sound of the gypsies singing as they washed their belongings in the brook. "Last night was not a dream," thought Candida, "I'm still with the gypsies and far away from home." This realization had a curiously calming effect on Candida as she thought about the constant arguing and fighting at home.

"But I'm not sure if I belong here with the gypsies." Candida pondered her choices and decided that she would stay as long as she continued to be treated with the respect and kindness she knew she deserved.

As the days went by, Candida began to feel increasingly comfortable with the gypsies—there were even times when she almost forgot she had another family—as the people here treated her as they treated one another—with much respect and love. Candida enjoyed the daily routine that she shared with the other children—playing in the forest (within view of the campsite), learning their daily school lessons, and then, following the evening meal, the entire gypsy camp would sit around a huge bonfire and sing and exchange enchanting stories about the gypsies and their adventures, and Candida began to find herself absolutely enthralled and captivated by these tales of their ancestors.

Leana, the young woman that Candida had been staying with, seemed in some way different from the others. She often kept to herself and spent a great deal of time creating beautiful pieces of jewelry out of smooth stones and wood and other natural substances she was able to find in the forest. She also took in wounded animals—looking after them until they recovered and then setting them free.

One night Leana made a rare appearance at the evening bonfire, where she told the story of a little girl who had been abandoned by her family at the circus and taken in by the gypsies who ran the circus. Leana described the feelings of hurt that the young girl had experienced at being left all alone and the strong sense of abandonment she had felt. She also described how the child had blamed herself for the family leaving her—that because she was "not good enough" and "evil," her parents and siblings did not want her with them. As Leana continued the story, it occurred to Candida that Leana was describing her own experience and that the gypsies had also taken her in and looked after her over the years.

Suddenly, Candida began to feel an affinity with Leana that she had never experienced with anyone before—but she was afraid—"What if Leana pushed her away? No, I must be very careful," Candida thought. "I will wait to see if Leana has any room in her life for me, and I will know in time whether it is safe for me to get closer to her." With that thought in mind, Candida realized that she was beginning to trust her own feelings more and more—that's right, even more.

It was that very night that Candida dreamt about an encounter with a hooded figure who was beckoning her to draw closer, and as she drew closer, the figure opened up one hand to reveal a small brilliantly lit object—but just as Candida shifted to take a closer look, she hesitated, as she could hear the figure saying, "Only move closer if you feel ready to do so, for once you step forward, you can never go back—your life will change forever." Just then Candida heard Leana's voice calling her to wake up, as she had slept longer than usual and was late for the beginning of the children's daily activities. Candida forgot about the dream until a few weeks later, when, following the nightly campfire one beautiful summer's eve when the sun was going down and the sky was tinged with purple and gold, Candida made her way down to the embankment—listening to the sounds of the animals and the birds preparing for the night—wondering what it would be like to be truly loved by someone.

At the water's edge, she encountered a figure eclipsed by a many-colored cape, singing softly with hands cupped, drawing in the cool water and then quietly sipping it. Then, all of a sudden, as if sensing the presence of someone, the figure quickly turned around and came face to face with Candida, who by now had jumped back in fright, not knowing what to expect. Upon seeing Candida, the eclipsed figure motioned her to come forward. As she moved very cautiously, step by step, she heard a voice whispering softly, "Candida, it's me, Leana—do not be afraid." Still feeling somewhat unsure, Candida continued to keep some distance. "Candida," Leana gently called, "I have something to give you."

Just then Leana placed a beautiful locket in the young girl's hands with the words: "I have been saving this locket for a very long time waiting to give this to you, and finally you are here." "I'm not sure I understand," replied Candida. Seeing Candida's puzzled expression, Leana encouraged Candida with the words: "Open the locket and look inside." Candida found two tiny photographs inside the locket: one was of a young child, who in some way resembled Candida herself, and the other photo she recognized as the young woman who had cared for her all these months—Leana!

Candida found herself feeling very curious and apprehensive at the same time: "Is this me?" she inquired, pointing to the photo of the young child. "Yes, and this other photo is of me," exclaimed Leana. "I don't understand," sighed Candida. "Look deeply into my face, Candida, and you will see the adult face—the face of your future," explained Leana, "for I have searched for you—for you are the child I once was—you wear the face of my past that I tried to ignore for a long time, until one day I decided I was tired of only knowing a part of myself, so I gave myself permission to remember you—to recall whom I once was. The more I remembered about you, the more pain I began to feel about your life—how you were treated, and how enraged I felt when I realized that you were unable to protect yourself. And I also felt betrayed and ashamed that you would have allowed yourself to be so badly hurt by our family."

"Then", Leana continued, "I began to feel guilty about blaming your pain on the family—maybe, after all, they were a loving family, and they treated you that way because you were not good enough. That's when I began to think that the child I once was, was a shameful creature—evil, bad, and ugly—how could anyone love me? You know, Candida, it is only in the last few months, since you have come to stay with me, that I have begun to question the way our family treated you, that I have begun to believe that I, in fact, did not deserve to be treated that way and that, instead, I deserved love and respect. My thoughts then shifted to you—how alone and unloved you must have felt. And so I decided that if I waited any longer to receive the love and respect I felt I deserved from my family, that I would not get it—and that here I was, a fully grown adult, who felt ready to take care of you myself—to bring you back to me so that you never feel alone again, where you would always have my love and respect to rely on. And now you are here!"

Candida, crying and laughing at the same time, looked up at Leana with giant-size teardrops splashing down her face, and said, "I have always felt that no one loved me because I am so ugly and evil, and that I would feel unwanted and alone for the rest of my life. Does this mean now that I will grow up to look and be just like you? You are so beautiful both inside and out." "You are a part of me and my life now, Candida, and I will always be there for you," replied Leana. "Does that mean I am finally where I belong—that you will take care of me and love me always?" Candida excitedly responded. Without hesitation, Leana replied, "Yes, I will be here for you, no matter what—your home is with me now."

Now Leana and Candida felt that they wanted to spend a great deal of time with one another, getting to know one another more intimately. So they would spend their days travelling by horse through the forest, with Leana helping Candida to learn the art of horseback riding. Leana would take time out with Candida to appreciate the ways of the forest animals, birds, and insects, giving her an appreciation of their lifestyles and choices, and at night, Leana would tell Candida wondrous stories about birds who helped deliver food to the poor and giants who let children play in their gardens. From the experiences they were sharing together, each began to feel more whole and more bonded with one another. Following one particularly magical day where Leana had been teaching Candida to communicate with some of the animals in the forest, and they had returned home feeling excited by what they had experienced together, Leana looked very lovingly at Candida and said: "Would you feel comfortable if I gave you a hug right now?"

Candida was able to reply very spontaneously and comfortably, "Yes, I would love that!" There was something very magical that occurred when the two embraced—each seemed to complete the other. Candida finally felt that she had found her real parent and that she would never feel lost or lonely again. Leana felt that she had found a missing part of herself that carried all her pain, shame, guilt, anger, and feelings of betrayal, but now as she was able to embrace the child, those feelings began to shift to a place outside of the child she once was, as she recognized that she had been deprived of a part of herself that desperately needed unconditional love and acceptance. Up until now, Leana had felt robbed of an essential part of herself, and now she felt whole again for the first time in her life. And as Leana and Candida held hands—each completing the other—they looked forward to being in one another's company—walking together toward the future down life's pathway.

And it's nice to know that just by moving forward from the present into the future at your own pace, when ready, you will find home, that's right, just like Candida did when she reunited with Leana.

⌘ ⌘ ⌘

CONNECTING WITH THE CHILD THROUGH PLAY: FOLLOW-UP EXERCISE TO "THE REUNION"

In order to anchor the transformations that have occurred in the above story, it may be helpful to suggest to the client at this stage of recovery to take some time during the next few weeks to connect with the child part of herself in some way. You may want to recommend that the client go at her own pace here. For example, she may be ready initially to relate to the child part of herself through old family photographs, where she could write about what it must have been like and felt like to have been that child, and in this way, she may start to develop some empathy toward that part of herself, even if she is not fully ready at this point to accept and reintegrate the abused child.

Further anchoring could be achieved through creating for the client two short tapes on initiating contact with the child through play. The first tape could be narrated in the following fashion:

> You might want to take some time now to revisit the child you once were. Imagine yourself walking down a pathway, and as you turn the corner in that pathway you start walking towards a street that looks very familiar. You then cross the street and find yourself in front of your home, the home you once lived in as a child. You walk up the stairs to the front door and knock and, to your amazement, the child you once were answers the door. She looks at you with surprise, appearing to recognize you in some way, and as you gaze at her, noting her features—the color and texture of her hair, the expression on her face and what she is wearing—other family members begin to gather around the child, inquiring, "Who are you and what do you want?" You reply: " I'm here to take the child I once was to play for the afternoon and then I will bring her back." The family agrees, perhaps somewhat hesitantly, and the child joins you on the porch.
>
> You walk down the stairs together and cross the street, following the pathway that leads to a beautiful meadow. You just so happened to have brought a ball with you so you start throwing the ball back and forth to the child, and she to you. At first you and the child stand a fair distance apart: you throw the ball to her and she tries to run up and catch it and then misses it; she throws the ball to you, and you also try to run up and catch it, but it was thrown too far away from where you had originally been standing.
>
> At this point, you and the child are now standing slightly closer together. This time you throw the ball to the child and she runs up to the ball, but not as far as before, and she almost catches it but not quite! The child then retrieves the ball and throws it to you but, alas, it lands short of where you are standing—so you move closer to where the child is standing and this time, when you throw the ball to her, she catches it and you make contact for the first time! What a triumph!
>
> It is time, now, to take the child home and she walks next to you down the pathway and, if comfortable, she may be holding your hand as you cross the street to your old home. As you leave her inside the front door, she waves goodbye to you, and you wave goodbye to her, connecting with some feelings that perhaps may be new or different for you in some way, planning to return, when ready, to revisit the child.

Usually it is our experience that at this point the survivor has a difficult time leaving the child back with the family; however, often there is a recognition that the adult may not be ready yet to take the child home with her.

The second short tape would describe the adult, when ready, permanently retrieving the child part of herself from the family home. Depending on what appeals to the child, you may want to suggest, for example, spending an afternoon with the child at the beach building sandcastles, and as a result, experiencing what it's like to be with the child, sitting close to her and communicating with her through the joint experience of building sandcastles—building dreams together. The client may be ready at this point to let the family know that she is taking the child with her to where she truly belongs. This is a significant turning point in her recovery, as she has decided that the child will not receive the unconditional love from her family that she has been waiting for all this time and that, now, the adult/parent part of self is ready to retrieve the lost child part of herself and gradually connect with that child unconditionally.

⌘　　　⌘　　　⌘

"ALICE SHEDS HER SHELL"

Although the following metaphorical story was created for a specific client, it will assist in providing survivors, in general, with the opportunity to prepare themselves for ultimately retrieving the lost child parts of themselves by first letting go of and then shedding the parts of the offender/family that she may have been carrying around all this time, which do not belong to her. This will allow the survivor, when ready, to begin to make room for the up-until-now lost parts of self.

This story was co-created with a survivor who was able to connect with some powerful images of herself caught in a black egg; her sister who had died of emphysema the year before, whom she depicted as a caterpillar smoking a hookah pipe; and her mother as the ever-gray presence, illustrated by the gray billows of smoke impairing the client's breathing, vision, and hearing. Up until the death of her sister, the sister had been the one to care for their ailing mother, and as a result of her demise, it was now the client's turn to caretake a mother she had some extremely mixed feelings towards, based on past childhood trauma. The powerful metaphors that the client created to describe her situation seemed to indicate that she was choking from an internalized message that it was now her turn to care for her needy mother—finding herself in a situation she had not contemplated, based on the belief that her mother would predecease her sister.

WITH EVERY BREATH YOU TAKE IN, you take in more and more space, almost as if your body is making room for new associations, feelings, thoughts, and imaginings—that's right—an opportunity to ponder and welcome new possibilities.... And it's nice to know that all you have to do is just focus—allowing each part of your body—yourself—to take in more and more comfort, letting your unconscious mind just drift and wander, while your conscious mind listens to a story about a woman called Alice.

Now Alice was a young woman in search of something—of what she was unsure. She would spend a great deal of time on the ocean shore communing with nature—speaking to the seagulls—thinking that some of the answers to her questions lay in intently observing the ways of the gulls—how they fly so high in the sky that their wings become tinged with gold from the sun—watching them form huge arches with their wings, only to then dip into the ocean far below, to cool down and dive for small fish. Their lives seemed so complete to Alice—their lot was not to question, but just to live out a blueprint, one that had been carefully created thousands of years ago by their ancestors. It seemed so simple: their own history could be found in how they express themselves moment to moment, until a new generation is ready to go through all the same motions and, once again, cyclically repeat what had come before.

Alice's life seemed so complicated in comparison to the seagulls, and yet so empty at the same time. She was searching for something that was missing from her life, but she was not sure where to find it. One day, as she ran along the shore, the wind in her face and her hair, she suddenly realized that she no longer had to find the answers, but that the answers would somehow find their way to her, that's right, easily and comfortably when ready.

That very night Alice had a dream—that from the waist down she was trapped inside a black egg—able to move only her upper torso, her arms, neck, and head. At first she felt stuck and then, as the dream unfolded, Alice felt herself becoming more and more mobile as she began to learn how to move around from place to place, by concentrating more and more energy into her lower torso, legs, and feet (i.e., going with the resistance), eventually being able to provide the momentum she needed to roll down the pathway that she found herself on.

Along the pathway Alice came across some strange and unusual sights as she turned the corner and encountered a huge caterpillar, its body wrapped around a tree, smoking a large hookah pipe. As Alice moved closer towards the caterpillar, the smoke from its pipe became so overwhelming that she began to choke, unable to speak as she struggled to breathe. Alice felt as if she could not see for most of the dream, her vision impaired by the caterpillar's billowing gray clouds of smoke. Between puffs, however, the caterpillar's only audible words were: "It's your turn now.... It's your turn now." With the caterpillar's words indelibly printed in her mind, Alice awoke, wondering what they could mean as she connected with feelings of intense pain in her shoulders.

That following night, the dream returned to Alice again, but somehow this time, she experienced a new sense of purpose; instead of feeling led down the old, all too familiar path, choking from the caterpillar's smoke, her vision and hearing impaired, she decided, quite independently, to follow a less familiar one instead. It was nice to know that this was her choice.... Just as she had come to this awareness, it occurred to her that she had always had choices and that she had, in fact, chosen to be trapped in the black egg. She also realized that the words of the caterpillar, which she had chosen to believe in, had acted as a smokescreen—blocking her connection to her own ability to think and to feel clearly.

In choosing another path, Alice created more and more distance between herself and the smoke, noticing that she began to breathe more easily and more deeply—that's right, it was nice to know that she could breathe unencumbered by the smoke, freely and comfortably, taking in the freshness of the air around her as she made her way down her own path, which happened to parallel the ocean. Something quite wonderful began to occur now that Alice began bringing more and more control back into her life—the black egg she was bound in began loosening, and eventually pieces of the egg shell started to dislodge themselves from her torso, gradually freeing Alice to find her feet again. At first she felt a little unsure and wobbly, as she freely stood on her own two feet for the first time in a long time—unencumbered by the hard, seemingly impenetrable shell that had surrounded her for so long. As she walked further and further along the path, her balance, vision, and hearing returned, and her gait strengthened as she continued to walk down her own path—her path of choice. And, just at that moment,

Alice became aware of the possibility of creating a new understanding of the caterpillar's words. "Yes," she thought, "it is my turn now, it is my time to take center stage in my own life, so that I can make decisions with my best interests in mind."

Alice awoke from her dream, bringing back with her a renewed sense of choice—experiencing for the first time what it felt like to feel unencumbered by her own sense of emptiness—discovering what it felt like to be in touch with her own senses: taste, touch, smell, sound that belonged to her and no one else—waking up refreshed and ready to commence a new chapter in her life.

⌘　　　⌘　　　⌘

FOLLOW-UP RITUAL TO "ALICE SHEDS HER SHELL"

In order to anchor the achievements experienced by the survivor from the above story, you may want to suggest to the client to take some time to look for any symbols, tokens, clothes, letters, drawings, furniture, books, and so on that the client feels "do not fit" or belong anymore, if ever, and, when ready, to dispose of these objects (or object) in some way. You may suggest having a burial service on land or at sea for the particular items that might have symbolized oppression, criticism, or terror.

In the last session following a series of 30 sessions with a group of survivors of sexual abuse, each member brought some memorabilia including artwork, letters, and poetry that were in some way connected with their offenders. The group jointly decided to have a bonfire at the beach where they had an opportunity to make some comments around letting go of the symbolic connections (i.e., the letters, poetry, art, etc.) to the offender and then saying the words; "And I'm taking back my power." This would usually be followed by tearing the articles into pieces and then throwing them into the fire.

Once the fire was out, the group facilitators, wearing specially insulated gloves, collected the ashes in a jar, providing the opportunity for each group member, if she wanted to, to take a small amount of the ashes and toss them into the ocean, repeating the same words as above: "And I'm taking back my power." This process proved to be an empowering ritual for all group members involved, acting as a clear, concrete indication of the internal transformations that had taken place within each survivor.

As a result of successfully managing to let go of what doesn't belong anymore, the survivor is then free, when ready, to create space in her life for the up-until-now lost parts of herself, particularly the abused child part of herself that she necessarily abandoned in order to survive. Now, with a newly developed empathy for self, the way is open for the client to take back and to reclaim what is rightfully hers.

⌘   ⌘   ⌘

DOLL EXERCISES AND GUIDED IMAGERIES

The goal of this exercise is to help facilitate an experience in which the survivor can connect in a compassionate and naturalistic manner so as to assist her in externalizing the trauma and in separating it from the "self." This allows the client to more safely work through the pain, fear, and panic of the abuse experience as it is done via a guided imagery and art exercise that accesses the historical information in a more indirect manner. The by-product of this exercise is often an entree into many positive memories and recollections that may have been unavailable to the client since the onset of the abuse.

This exercise is useful with groups as well as in an individual counseling setting. The advantage of the group experience, as previously stated, is the power provided through peer support and validation while experiencing the exercise.

Step I

The first part of this exercise is the induction in which the survivor recalls herself at the time of the abuse. The use of the third person is most important here.

Explain to the client(s) that the purpose of this guided imagery is to help reacquaint her with herself at the time of the abuse, but that she need only go as deep or as far as she feels ready to. Try to leave the instructions as vague as possible so that each individual can experience her own natural process.

SAMPLE GUIDED IMAGERY

AND YOU CAN JUST TAKE A FEW MOMENTS to relax your body as you sit there, taking a nice easy breath, as deeply as you can, comfortably listening to the sound of my voice on the outside, while you can hear your own breathing inside, allowing your mind to wander wherever it needs to go (*pause*), knowing that you need only be in touch with as much or as little as is right for you now, allowing your unconscious mind to interpret this experience in whatever meaningful way it chooses. Knowing that you are not alone and that you can keep your eyes open or closed and your feet firmly planted on the floor or in any position that you feel most comfortable and secure, feeling free to participate as much or as little as you wish. Nothing you really have to do, just simply being here and drifting. That's right.

And you can let your mind wander to any image or impression of that child or girl at a time from the past when there was abuse happening. I don't know how old she might have been or what grade she might have been in, just allow any impression that seems to pop up to just happen (*pause*) that's right. And how tall was she? (*pause*) Remembering to breathe, that's right. And what was she wearing at that time? (*pause*) What colors or textures were her clothes? (*pause*) And how did she look? What color was her hair? (*pause*) And what about her face? (*pause*) What kind of expression would there be on her face, in her eyes, and what color were those eyes? (*pause*) And how about her mouth? (*pause*) And what else about her face? (*pause*) What about her expression stands out? Remembering to breathe and that you are not alone (*pause*) And how did she feel at that time? And how did she feel at that time? (*pause*) (*repeat*) and what did she feel? (*pause*)

And did she have a favorite toy or pet? (*pause*) And where was she then? (*pause*) And were there any sounds she can remember? Maybe a favorite song or story (*pause*). And what can she hear? (*pause*) And is there anything else she can remember? (*pause*) And can she smell anything? (*pause*) And are there any scents or smells? And is she aware of any textures or colors that stand out? Remembering to breathe and to only go as far as you need to go (*pause*). And is there anything else about her that is important? And just take a moment to identify anything else that is significant, breathing as comfortably as you can, that's right (*pause*).

And is there anything else about her that is important? And just take a moment to identify anything else that is significant, breathing as comfortably as you can, that's right (*pause*). And when you are ready, gradually orienting back to the room, making eye contact with someone else and taking a stretch and a nice comfortable deep breath.

EXERCISE

With the materials provided (unfinished doll, construction paper, glue, markers, crayons, plain paper, scissors, etc.), instruct the client(s) in the following manner: With paper dolls approximately 24" long "construct a doll that is representative of you at the time of the abuse in any way that you choose." (Figure 5.1 is an example of an unfinished doll.)

When the doll is finished, allow the survivor time to process the experience and the doll that she constructed. If this is being done in a group setting, it is important to manage the time so that each participant has at least 5 minutes to process this exercise.

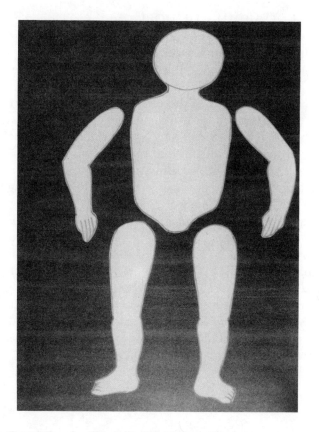

Figure 5.1 Example of a Blank Doll (arms and legs are separate as some survivors choose to omit various body parts).

Step II

In a subsequent session when the therapist judges that the client is ready for the next stage (we recommend enough time to adequately process the Step I experience), another guided imagery is employed: The survivor is instructed to recall her doll from Stage One and to begin to think about it in a slightly different way.

Sample Guided Imagery

(Employ a brief relaxation induction first)

AND THINK ABOUT THE DOLL and the person she represents *(pause)*, remembering how she looked at that time *(pause)* and how she felt, all of those feelings and experiences, just allowing yourself to drift in whatever direction you need to, but only as far as you can safely go *(pause)*, that's right. And remembering that you are not alone, and remembering the support of the chair beneath you, breathing easily, that's right. And as you remember that doll/person, dressed in that particular way, I'm wondering what else you can notice about her, about how she is in that body and in that mind? *(pause)* And I don't know when you will be able to notice something unique about her, it may be now, or in a moment from now, but wouldn't it be interesting to see her in a slightly different way? *(pause)* Wouldn't it be interesting to be able to appreciate something about her that you haven't previously been aware of *(pause)*, perhaps appreciating her ability to survive her abuse for the first time *(pause)*. Just thinking about all of those resources and abilities that may not have come to mind before *(pause)*. And what can you appreciate about her? Taking a few moments of clock time to notice something you may not have noticed before...that's right, anything that comes to mind *(pause 30 to 60 seconds)*. And when you are ready, take some easy breaths and reorient back to the room, looking around you and remembering you are not alone.

Exercise

Say to the client(s), "With the materials provided, construct a doll incorporating something that you may not have noticed before; it might be in the form of a symbol, characteristic, or expression that represents some of her strength or resourcefulness—anything that seems relevant to you now." Again, the instructions are as open to individual interpretation as possible. Allow time for processing and talking about the experience.

Step III

A third guided imagery is now utilized to help elicit some future possibilities and a focus for the self of the future. This presupposes and seeds the idea of resolution, of having an experience of the self as separate from the abuse, and of a hopeful future. The survivor is now asked to imagine herself in the future, as she would like to be.

SAMPLE GUIDED IMAGERY

(*Employ a brief relaxation induction first*)

A ND AS YOU ARE SITTING THERE listening to the sound of your own breathing inside and feeling the support of your body resting in that position, wouldn't it be interesting to see yourself sitting there from a different perspective. From a different viewpoint, as you are there now, but also as you can be in the future. A different sense of yourself, the same self, but another self (*pause*), just as you have been aware of a different self from the past, you can now be aware of a different self in the future (*pause*). I am reminded of what it is like to look at oneself in a three-way mirror, like the kind you might find in the changing room of a clothing store (but without the horrible lighting). When you look into that mirror you can see yourself from three different perspectives. You know how you have been in the past and you are now aware of many of the strengths and resources that you possess, which have carried you through to the present. Wouldn't it be interesting to experience yourself as a future possibility, so many options, so many new perspectives? (*pause*) And think about how you would look, what sort of expression would you have on your face? (*pause*) And how will you be carrying your body differently? (*pause*) And what will that aura that you are projecting be saying to others? (*pause*) And how will you sound? What will be different about the way you speak and the quality of your voice? (*pause*) And how will it feel to be that different yet same person? (*pause*) What will you be saying to yourself that will be different? (*pause*) And what will that different you be doing? (*pause*) And where will you be? (*pause*) And how will you be? (*pause*) Will you be alone or with others? (*pause*) And what will it be like and what will she be like? (*pause*) And what will you be like? (*pause*) And how will your experience be different? (*pause*)

And you can take a moment or two of clock time to experience that fully, in any way that is right for you. With a deep sense of appreciation for all of that courage and resourcefulness that you may not yet be aware that you possess. But it's important to remember that your unconscious mind knows so much about you and your abilities and you can begin to be aware and to share that information with yourself in a more conscious manner (*pause*), that's right, even more comfortably in a way that's meaningful to you. (*pause 1 or 2 minutes*) And when you are ready, you can gradually reorient back to the room, bringing with you anything that's important for you.

Exercise

You can say the following to the client(s): "With the materials provided, construct a doll of the you—the you you would like to be." Allow time to process the exercise and imagery.

In conclusion, the process from Doll I to Doll II to Doll III is, in our experience, a fascinating transition, which generally initiates lively discussion and seeds future possibilities. It is interesting for the survivor(s) to view these three dolls and their progression from past to present to future (see Figures 5.2 and 5.3).

⌘   ⌘   ⌘

MASK INDUCTION AND EXERCISE

As discussed earlier in the chapter, the goal of this exercise is to help uncover many of the fears and feelings associated with the abuse that have been covered up, stuffed down, or masked by the survivor at the time of the abuse. The client can therefore begin to externalize and let go of those feelings while at the same time realizing that she has the ability to free herself from the secret as well as being able to appreciate the limiting effect that this has had on her both at the time of the abuse and thereafter.

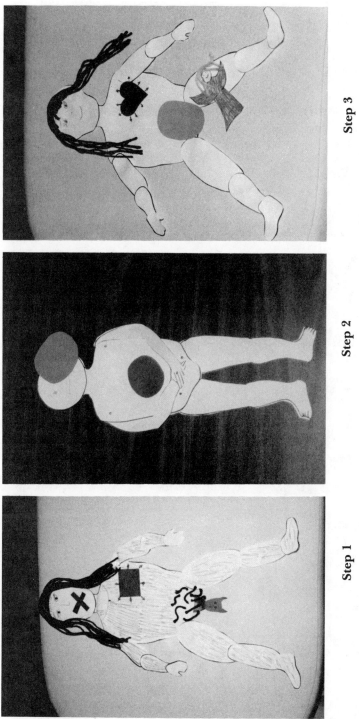

Step 1   Step 2   Step 3

Figure 5.2 Doll Exercise.

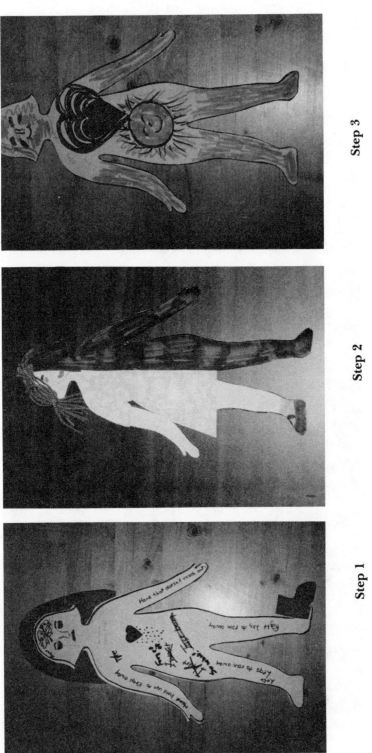

Step 1   Step 2   Step 3

Figure 5.3 Doll Exercise.

Group Experience. *We feel that this exercise is most helpful when used in a group setting so that the survivor has the interaction and validation of her peers while processing the feelings and material. However, this exercise and guided imagery are also very beneficial and effective when used in individual therapy sessions where the therapist can help witness and validate the processing of the exercise.*

Mask Induction

A S YOU ARE SITTING THERE listening to the sound of my voice outside, wouldn't it be interesting to just allow your mind to wander as you are aware of the support against your back and under your feet—it's so nice to feel supported and comfortable as you sit there. Feeling free to make any adjustments that seem right for you at any time you are ready. And keeping your eyes open or closed, whatever you feel most comfortable doing, and you can focus on something in the room if you like or you can focus on the sound of my voice, knowing that you are not alone and that you can come back to the room whenever you need to. That's right. And you can listen to the sound of your own breath as it enters your body comfortably and slowly. That deep satisfying breath that nurtures you with each inhale and lets go of whatever you would like to let go of on every exhale, that's right, finding your own unique rhythm and pace. Accessing all of those strengths and resources that you have on an unconscious level that you may not have realized were there (*pause*).

Just allowing your mind to wander and wonder at all of that knowledge that you have within. All of those experiences that you can safely and comfortably access. Remembering only what you need to remember and letting go of the rest (*pause*). I am reminded of a recent art exhibition I visited called "The Voice of the Mask"; as I wandered through the gallery, I was entranced by the beautifully constructed masks, noticing their texture and shape. Wondering at all of the brilliant colors—bright red, green, yellow, orange—and the expressions on their faces—sadness, surprise, fear, shock, wisdom, and timelessness. These masks were symbols of the individuals who had worn them, a culmination of their experience and persona. What a strange sensation to wear a mask. Once at Halloween I can remember wearing the mask of a cat and feeling quite detached from my usual self. There, and not there, seeing through my eyes and yet feeling as though I was someone else (*pause*). Visible but invisible (*pause*) present but not present (*pause*).

As you are sitting there hearing my voice outside, I'm wondering what it would be like for you to think about that face you present to the world on the outside. What does her persona look like as she presents herself to the outside world? What kind of expression does she have? (*pause*) How old is she? (*pause*) How does she look and seem to others? (*pause*) Remembering to breathe. I don't know when you might begin to notice something about that face that others see? And what about underneath that mask? How does she really feel? (*pause*) How old does she feel? (*pause*) How does she sound to herself? (*pause*) And how *does* she feel underneath that mask she presents to the outside world? And what expression does she have on her face, what emotions? (*pause 30 seconds*)

Remembering to breathe deeply and only going as deep as you can comfortably go, that's right. Keeping your eyes open or closed and listening to my voice knowing you are not alone. Just letting any images or feelings or thoughts float and drift through your mind. Just seeing, experiencing, feeling, or hearing whatever is important right now and back then, that's right (*pause*). And as I was walking through that exhibition, I was struck by all of those images and impressions triggered by those masks, and I was struck by all the symbols those masks represented—symbols of transformation and change...and you can take a moment of clock time, all the time you need and integrate whatever is important for you from this experience, bringing back some important information or letting go of anything you need to let go of...safely and comfortably...that's right. And when you are ready, gradually reorienting back to the room, breathing comfortably, feeling your feet on the floor, stretching and looking around you, noticing something or someone that catches your eye. Remembering to breathe at your own pace, easily, that's right.

Mask Exercise

After reorienting the client(s) back to the room, the therapist can ask the client or group to construct a two-sided mask: (for example, see Figure 5.4) on one side, the face that she presented to others, on the other side, the face or mask that was hidden, the expression and emotions that were experienced on the inside and perhaps never shared or acknowledged heretofore. The therapist should suggest that the mask can take any form or image that comes to mind. It could be a person or an animal, any form of expression is okay. Sometimes it is less threatening for the survivor to use symbols such as animals to personify the feel-

Expressing pain and rage

Feelings on the inside

Transformation ——→ how survivor *would like* to feel and be

Figure 5.4 Mask Exercise.

ings. For some survivors, the concept of a two-sided mask may be premature. Figure 5.4 is an example of a client who had difficulty with the concept of a two-sided mask, but was clearly ready to acknowledge and express her preiously buried feelings of pain and rage. This particular example emphasizes the therapist's need for flexibility around all exercises.

The therapist will need to have art supplies such as construction paper, plain paper, glue, scissors, markers, and crayons. We have also found it beneficial to have such things as feathers, wool of different colors (often used for hair), glitter, and various odds and ends that can be creatively and symbolically utilized.

After the masks are created, each person in the group, or the individual with the therapist, should have an opportunity to talk about her experience. There is no right or wrong way to interpret this exercise: whatever is expressed needs to be validated and processed in a nonjudgmental way.

⌘ ⌘ ⌘

CELEBRATION AND TRANSFORMATION RITUALS

The following are suggestions for rituals which we have co-created with many of the survivors we work with. Many find them to be helpful in marking the healthy changes and growth that have taken place in their healing process. We found that doing these kinds of ritual helps to make the healing experience more concrete and valid. It can also anchor the breaking of old patterns and the introduction of new and personally relevant traditions.

We encourage you to co-create your own rituals to complement the particular process that is unique to each client.

The Rebirthing Party

Many survivors describe occasions such as birthdays as not particularly happy events. We often reframe these occasions as opportunities to celebrate herself and her newfound, more tolerant, appreciative connection with the "self" she was at the time of the abuse.

Suggest to the client that she choose a day in the calendar to celebrate her emancipation from the abuse (the day she reclaimed her inner self or inner child as the adult self). This transition can be marked by honoring her self with a rebirthing party, which includes trusted friends who have supported her throughout the recovery process.

The client may want to create a cake with all of the child's favorite ingredients and candles to make special wishes for the now more hopeful future. Messages of appreciation to the self and from others can be included in this celebration ritual. This celebration may take place at a location that has special significance for the survivor, such as the beach, outside in nature, or at the home of a treasured friend or supportive family member. Favorite music may be played, and those present may participate in some significant activity. Again we encourage you to individualize and co-create this experience with your client so as to incorporate the details that are meaningful to her.

Renaming the Transformed Self

As mentioned in Chapter 3, at this stage of the healing process many women choose to change their names as part of the process of reclaiming the child part of the "self." We are always supportive of this choice and often suggest it be celebrated with a christening ceremony where close, trusted friends, who have been supportive along the way, are invited.

Some women arrange to have these ceremonies in environments that have symbolic significance to them. One client had the ceremony on a friend's boat, and on completion of the ritual, which included a prepared speech by one of the only members of her family who acknowledged the abuse, she threw symbolic remnants of her past into the ocean. Another survivor had a renaming transformation ceremony that was presided over by a local "Shaman." During the ritual, she wore the mask she had created during therapy. At the culmination of the ceremony, she discarded the mask and was introduced and blessed by the Shaman using her new name. Again, the possibilities are endless, and creativity and imagination are always encouraged.

"HUSH—PART THREE"

This metaphorical story is a continuation of the previous two in which Hush encounters many of the same issues and feelings that are characteristic at Stage Three of the healing process. While this metaphor was initially developed for one client, we have used it in many groups and with individuals and have found it to be effective for those who are dealing with their recovery at this stage.

THROUGHOUT THE AUTUMN, Hush began to feel moments of spontaneity and just plain fun. At first, she felt guilty for allowing herself to be playful. It was almost as if, if she let herself go and have a good time, something bad might happen. She still struggled with feelings of low self-worth and sometimes she had very strong mood swings, which left her feeling a little crazy and always feeling ashamed and guilty for expressing her feelings in what she thought was a too-extreme manner.

Hush had periods of time when she felt extremely angry—it often seemed for no apparent reason. One day Hush saw Raye studying her mask (her most prized possession). She immediately grabbed it from her and told her not to touch or go near her belongings. To Hush, her backpack, filled with the only possessions she owned, was to be fiercely guarded: she was very suspicious of anyone who showed any interest or curiosity in her. Raye, who was genuinely admiring her mask, was very apologetic about touching Hush's belongings without permission. This in turn made Hush feel embarrassed and ashamed of her reaction. She became very depressed and retreated into her corner of the den, where she remained for several days.

Eidolon, who was aware of this incident, came to talk to Hush about what had happened. Hush explained how she was feeling and Eidolon helped Hush to realize how natural it was for her to be protective of herself and said, "It is very positive that you care about your belongings in such a way—those prized things are like an extension of you—that tells me that you are beginning to have a stronger sense of yourself. It's natural for you to be very wary and protective after everything that you have been through. It just takes time and practice to learn how to react to everyday situations that may have reminded you of things that happened in the past. Eventually, your reactions will even out and you will learn how to set clearer boundaries for yourself." Hush was relieved at hearing this information and that Eidolon still liked her even after what had happened.

That night Hush talked to Raye about what had occurred and they worked out some new ways of being denmates that would be more comfortable for each of them.

Crystal and Dot were also experiencing some discomfort in becoming accustomed to sharing both their external and internal environment with others. Everyone who had come to this sanctuary struggled with the fear, as well as the joy, of learning how to give and receive friendship. Hush, Crystal, Dot, and Raye all had times when they doubted they were capable of simply being with anyone else without all of the self-critical thoughts and fears that were associated with learning how to be close to another being.

One afternoon while helping Eidolon harvest the vegetable garden, Crystal and Dot (who were in silent competition to see who could harvest the most the fastest to impress Eidolon) began arguing. Dot, who often had a critical tongue, made some comments to Crystal in the heat of the moment, which triggered some of Crystal's most vulnerable feelings. All she could think about was that she had to get out of that garden as fast as she could. She remembered how she had been blamed for everything by her family in the past, and all she could think about was running. She took off into the woods without really thinking about where she was. Eventually, she stopped running and sat down in a frozen state, totally unaware of her surroundings or her own safety.

After an hour or so, the others became very concerned—it would soon be dark and Crystal had still not returned. Eidolon sent for a friend of hers who was good at scouting and knew the woods well, but she wouldn't be able to come till the next morning.

Hush was so upset at the thought of Crystal alone in the woods that she decided to go and look for Crystal by herself. Eidolon advised against anyone venturing into the darkness without the guide, but Hush impulsively ran into the woods after Crystal.

Hush found herself anxiously wandering around in no definite direction. After a while she realized that she was utterly lost in the dense forest. She sat down on a log and began to feel overwhelmed. She had done this before, and it seemed like an old nightmare repeating itself. She felt a familiar sense of panic taking hold of her. Just like the time she was lost on her way to Eidolon's, she had that old sense of badness inside of her. "I'm so stupid, I don't deserve to find my way back. How could I ever have thought I could help find Crystal. I'm so useless, I'll just bring her more bad luck."

This time, however, Hush also remembered that she had been able to find her way out of the woods and back on the right path with the help of the contents of her backpack. But Hush had left in such a hurry, she had left her backpack behind. For a moment she felt sick to her stomach. Her heart was beating so fast she thought she would faint.

She tried to remember some of the things her Aunt Kit used to tell her. Take some slow deep breaths, look around you and focus on something close by, think about something, someone, or somewhere that helps you feel safe. She heard her aunt's voice telling her to "trust your-self and your ability to go where you need to go. Try and let go of all of these old troublesome feelings and remember that you have all of the tools you need at hand."

Hush thought about her mask and how it always helped her to feel safe. But she had left it behind in her backpack. Hush forced herself to picture the mask in her mind; she saw that confident expression and those familiar colors. She could feel the mask against her face as it became part of her. She remembered how she *could* feel safe and even a bit courageous when she wore her mask and soon she was able to calm her anxiety.

She began to understand that she had reacted to this situation in an old familiar way. It had reminded her of how she used to feel. But she also realized that she now had the ability to act and feel differently and that she could make some new choices.

After Hush calmed herself down, she remembered that she had found her way out of these woods before. If she had done it once, she could surely do it again. She closed her eyes and tried to remember how she had found her way before. The moon was quite bright that night and after orienting herself, Hush trusted her instincts as to which direction to take. After walking in one direction for about an hour, she thought she heard something familiar. A moment or two later, she came across Crystal who was sitting on the forest floor in tears.

Crystal was so happy and surprised to see Hush, it seemed too good to be true. Hush assured Crystal that she was real and they talked to-gether for several hours until sunrise. In the light, they were more eas-ily able to find the right path back to their community.

On their return, there were so many emotions and feelings to be understood and sorted out. Eidolon told Hush she was very impressed with her ability to conquer her old fears, and she suggested that Hush's successful adventure would be a meaningful one to share with the oth-ers. Hush's first reaction was self-doubt. Why would anyone else be interested in what she had to say? But Eidolon reminded Hush of all the resources and skills she possessed. Hush had a great idea. She could help the others make masks for themselves—masks to help them each experience what it would be like to conquer their most persistent troublesome feelings.

She consulted the others about her idea. Much to her surprise, they all thought it was a wonderful plan. Everyone had admired Hush's mask since she had joined them, and they were each eager to learn how to create their own unique masks to help them uncover and deal with many of the overwhelming emotions that often left them feeling out of control. Perhaps they too could learn how to feel different. They were all now in a different place where they could more safely feel and be supported, a place where they could make some new choices.

(*To be continued*)

And you can take a few moments to integrate this information in any way that fits for you (*pause*).

It's nice to know that you can begin to be aware of your own inner voice that can help to guide you in a direction that's right for you.

When you are ready, you can gradually reorient back to the room, taking some easy breaths and remembering whatever you need to remember and letting go of whatever you need to let go of.

CHAPTER 6

Stage Four: Empowerment and Evolution of the Sexual Self (Part A)

As the reintegration and redefinition of the self continues, the survivor is better able to deal with her life in the present. She has now had the opportunity to face the most disturbing aspects of her past abuse, and with the help of the therapist and her peers in the group experience, she can restructure her life in a way that is meaningful to her. By this time she has gained some new tools and methods for externalizing and controlling the overwhelming feelings and she can begin to incorporate into her life some new ways of dealing with previously out-of-control behavior.

Stage Four is a continuation of the reintegration process. Now that the survivor is better able to separate her own "self" from the offender and understand that the responsibility for the abuse rests outside of herself, she is at liberty to redefine herself in relation to others. The therapist can exercise this opportunity to help the client construct some clear and personally relevant boundaries. As more exact boundaries are defined, the survivor usually begins to recognize and to face the many complex feelings she has in relation to members of her family of origin, partner, and children.

We understand this stage as a two-part process. Part A of Stage Four is concerned with redefining the self in relation to others. The survivor is renegotiating and redefining relationships and is also dealing with trust issues and how her awareness in general can empower her to reshape her future both internally and externally.

Part B of Stage Four is a more future-oriented "taking-action" phase, in which the survivor is generally more proactive. She is concerned with redefining her sexuality and with the big picture, both personally and in a societal sense. Part B will be covered in Chapter 7. The following are the substages of Part A:

I. Prevalent Psychological and Physiological Symptoms
II. Understanding How the Abuse Continues to Affect the Survivor in the Present
III. Lifting the Cloak of Self-Blame and Dealing with Family and Trust Issues
IV. Creating Boundaries
V. Externalizing the Expression of Grief and Loss and the Empowerment of Self

Following our discussion of these substages, we will present Metaphors, Exercises, and Rituals, which will help the client reinforce and anchor the healing tasks that challenge her at this juncture.

I. PREVALENT PSYCHOLOGICAL AND PHYSIOLOGICAL SYMPTOMS

In Stage Four (Part A and Part B), the survivor continues to experience very intense emotions, which are often characterized by many of the old psychological and physiological symptoms, such as dissociation, sleep disturbance, anxiety attacks, and extreme fatigue. However, there is a dramatic increase in the stable periods that lie between these intermittent setbacks.

The back and forth nature of the healing process in the context of sexual abuse is often very frustrating to survivors (not to mention therapists). Clients feel they are making great headway and then out of the blue, they encounter the old demons again. In our view, these setbacks often indicate transition points in recovery similar to the various developmental phases in early childhood when a child sometimes regresses or revisits old familiar behavior before leaving it behind or outgrowing it. The therapist can utilize this opportunity to help the survivor reframe these setbacks as transition points that provide the opportunity to practice many newly acquired coping strategies. It is also important to help remind the survivor of how far she has come and to notice that these events are becoming less frequent than before.

By now, the survivor has practiced utilizing many new tools and previously unacknowledged resources and skills that enable her to be less vulnerable to those old ways. As a rule, one of the benefits of the un-packing and unstuffing of emotion is an improved feeling of well-being, both physically and mentally. The survivor generally begins to pay more attention to her health and to treat her body accordingly.

II. UNDERSTANDING HOW THE ABUSE CONTINUES TO AFFECT THE SURVIVOR IN THE PRESENT

At this stage of recovery, the survivor is more connected with her adult self and therefore is able to more clearly understand how the abuse affects her relationships in the present. Depending on individual cir-cumstances, this may include partners and children as well as friend-ships and work relations. In our experience, this always includes her relationship to her family of origin and to the perpetrator who may be part of that family.

The therapist and the survivor can now explore the impact of how the abuse was treated in the context of the family. The family of the abused survivor frequently urges her to forget about the past, forgive them (and that includes the perpetrator if he/she is a family member, as is often the case), and get on with her life. There is an implicit mes-sage here of minimizing the effects of the abuse, and the survivor often revisits her feelings of guilt and confusion in regard to her inability to let go of the past. It is the therapist's task here to once again confirm the effects of the abuse and to encourage the client to identify her *own* needs and experience with regard to her family.

Now that the survivor can more safely feel and identify the long-buried responses to the abuse, the therapist can help her realize that her reactions are healthy outlets to be respected and not minimized. For the first time, many clients can examine the nature of the family environment and the roles family members played in keeping the secret or in perpetuating the abuse. Some women realize for the first time that they *were* treated abusively by their family.

Andrea, a 34-year-old survivor, had been abused by her sister's hus-band at the age of 14. In a very vulnerable state, she had moved in with her sister after the death of their mother. At the age of 15 An-drea became pregnant with her first child. Andrea's sister and the rest of the family blamed Andrea for the pregnancy and for seducing her brother-in-law. She was thus stigmatized and expelled from the family. Having nowhere else to go, she moved in with her abuser and subsequently had another child with him. The relationship continued for an additional four years.

Andrea describes that period of her life as if she was in a "dream world, observing [herself] from a distance." It wasn't until she entered therapy at the age of 34 that she realized she *had* been sexually abused by her brother-in-law and that *she* was not responsible for that abuse or for the subsequent isolation from her family.

After a year of individual and group therapy, Andrea was able to look at the dynamics of her family from a different perspective. As many years had passed since the separation of her sister from the perpetrator, Andrea was able to reconnect with her family and work through much of the pain and abandonment she experienced. Andrea's sister, after doing her own work around relationship issues, was able to take responsibility for her past actions in relation to Andrea. In a few joint therapy sessions both sisters were able to more clearly understand how they had each been manipulated by the tactics the offender used to rationalize his behavior.

Coming to terms with how she related to her two children was a more complicated undertaking for Andrea. She struggled with conflicting feelings toward her children. Andrea had numbed herself with alcohol and drugs for many years. The pain she had lived with for so long could no longer be stuffed down. During the year of therapy she had also become sober and she began to understand how her relationship with the offender as well as her coping behaviors had interfered with her attachment to her children. There was a great deal of confusion surrounding the conflicting feelings she experienced in relation to them. The therapist was able to help her understand the love/hate relationship she had with her children in the context of her relationship with the offender and she was eventually able to bring them into therapy sessions with her to begin to clarify, explain, and restructure her relationship with them.

Each family situation is unique, and we believe that it is the client's right to choose how she wants to handle family relationships. Many survivors have long ago distanced themselves from family members, while others have had a continual battle to be accepted by them. There is often a strong need to try again to reconnect with family at this stage of therapy.

Terry, a 30-year-old incest survivor, had moved across the country at the age of 21 to escape her abusive past. After two years of therapy, she began to make contact once again with her mother and sister. This decision grew out of the awareness gained—resulting from the anger and rage she began to experience with more intensity—at the end of a Phase II survivor group. The subject matter at the end of the group concerned relationships and the identification of unmet needs. Terry began having flashbacks again concerning the physical and emotional abuse she experienced from her mother and from her father (the perpetrator). Terry began to correspond with her mother at this time and felt that she wanted to attempt some kind of resolution to their relationship.

There was a great deal of anger surfacing not only concerning her mother's lack of protection and support for her in relation to the sexual abuse, but also in general within the family. Terry began to realize she was the scapegoat for all the family's problems. A frequent theme of any conversation about her experience was the excuse that "if she hadn't been such a difficult child, the family would have been happier and much of the abuse wouldn't have happened." During this time Terry was struggling to externalize her feelings of anger and loss and wrote a series of poems in her journal about her family-of-origin experience and about her mother in particular:

> Why won't you help me?
> I must really deserve this
>
> He comes to my bedroom
> My sister is scared
> She gets up
> And climbs into your bed
>
> Why do you comfort her
> And not me?
> I must deserve this....

Terry

It is common at this time for the survivor to revisit many of the old feelings of shame, guilt, and anger. However, there is now a different understanding of these feelings. Because the survivor is better able to separate and externalize her emotion and pain, there is now a feeling of more personal power and the possibility for resolution of these feelings.

Terry began to realize that although her mother admitted she had been abusive and unavailable to Terry, she was still minimizing her abuse experience and protecting Terry's father who was now ill and dying. Terry's sister was able to give her a bit more support than her mother as she had recently begun to remember many of the abusive incidents of her own childhood. To Terry, this was reassuring but not enough; she felt the need to go back to her family home to confront her father and mother.

In a situation like this, it is important for the therapist to prepare the client for the possibility that the outcome of such a confrontation may not be the desired one. We talked through the various possible scenarios including Terry's "worst case scenario." We also explored some practical measures in case things didn't work out as she had hoped. We discussed the survivor's natural need to be parented in a safe and loving way and that this parenting may never be possible for Terry in the context of her family of origin. It is important for the therapist to be both supportive and realistic about the nature of the relationship that is or is not possible when incest has occurred within a family. In Terry's case we explored her feelings of abandonment and the polarity of her emotions, that is, the need for revenge and restitution on one hand versus the child's need to be loved and protected.

Terry's homecoming was a mixture of frustration and satisfaction. Her father gave her an "empty apology" mixed with excuses and blame attached to his alcoholic behavior. Terry's mother was a bit more supportive but still held the attitude that it was time to let go of the past and get on with her life. Terry's sister was more supportive and this was the most meaningful aspect of her visit—as they were able to get reacquainted and hopefully begin a new relationship with each other that could become more mutually satisfying. For the first time, they had been able to remember and share some happy moments from their childhood. Terry was pleased that she could now remember and accept some happy times and, for the first time, acknowledge some of the closeness she experienced with her father and mother before the abuse began (approximately at age 5) in addition to all of the negative memories from her past.

On her return from this visit, Terry felt encouraged about her encounter with her family even though she didn't get exactly what she needed from it; she had been prepared for that and now felt ready to do more work focusing on herself and her future. Terry was now preparing herself for the possibility of healthy relationships in that future.

At this time we began to do hypnotic work to help her place some personally relevant boundaries around her future relationship with her family and to deal with the past in a way that acknowledged the pain and isolation, while also setting the stage for future growth and fulfillment. Terry expressed a strong need to be free from "the ghosts of her past," which she felt were still limiting her choices for the future. The metaphorical story "The Attic and the Drawbridge," found at the end of this chapter, was co-created with Terry to assist her in respectfully putting her historical experience in perspective by letting go of the responsibility and burden of the abuse and identifying her own needs in order for her reintegrated self to be able to emerge and blossom.

III. LIFTING THE CLOAK OF SELF-BLAME AND DEALING WITH FAMILY AND TRUST ISSUES

As demonstrated in the previous two case examples, by and large the survivor no longer feels she has to assume responsibility for the abuse within the family circle. She can begin to lift the cloak of self-blame that has overcast her life heretofore. The client can now shift the responsibility of the abuse to an outward expression of anger, loss, and grief toward the perpetrator and caretakers who did not protect her.

At this point in therapy, the therapist can help the survivor to enter a process of making distinctions about whom she can trust and accept in the family. Sometimes there may be no one. This process can assist her in acknowledging and trusting her own instincts and judgment, which may have been overshadowed in her previously eclipsed self. With her burgeoning ability to trust the self, the survivor is now better able to make choices about which family members she would like to maintain relations with and the nature of those relationships.

Many issues arise at this time for the survivor. One of the most intense is that of confronting the offender. As we saw in Terry's case, this was something she felt she had to do in order to end the abuse cycle and begin again. There are many conflicting viewpoints on the subject of confrontation. We are of the opinion that it must be completely up to the individual, but it is the therapist's job to clearly and realistically help the client weigh the pros and cons according to each individual situation.

Writing exercises and journal writing in general are very useful at this time. We encourage survivors to identify and to explore ways in which she can further externalize the blame and shame of the abuse and focus it back on the perpetrator. Each individual must decide which way is right for her. "The Emerging Voice" is an induction written to help the survivor tune in to her own needs and emerging identity. This can seed the necessary awareness, exploration, and identification of her values and belief systems that will assist her in making the writing exercises at the end of this chapter more focused and relevant. (See Value-Clarification Exercise and Letters to the Offender.)

In cases where family members or perpetrators are deceased, writing exercises can afford the survivor the opportunity of saying and doing what she needs to do in order to move on. Writing is also much less threatening and reduces the risk of retraumatization. Writing letters to the offender, which may or may not be sent, is an effective tool that may be utilized at this time. We have incorporated letter-writing exercises to the offender and to the self in the latter sessions of our Phase II group. (Please see Letters to the Offender at the end of this chapter.) Again, we feel it is important to emphasize how valuable it is for the survivor to be able to discuss these issues with her peers. Being able to hear about others' situations and decisions regarding such matters can assist her in her own decision-making process. Because women are often at slightly different places in their individual recovery, the group process offers survivors varied life experiences to draw from, which can help each woman to decide what is best for her. Many women decide to lay formal charges after understanding and expressing their feelings towards the offender. For some, resolution results from the verbalization of the experience as facilitated in the letter writing or in the writing process in general.

At this point in the healing process, family therapy is another option under certain circumstances. There are some criteria that we think need to be present in order to do family therapy. The most important factor to consider is who will be participating in the sessions and what is the desired outcome? In many cases the survivor's family may pressure her to include them in therapy in an effort to minimize the nonoffending family members' roles in the abuse cycle. The ulterior motive sometimes is to pressure her into forgiving the offender if he/she is a family member. Again, it is the role of the therapist to help the survivor sort through the intent behind the therapy and to clarify the goals of any such sessions.

In the case of Andrea, her goals were to reestablish contact with siblings and to improve relations with her children. These types of interactions can be mutually beneficial and healthy if all parties have similar goals.

It is helpful at this stage of the healing process to explore the issues of abandonment and how realistic it is to reestablish relations with the nonoffending parent if that is a possibility. Terry struggled a great deal with this issue and finally came to realize that her mother was never going to respond to her with the unconditional love and nurturing that we are programmed to believe is our birthright in this society. She also became aware that her mother (as is often the case) was a survivor of sexual abuse herself. Under these circumstances it is important to allow the survivor to articulate her feelings without having to feel guilty about their expression in view of her mother's past.

In summary, it is our opinion that in some situations, family therapy can be healthy and cathartic if the focus is on developing new boundaries and better communication patterns as opposed to patterns that involve continued blaming and minimization of the past abuse—and only if it is the choice of the survivor according to her own goals and timing.

The subject of trust is one that becomes more and more relevant to the survivor at this time. As a result of her abuse, there may be no one in her family that she had a trusting relationship with. Generally, she is now more cognizant of the impact that her lack of trust has over her relationships with family, friends, or partners. As previously stated, we encourage the client to begin to listen to her own instincts about whom she can trust. By-products of the coping skill of hypervigilance are often an acute ability to sense danger and to anticipate future events. We often utilize and reframe this skill in an effort to help the survivor realize that she can learn to listen and to trust herself. This skill combined with practice in setting boundaries and delineating for herself what is best for *her* are important tasks in Stage Four.

We believe it is paramount at this time to help the survivor revisit her many accomplishments so that she can continue to appreciate how far she has come and to validate her courage in facing the abuse. Please see "The Eucalypt Tree" metaphorical story at the end of this chapter, which we often use to help remind the survivor of how she is choosing to begin again and exercising her own power for regrowth and redefinition.

IV. CREATING BOUNDARIES

Creating boundaries for the self and learning how to say "no" to others can be a very liberating and empowering experience for the survivor. Clear boundaries are something the survivor has rarely experienced in her development. The act of sexual assault is a very powerful message to her of the violation of her primary boundary, her body. The environment that sustains the abuse seldom condones the existence of boundaries, because their existence would threaten the power imbalance that is necessary to maintain the secrecy and isolation.

Survivors speak a great deal about their lack of privacy and rights within the family. One must have a more clearly defined sense of self in order to establish limits. The survivor has rarely had the option of choice or the opportunity to define her self. It has been unsafe for her to say no and many women have never realized they had the right to say "no." As one client said, "I didn't realize I could say no to anything I was expected to do, let alone to [say no to] sex."

Learning how to say "no" can help the survivor to externalize her guilt and shame. She usually bore the responsibility for much that was not right in the family. As Andrea said, "I no longer had to be the family scapegoat. I always blamed myself for everything, but now I realize I was just a kid with all the needs and desires kids have. But with no one to understand that and nowhere to just be me."

One place the survivor can learn about boundaries is with the therapist. Therapy offers a variety of opportunities to establish and illustrate healthy boundaries. Simple things like appointment times, payment, and respectful listening skills can be used as examples.

The survivor group experience is also an extremely effective tool for experiencing boundaries first hand. Establishing rules for the operation of the group is good practice for learning to set personal limits. The way group members learn to negotiate their relationships within the group, resolve conflict, or simply say what they feel or express an opinion is an extremely valuable learning experience.

In order to establish boundaries, one has to understand one's own value system and to understand and to define one's needs and expectations about any particular subject or situation. The survivor may be exploring these distinctions for the first time. We have found, therefore, that it is helpful at this time to work through a series of writing and value clarification exercises (see Value Clarification Exercises at the end of this chapter) to help the survivor understand her own needs and limits and to help her distinguish which of these values and expectations she wants to "own" for her own reasons and which are holdovers to be discarded from her past. The previously mentioned metaphorical story "The Attic and the Drawbridge," found at the end of this chapter, also seeds the notion of creating boundaries and prepares the client for this concept on a metaphorical level.

It is often both frightening and exciting for the survivor to learn to set comfortable limits for herself and in relation to others. This process can also help her to evaluate whom she can feel safe with and trust. In understanding one's own value and belief system and consequently in defining one's personal boundaries, the client can introduce a new level of safety and predictability into her life. Predictability is generally something quite foreign to the survivor's experience. In our opinion, the feeling of personal safety and the development of trust in any relationship are next to impossible to attain without the ability to institute and to understand one's own relevant framework. Thus, a sense of predictability and empowerment can eventually lead to a higher level of safety and trust of the self and of others.

The process of developing self-trust and trust in relationships is one that begins in the healing journey, but it should be noted that this concept continues to endure as the survivor progresses in the real world outside the therapeutic relationship. As with all of us, this development is a life-long process. Although the therapist can assist the client during more difficult times of recovery, much of the work in negotiating relationships with partners, friends, and family will take place after she has returned to the mainstream. We see our role by the end of Stage Four as one that is ultimately needed on a less frequent basis, sometimes for sporadic appointments or the occasional check-in.

V. EXTERNALIZING THE EXPRESSION OF GRIEF AND LOSS AND THE EMPOWERMENT OF SELF

At this stage of the healing process, the survivor's personal story has gradually unravelled. Its pieces progressively reintegrate into a renewed sense of self. As feelings are externalized, experienced, and connected to the self in a personally relevant manner, the survivor can gain perspective and take more definitive action concerning her future. Many women at this time experience newfound energy to deal with the past and make plans for the future. As the survivor reexamines her values and beliefs, we have found that some common themes emerge. One of the most significant of these is the understanding of grief and loss. Some other key issues, such as anger at society for not protecting its children and the commitment to self and one's children to end the cycle of abuse, will be covered in Chapter 7. This is a time of facing the past in new and different ways.

The survivor must grieve her losses in order to achieve a sense of identity and well-being and she has to constructively focus her anger and reintegrate the various pieces of her life, including relationships with significant others, in order to realize her future with all of its challenges and opportunities. Ours is a society that has a great deal of difficulty acknowledging and managing grief and loss. Too often we are told to "cheer up," "put it behind you," and "forget about it." These messages are very strong and often serve to trigger old guilt reactions. It is therefore important for the therapist to support and to encourage the client to identify, understand, and grieve the losses she has incurred.

It is generally easier to accomplish this now that the survivor is more aware of her abuse and the emotions and reactions resulting from it. The therapist can now help her to understand the various stages of grieving. This is usually very validating and helps her to further make sense of a lot of her confusing and often-conflicting emotions.

We have found the use of the Kübler-Ross model (see Kübler-Ross, 1969) to be helpful at this time in explaining the grief process. It is also very important to be aware of grief and loss in terms of the developmental stage the survivor was at when the abuse occurred. We refer readers to a book called *But Won't Granny Need Her Socks?* by Donald W. Knowles and Nancy Reeves (1983), who clearly and sensitively describe these developmental stages in the context of grief and loss.

In our groups we spend a few sessions understanding grief and loss to help the survivor begin to identify her own losses. The group is a valuable resource for dealing with these issues. Again, in hearing others' stories, feelings, and experiences, the survivor is able to validate and to speak out about her own history. The peer support is very powerful and the client realizes that many previously minimized responses are very real and deserve to be honored and mourned. Journal writing is very effective at this time to help the survivor gain perspective and work through the myriad of feelings and emotions left over from the abuse.

Many women in the groups find it helpful to read some of their writings in the presence of others. We often give homework assignments to our clients, either in individual therapy or during group, to write letters to self and others concerning their losses. An example of such an exercise can be found at the end of this chapter in the section on Grief and Loss: Exercises and Rituals.

Terry, the previously mentioned client, wrote a series of poems concerning her losses and found it very therapeutic to read them aloud during a group session. Terry was thus able to gain the recognition and support from her peers that she did not receive from her family of origin.

> What I have lost
> Cannot be measured
> Cannot be recompensed
> Cannot be saved
> Can only be grieved for
> In a very profound way
>
> I open my eyes
> And suddenly
> I am feeling so sad
>
> There's a world out there
> I did not see it
> I did not hear it
> I did not feel it
> I could not smell or taste it
> I was swept away by my own pain
>
> An eclipse that lasted 23 years
> A storm that blew right through me
> And uprooted everything in my heart
>
> Hang on
> I hung on
>
> Terry

At this point in therapy we have found the use of ritual to be an exceptionally valuable tool to acknowledge the grief and loss remaining from the abuse and, in particular, to mark the transition from past to present and future. One exercise and accompanying ritual we have found particularly cathartic is the construction of a *grief doll.* The client is asked to make a symbolic representation of her grief in the form of a paper doll. The instructions are fairly vague so as to encourage each individual to place her own unique interpretation on the doll. We give some suggestions that *may* be followed, such as using various parts or appendages to represent certain losses or events to be mourned. (There are further details at the end of this chapter.) This affords the survivor an opportunity to concretely and symbolically take action with regard to the incurred losses in her life.

After the dolls have been constructed, the therapist suggests that the client do something symbolic with the grief doll to both acknowledge her experience and mark it in some personally meaningful way. One group we facilitated chose to have a collective ceremony at the beach where each woman read something she had written for the occasion, after which some group members chose to burn their grief dolls as a symbol of the end of one phase of their lives and their renewed hope for a new and brighter future. The use of this type of ceremony or ritual can therefore mark the end of the old ways of the past and seed the notion of new beginnings. The advantage of a ritual with witnesses in the form of peers from a survivor group, or trusted friends or family members, is that it can demarcate the shift in old negative patterns, behaviors, and feelings on both an internal and external level, thereby reintegrating the survivor back into the mainstream—perhaps for the first time.

METAPHORS, EXERCISES, AND RITUALS

"THE ATTIC AND THE DRAWBRIDGE"

This metaphorical story was co-created with a particular client to address the need to put in place a new perspective on the survivor's historical experience. The therapist can help facilitate this by encouraging the client to let go of the burden of responsibility for the abuse, identify personal needs, and set the stage for the development of new and personally relevant boundaries to assist in the process of reintegration and the realization of future potential.

A S YOU ARE SITTING THERE hearing the sound of my voice, wouldn't it be interesting to allow your mind to wander and explore all the possibilities ahead? And you can go inside, comfortably, and know that your unconscious mind is such a valuable storehouse of ideas, experiences, and resources to be sorted through and utilized in any way that you choose.

It's important to remember that you *can* let go of so many old and uncomfortable ways that are no longer helpful or necessary. And as you are sitting there in that position, focusing inward, it's nice to know you can let go of whatever you need to and simply be, while reorganizing and reintegrating all that you will need for the future.

I am reminded of an experience that Coral, a friend of mine, had while clearing out the attic of her childhood home. Coral's parents were moving after over 20 years of living in the same house. So Coral went back to her former home to help clear out the attic, which contained many of her belongings from childhood.

Coral described this as being both a painful and a liberating process. As she climbed the stairs and unlocked the door, Coral was struck by how suffocating the air was. She could barely see in the dim light and she was acutely aware of the floor creaking beneath her feet as she felt her way around up there. After locating the shutters, she was able to shed some light on the situation in order to be better able to focus on the task at hand.

Coral realized that there were years and years of her life strewn about that attic. She began sorting through the various piles of belongings, each one triggering a variety of memories and associations.

She alternated between the boxes on the left side of the attic and others located on the right side. Eventually she found a long-forgotten chest containing some old favorite books, a treasured teddy bear who had been a tremendous source of comfort and security, and a long-lost diary containing many painful childhood experiences. Clutching her teddy bear, Coral began to read through some of the entries in her diary. She was flooded with many of the emotions she had experienced in her past.

Coral's childhood had been a painful one. She had always felt like the "black sheep" of the family. Her brothers and sisters had often scapegoated her, and as she read through the old diary, those feelings of isolation and rage began to surface once more. But Coral was now better able to understand and to deal with these previously overwhelming feelings. She knew that if she didn't stuff them back down, but let them surface instead, soon she would find the right way for her to express the anger she felt toward her family for those hard times. Her main goal in coming back home was to find some way to make peace with her past—in a way that didn't minimize what she went through but allowed her to move on so she could be free from the old ghosts.

As she read through her diary, she realized that she had never felt free to be herself. She read some comments on old report cards that referred to her shyness and social isolation, but much to her surprise, she also found many positive comments which spoke to her future potential and creative imagination. It's amazing how the negative can so often overshadow the positive.

That night while Coral slept in her old bed, she dreamed she was at that difficult age again, being teased and excluded from games her siblings were enjoying. She remembered being separated and subsequently left behind at the beach one day. At first she was terrified, but then she had become absorbed in playing in the sand. It felt so good to feel the warmth of the sun against her body and she enjoyed squishing the moist sand between her fingers as she built her sandcastle. She spent a lot of time constructing the foundation for her castle. She collected stones and shells to make that substructure sound, and by the time she completed the walls and turrets, the tide was quickly approaching. Soon Coral's castle was completely submerged and she began to cry, remembering that she was all alone. There was an older lady who had been watching Coral for some time and she introduced herself as Rosemary and asked if she could help. Coral nodded and told the lady that her castle was ruined and that she was all alone.

Rosemary began telling Coral that she had seen what a good job she had done building the castle foundation and that she was sure that the foundation would be intact when the tide went out again. Just then Coral's sister came by and found her; while walking over to Coral, she stepped on the castle turrets that were mostly submerged and toppled the remainder of the castle.

The next day Coral and her sister returned to the beach and much to Coral's surprise, there was the substructure of the castle—intact. Coral excitedly began to rebuild her castle. This time she also built a moat around it to make use of the tide as it approached. She was thinking about who would live in her castle. Her sister told her that everyone who lived in a castle lived "happily ever after"; they were all perfect and no one fought or worried about anything. This seemed hard for Coral to believe as she had never experienced anything but trouble in her life. Rosemary, the lady from the day before, had also returned and began to tell Coral about castles she had visited in Europe and how they were built with such strong walls and with moats to protect them from those who might invade the castle and surrounding territory.

Coral found this fascinating and asked Rosemary about haunted castles. Rosemary said that in England there were several castles that were haunted by spirits from the past. Coral said she didn't want any ghosts to haunt her castle. She asked Rosemary what she could do to make sure that her castle wasn't invaded by anyone—ghost or human, whom she didn't want to be there. Rosemary told Coral about drawbridges. She said they were designed to keep out unwanted visitors or enemies and that they could be lowered when one was ready to receive trusted friends and raised again when one wanted to be alone or undisturbed while going about one's business. Coral thought that the idea of a drawbridge was wonderful and she intended to put hers to good use. She thought long and hard about whom she would lower the drawbridge for and why (*pause*).

And you can take an easy, satisfying breath and allow your unconscious mind to listen inside, in its own unique way, while your conscious mind can listen to the sound of my voice outside or simply drift off any place it wanders (*pause*).

The next day Coral climbed the attic stairs with a new sense of purpose. As she sorted through old belongings, she was able to let go of most of the debris. She separated all of those old hand-me-downs that had never really been "her."

Coral no longer found it necessary to read through all of the painful details in her old diary. She had the urge to tear out some of those pages and concentrate on the others that contained evidence of some of the positive memories, pictures of her best friend, report cards with supportive comments, and some of her own poetry.

Coral began to daydream about herself as she would like to be. She imagined herself with an attitude of confidence, a look of strength on her face and in her eyes. Her voice sounded different, less tentative and more resolute. She thought about what she would like to say to her parents and siblings about how she felt growing up so isolated.

Coral realized that she now had the ability to make some different choices for herself and she also understood that she might never hear the words of recognition or receive the comfort from her family that she so desperately needed. But deep within herself she heard a voice that she recognized as her own, a melodic, wise voice, reminding her that she had the ability to redefine her life in her own terms and that even though others might not accept or validate her new choices, she could finally begin to honor her own needs, hopes, and wishes for the future.

And you can take a few moments of clock time and listen to your own voice inside, (*pause*), pause and be aware of all of your own resources.

And you can give yourself a message of appreciation and love for all that *you* value and merit now and in the future.

⌘ ⌘ ⌘

LETTERS TO THE OFFENDER

The following writing exercises are examples of some we have used with individuals and in groups to further explore the nature of the survivor–offender relationship. The intent is to gather personally relevant information that the client can then utilize in any way necessary to respond to the offender either directly or symbolically. In doing so, she can further separate her self from the offender and place the responsibility where it belongs and thus move closer to resolution and restitution.

Personal Inventory in Preparation for Writing to the Offender

This inventory can be given as a homework assignment to be answered over a period of time and then discussed and processed with peers in a group setting or with the therapist in individual therapy. We have found this to be a demanding but enlightening process that sets the stage for the next exercise of writing a letter of disclosure to the offender. It is important for the therapist to remind the client of the new skills and abilities she has acquired to help her deal with anxiety or panicky feelings. Relaxation exercises are recommended at the beginning and at the end of such intense sessions.

In preparation for writing a letter of disclosure to the offender, answer any or all of the following questions that seem relevant to you:

1. What was the offender's relationship to you? That is, was he/she a member of the family, a sibling, parent, family friend or neighbor, etc.

2. How did your relationship with the offender affect other relationships in your life?

3. How did the offender ensure the secret was kept?

4. What tactics or methods were employed by the offender to establish control over you?

5. Describe your relationship with the offender. How did the relationship change over time? How long was the relationship?

6. Were there any aspects of the relationship that were positive for you?

7. If there were some good parts to your relationship with the offender, was or is that a source of guilt, shame, confusion, or "craziness" for you? If so, please explain.

8. In what ways did you have to alter or deny the truth in order to keep the secret?

9. What messages did you have to give yourself in order to survive the abuse?

10. Do you feel any ambivalence about the offender's responsibility for the abuse? If so, write about how you or others may minimize or excuse the offender's behavior and why that happens.

11. Write about any other feelings, dilemmas, or experiences this relationship has caused you.

Letter to the Offender

The main intent of this letter is one of expression and release—mailing it is not necessary and would warrant further discussion and preparation.

We have found it most beneficial for the survivor to read her letter aloud to her peers (in group) or to the therapist or trusted friends. The reading of the letter to other(s) seems to validate the content and to serve as a release of responsibility for the abuse. This is generally a very empowering experience.

The following are the general directions that you can give to the client(s): "Keeping in mind the information, feelings, and responses you are aware of with regard to your relationship to the offender, write a letter (or letters) of disclosure to the offender. Express whatever you need to in any way that fits for you. You may want to include a discussion of your concerns about how the offender may choose to react or respond to your disclosure." For further examples of empowering exercises for dealing with the offender, see Dolan's *Resolving Sexual Abuse* (1991).

⌘　　　⌘　　　⌘

"THE EUCALYPT TREE"

Due to temporary setbacks in the survivor's healing process, it is important for the therapist to remind her to take stock of how far she has come. It is easy for any of us to lose sight of our accomplishments and progress during a languid period.

We use the following metaphorical induction toward the end of the healing journey when the client often experiences frustration and anger at how much struggling she has had to do and how much there may be ahead of her.

After the survivor experiences the metaphor and speaks about it if she chooses, it is a good time for the therapist to encourage her to further celebrate how far she has come. This could be done any way she desires. We often suggest that the client do something concrete for herself that is a symbol of her growth that can continue to remind her of how far she has come. Some women have planted trees or herb gardens to acknowledge their progress, others have bought themselves plants or keepsakes. It is often helpful to give the client(s) a homework assignment to find a way to mark and celebrate her progress thus far.

A S YOU ARE SITTING THERE, feeling the support beneath you and taking in some nice easy breaths, as deeply and easily as you can, just allow your mind to drift and wander anywhere it needs to. And you can hear the familiar sound of that nurturing breath as it enters your body, going to any of those tight or uncomfortable places and easing any of that tension; that's right—breathing more easily and comfortably. It's important to know that your unconscious mind remembers so much about you and how far you have come. All of that courage and power that you have inside you. All of that strength and tenacity that has helped to keep you on the path to healing and awareness. And wouldn't it be interesting for your unconscious mind to be able to share some of that knowledge with your conscious mind. You might think about or remember something that you have accomplished or discovered along the way. I don't know when you might acknowledge or remember that information; it might be now or later today or it could even happen in the coming week. But it's nice to know that you do have so much to appreciate about yourself and your journey that you can transfer to your conscious mind.

And as you are sitting there listening to the sound of my voice outside and hearing and experiencing some important things for you on the inside, I am reminded of a trip I took to Australia a while ago. In Australia they have an abundance of "Eucalypt" trees (as they call them down under). Over many hundreds of years, the Eucalypt has made an amazing adaptation to the frequent electrical storms that occur during its growth cycle. The tough, strong Eucalypt pod, which contains these valuable seeds vital for regeneration, requires the heat of the fire in order to burst open and disseminate those seeds, thus enabling new growth and preservation of the species. It's amazing how nature instinctively adapts to its constantly changing and often dangerous environment. And it's important to remember how far *you* have come in your healing journey. And to notice and appreciate your ability to redefine and reintegrate all of those unique and valuable parts of your self. You have the ability to sort through and redefine those pieces of you that may have been forgotten or neglected.

So take a few moments of clock time, all the time you need to think about how far you have come. You might want to just allow your mind to wander and let your unconscious select and remind you of some of your accomplishments (*pause 1 minute*). And just allow yourself to experience that even more fully (*pause*). And wouldn't it be interesting to see yourself in a slightly different way. Maybe some place that you would like to be in the future, next week, or tomorrow. Where might you like to be? And how would you know there was something different about you? Maybe the way you are holding your body, or you might have a confident or comfortable expression on your face? How would you sound to yourself? What positive message could you be saying to yourself? And how would it feel to realize that you are courageous? And how would your face look and feel with an expression of power and confidence displayed there? (*pause 1 or 2 minutes*) And just allow yourself to experience that even more comfortably.

And you can take another moment of clock time to integrate this experience in any way that fits for you (*pause*). And when you are ready, you can give yourself another message of self-appreciation for all that you have accomplished...that's right. Allowing that sense of love for you, and all that is unique to you, to permeate through your entire body—from the top of your head, circulating throughout your entire body, every cell and every artery and vein, to the tips of your toes (*pause*). And when you are ready, you can gradually reorient back to the room bringing with you a sense of strength, power, and self-appreciation for all that you have accomplished and the great distance you have traveled.

⌘   ⌘   ⌘

GRIEF AND LOSS: EXERCISES AND RITUALS

As previously stated in this chapter, the identification of the survivor's incurred losses and her subsequent grieving is a key turning point in the healing process. The following are examples of writing and art exercises we have found useful in dealing with these issues. These writing exercises can be used in individual or group sessions.

Letters of Acknowledgment

Both of the following exercises, as well as discussions with the therapist and peers about grief and loss, can help prepare her for the construction of the *grief doll* mentioned earlier in the chapter.

We have found it helpful to hand out to the client during the session printed instructions for the letter writing on it. As with any exercise, the timing and choice to do the writing must respect each client's individual healing process. These letters may or may not be mailed according to each client's wishes.

Letter 1

The therapist can ask the client to write a letter in the following manner: "Write a letter of acknowledgment to yourself concerning the losses you have suffered as a result of your abuse. Consider the effects these losses have had on your life in the past and in the present."

After the client has written this letter, the therapist can help her to debrief the content and responses from this experience and to understand them in the context of the abuse and in relation to the grieving process. We would then recommend that another letter or letters be written that may help the survivor identify, express, and externalize many of the intense feelings and emotions toward those responsible for the abuse and/or those who did not protect or meet the needs of the survivor at the time of the abuse and thereafter.

Letter 2

The therapist can give the following directions: "Write a letter to anyone else from your past or present whom you would like to understand how the losses you have incurred have affected you."

The Grief Doll

After the survivor has a clearer understanding of the grief process and/or has identified the losses and issues associated with it, the construction of a *grief doll* can help her to more concretely and symbolically resolve these issues.

In our opinion, this exercise is most effective when done in a group setting; however, we have also used it successfully with individual clients.

The therapist will need to have blank paper dolls of approximately 24 inches in length as well as various art supplies, such as construction paper, scissors, glue, odds and ends like beads, buttons, feathers, yarn, markers, glitter, and so on.

Some clients may ask for more detailed instructions, but we find it is important to encourage them to just let the doll create itself—once they begin, the results are quite amazing. We always stress that it is the content, not the artistic skill, that is most important (see Figure 6.1).

The therapist can instruct the client or group in the following manner:

> Think about the many losses you have suffered as a result of being sexually assaulted. There may be some that you have identified which are most significant to you. Or you may have some more generalized affects that continue to intrude in your life that you would like to express in a more concrete manner. Take a couple of moments, either with your eyes open or closed, and think about those losses that are most significant to you. Remembering to breathe as comfortably as possible, just allow your mind to wander and think about what it would be like to make a grief doll. How could you express the grief and the sorrow you have experienced, in the form of a grief doll? It might be interesting to think about various parts of that doll as representative of some of the parts of yourself, those parts that you can now reintegrate into your life in a different way, a way that fits for you.
>
> You may want to consider different parts to signify different emotions or different ages, or you might have one or more dominant aspects of your grief that you would like to express and/or symbolize. Just allow your mind to explore your own grief process, and when you are ready, take one of the paper dolls and create a symbol of your own unique process and experience in any way that fits for you.

Grief Doll Ritual or Ceremony

As we have previously stated, the use of ritual or ceremony is an important marker that can demarcate transition on an internal and external basis. At this fourth stage of the healing process, this is very important so that the survivor can delineate a shift from the past to the present and future.

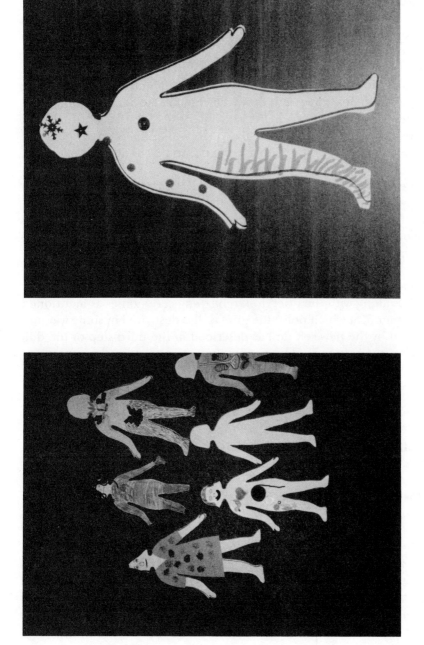

Figure 6.1 Grief Dolls

On completion of the grief doll, we suggest to clients that they might like to do something symbolic to grieve their losses. Either in a group or individual setting, it is helpful to facilitate a discussion about their individual dolls and what they represent to them. The therapist can then suggest that the client think about some way that she would like to express her process of mourning.

Many groups like to have a collective ceremony. We have found it helpful to do some meditation or visualization about this while holding the grief doll. It is important that each client make her own choice and not feel pressured into such an event. We give examples of rituals that others have performed, but we always stress that this is a very personal choice. It may take some clients weeks or months to decide on a ritual, while others immediately know what they would like to do.

One client constructed a doll with a series of symbols on various parts of its body, signifying parts of herself that had been lost and "damaged." She chose to remove these symbols from the doll (at various points in time over a 3-month period) and burn them. When each of these symbols was discarded from the grief doll, they revealed a new symbol beneath them which signified new and healthier parts of the self.

Some common themes for rituals are the burning of old diaries or journals along with the grief doll, rebirthing ceremonies as mentioned in Chapter 3, at which point the grief doll is destroyed in some way and replaced by the new self doll as described in the third step of the doll exercise in Chapter 5. The possibilities are endless and as unique as each client.

⌘　　　⌘　　　⌘

EMERGING VOICE: INDUCTION FOR RELAXATION AND NEW POSSIBILITIES

The following induction is designed to help the survivor to further integrate the various aspects of herself that she has been identifying and reclaiming in the healing process. This can be used with groups or in individual settings. We find it helpful as an introduction or as an adjunct to the exercises concerning boundaries, values, and beliefs.

The therapist does not have to debrief this experience. We have found it important for each client to make their own interpretations. Some may wish to speak about it and others may not. Some clients will say they don't really remember much and perhaps don't think anything particularly significant took place. It is important for the therapist to validate whatever happens as each client's unconscious has its own process.

A ND AS YOU ARE SITTING THERE hearing the sound of my voice outside, you can take some easy breaths and go inside. Listening to the sound of your own breathing. Paying attention to your own unique rhythm, the rhythm of your breathing and the rhythm of your heart (*pause*). Feeling supported by the back of your chair, or just allowing yourself to sink into that support wherever you are. And you can feel your body in that position as you sense the beat of your heart and are aware with every breath you take into your body that you need only take in what you can, comfortably. And as that breath circulates throughout your body, it's nice to know that each breath can nurture you, filling, replenishing, and helping you to let go of all the tension and stress in your body and mind on each exhale. Letting go of what no longer fits or feels right. And listening to your own unique experience, you *can* hear yourself on so many different levels, just as you can hear the sound of your own breathing inside and the sound of your own voice outside and within.

Wouldn't it be interesting to be more in touch with your inner "self?" To feel comfortable having a dialogue with your inner self in a new and more understanding way? And how might that voice inside you sound? (*pause*) And what qualities would that voice reflect? What parts of yourself would you like to express more fully, differently? (*pause*) And what aspects of yourself might you like to alter in a way that feels right for you and sounds right for you?

There are so many mixed messages out there about how you *should* be. How would you like to be? How would you like to be able to express yourself differently? (*pause*) How would it be to find your own unique way to express that?

As you are thinking about that, over there, wouldn't it be interesting to view yourself over here in a different way? How would that independent spirit express itself? (*pause*) And how would your expression be different? (*pause*) How would it feel to be more at ease with yourself? More purposeful? (*pause*) How would you like to express your own unique femininity, without fear of judgment? Finding your own way to integrate those characteristics or parts of yourself that have sometimes been referred to as masculine or feminine.

What color might that newly and uniquely integrated self be? And if it had a shape or a texture what might that be? (*pause*) And if it had a sound or a symbol, what might that be? (*pause*) And you can color your style and experience in any way that reflects your unique and diverse manner. Choosing the richest hues and textures that you can embroider into a flexible tapestry of experience, your own interesting way of interpreting those values and beliefs that express *your* way of being with yourself and with others (*pause*).

And you can take a moment of clock time to allow that to develop even more (*pause*) It can be very interesting to allow your unconscious to take you on a creative journey—opening up new possibilities. Rediscovering that independent spirit that can be more at ease, more colorful, more expressive, that's right (*pause*).

It can be fun to try on different clothes and costumes until you choose the ones that, for whatever reason, you feel the most at ease wearing. Until you hear that voice deep within you say, "That's it, I like this." Or listening to a variety of music and being aware of that certain melody that you react to in a way that is uplifting, moving, or inspiring (*pause*).

And I don't know when you might experience a different level of comfort and understanding within yourself. It may be as you become accustomed to hearing that inner voice within you. Or you may catch yourself listening and understanding in a new way, trusting and validating this emerging voice as you become more familiar with all of those different aspects of your self that you can now be appreciated even *more* fully.

And you can take a moment of clock time to hear that voice within give you a message of self-appreciation for the courage, strength, and unique abilities that you possess. That's right....

And when you are ready, you can gradually reorient back to the room, taking some easy breaths and reconnecting with your surroundings.

⌘   ⌘   ⌘

VALUE CLARIFICATION EXERCISES

Once the survivor has a clearer understanding of her oppressive and often paradoxical relationship with the offender, she can now begin to set clearer boundaries for relationships with the offender, if that is a current issue (as in the case of incest), and with other relationships in her life.

In order to set effective boundaries and exercise autonomy, it is necessary for the client to redefine and reevaluate her own value and belief system. The follow-ing are some sample exercises we have found helpful in achieving this goal. These exercises are appropriate for use individually or in a group setting.

Questions Identifying Values and Beliefs

1. In your family of origin, what values, ideals, or beliefs were emphasized while you were growing up? For example, how important were issues of money, education, religion, honesty, work ethic, traditional roles of women and men, social respon-sibility, etc.?
2. In your family of origin, was it acceptable for you to:
   • express emotions such as anger, fear, etc.?
   • feel responsible for others' behavior and feelings?
   • have a caring, open relationship?
3. How do you feel about these values and beliefs now, in the present?
4. Which of these currently fit for you? Which are no longer rel-evant?
5. What other values or beliefs would you like to add?
6. What values or beliefs would be important for a partner, friend, or anyone else of significance in your life to possess?
7. How did your relationship with the offender affect how you experience your own sexuality?
8. How would you like to experience your own sexuality?
9. What does it mean to you to be a woman? What is your defini-tion of femininity? What is your definition of masculinity? How could you integrate these concepts in a way that fits your per-sonal style (physically and emotionally)?

Clarification Exercise for Needs and Expectations

1. How do you know when it is safe to express what you are feeling?
2. How has your experience in past relationships affected your ability to trust?
3. How do you know whom you can trust, that is, what do you

need to consider before you decide whom you can trust in any particular situation?

4. How do you express your anger?
5. How would you like to express your anger?
6. How will you know when another individual respects you?
7. How will you know when you feel safe with another person?
8. Does the gender of another person affect how safe you feel with them?
9. How will you know when you can trust someone sexually?
10. Is it okay for you to express your vulnerability to another? If so, why and how could you do that?

Personal Needs Assessment

Think about what you need to feel personally empowered. For example, I need:

- independence/autonomy
- career
- intimacy
- belonging
- safety
- trust
- fun
- intellectual stimulation
- creative outlet
- sensuality/sex

What do you need and/or expect from a relationship with another person, partner, or friend? For example, I expect from a relationship with my partner:

- monogamy
- intimacy
- trust
- honesty
- acceptance of my past
- equal distribution of housework

⌘   ⌘   ⌘

SETTING BOUNDARIES EXERCISE

Now that the survivor has had some time to explore her value and belief system, she can begin to think about setting some clearer boundaries for herself that can assist her to better define herself in relation to others.

It is important to note that the therapist needs to be cognizant of each individual's timing with regard to this and other exercises. For some, setting boundaries is a slow process. Discussion of the feelings and reactions of the client and the anticipated response of others to setting boundaries are important. The therapist needs to help the survivor judge the appropriate timing for the implementation of this new phase of development.

The therapist can instruct the client(s) in the following manner:

Take a few moments to reflect on a situation(s) in which you felt you were taken advantage of. This could be in your workplace, a social context, or in relation to your family, friends, partner, or children.

Are there any specific situations that come to mind when you frequently felt (or feel) pressured into doing something you don't want to do?

How do you feel after you do something you were pressured into? How would you like to feel?

Take some time and think about setting some boundaries for yourself that might help you more clearly honor your own needs and expectations of yourself and others. You may want to start with one boundary to begin with, or you may be ready to set more. Sometimes it helps to make a wish list of personal boundaries and set goals for yourself as to when you feel ready to attain them.

MY WISH LIST OF PERSONAL BOUNDARIES

- Which one or ones do you feel ready to practice currently?
- When will you know you are ready to set another boundary for yourself?
- How will others know you have these boundaries?
- What can you do if others ignore your boundaries?

Remember—we are all creatures of habit. If you don't succeed right away, just keep trying. It's like anything else—it takes practice and persistence.

⌘   ⌘   ⌘

"HUSH—PART FOUR" (STAGE FOUR, PART A)

Part Four of the Hush metaphor continues the story of Hush to help illustrate the issues and development of the survivor at this stage of the healing process. The story of Hush, although originally co-created with a particular client in mind, has proven to be highly appealing to survivors in general. We often individualize some of the feelings and responses to fit specific cases. However, we also have found the metaphor to be open-ended enough to allow clients to apply the concepts and draw their own meaning from it in their own unique and personally relevant way.

This metaphorical story can be used with individuals or in groups.

FOR SEVERAL DAYS after Hush's most recent adventure in the woods, she began to experience something different. At first she didn't really understand what was going on inside of her—she was accustomed to fearing or worrying about old sensations in her body. But those old panicky and overwhelming feelings were becoming less frequent now. These new feelings were different. There was an unfamiliar sense of anticipation and premonition coming from deep within. She could almost hear a voice inside herself.

Eidolon suggested that perhaps she should practice listening to that voice, dialoguing with it. This was not easy. She had spent so much time trying to turn off the many confusing thoughts inside. Hush found it more comforting to talk to the others about these feelings. It became clear, once again, that she wasn't alone in her experience. Raye began to speak to her about her own emerging emotions. It seemed she was engaged in her own internal dialogue that waffled between wanting to run away and be by herself with her old familiar thoughts and a new need for being included in a more social way.

One day while Hush and the others were taking a walk, Dot reminded Hush of her offer to teach them about mask making. The time seemed right and Hush spontaneously asked each of them to begin to collect items from the forest that they would like to use in the construction of their masks. The process of collecting treasures from the forest turned into quite an adventure. Each one was very focused and curious in this process. When they were finished, it was interesting to see the diversity of choices among them.

Hush's original mask had been crafted with a specific purpose in mind. But now, it seemed more appropriate to suggest to each of her friends that they think about what they would like to express about themselves at this point in time. It seemed that the mask making had taken on a life of its own, with Hush giving pointers about the practicalities and tools that she and Aunt Kit had utilized long ago while creating her first mask.

At various times in this process, each individual was confused about what was emerging from within. Eidolon suggested that they might want to let their masks represent some of the polarization each of them was experiencing. The need to be included and cared about versus the draw toward isolation. The fear of anything new versus being stuck in the old. Blaming the self versus placing responsibility where it truly lies. Feeling shame versus pride, guilt versus honesty, doubt versus trust.

As each mask took on its own identity, the need to articulate the emerging characteristics led to a lively discussion and interpretation of each individual's history. Crystal was able to speak more clearly about her feelings of shame and guilt. Her mask, like Raye's, was two-sided. On the inside, her expression of those old feelings were dark and melancholy. The other side, in sharp contrast, had a bright luminescence that reflected a lightness and creativity that initially surprised her.

Raye's mask had an outward expression of hope and courage; it seemed to invite the onlooker to engage in a lively dialogue, while on the inside, some of those old feelings of loss and abandonment were struggling to be released and understood.

Dot's mask was one of transformation. On the left side was a rather shy, doubtful but vigilant expression, while on the right side, was a whimsical warrior whose mouth seemed ready to release a unique protest for all of the injustice suffered personally and by those around her.

Everyone was amazed at how liberating it felt to express what was going on inside. There was also a different kind of energy in their discussion. Dot became quite angry at one point while speaking about her mask. Hush and Crystal began to experience feelings of sadness and loss. Eidolon was able to help the group identify what was happening. She told them about how natural and healthy it is to feel anger and grief at the loss and pain they had endured in their pasts. Raye was able to speak about how lost and abandoned she had felt for so long—how she longed for a real family whom she could trust and who truly cared about her.

For the next few weeks, Eidolon helped each of them understand and articulate their individual losses. It soon became even more apparent how much they all had in common. They all thanked Hush for introducing them to mask making. Eidolon suggested to Hush that she might consider utilizing her unique abilities and creativity by teaching others how to make masks.

Hush began to think a lot about her future. She had always planned to leave the village and seek out other lynx. But maybe she would settle here for a while. Dot, Raye, and Crystal had also been thinking about what to do next. "You all have so much knowledge and experience to share," said Eidolon. "As you continue to reclaim your own voices and express your own identities, you will know what is right for you."

Hush and the others realized that even though they didn't always get along with one another—they were all very different in many ways— they shared a strong bond, and they respected and were beginning to trust each other more all the time. They spoke about how they felt like a family, and they all decided that they could each adopt one another and create for themselves what each of them had been longing for in a family.

This was a very new idea. It needed a lot of consideration. Each of them began to explore what having a family meant. Hush talked about her fantasy of a family. Dot and Raye spoke about their concerns and how difficult it was for them to trust and to feel close to others. They explored many different possibilities and ways of becoming each others' family. Eidolon encouraged them to take their time and for each one to listen to their inner voices and eventually they would understand and negotiate what was in their best interests.

One decision they made was to have a celebration in honor of how far they had come. It was decided that they would wear their masks for part of the celebration to acknowledge all they had experienced as well as their hope for what was to come.

Hush decided to make a new mask for this important event. She wasn't exactly sure about how this one would differ from the one she and Aunt Kit had made. She felt excited about creating a new mask. Hush decided to go out for a walk and select some new materials to construct her mask. She picked up her backpack filled with all those tools she had been carrying around for so long. She wasn't exactly sure about how she would use them, but she began to experience that new and unusual feeling again. She recalled her aunt saying to her "that you may feel more confident and in tune with yourself before you consciously realize what is happening."

Kit was right. Hush was feeling different than ever before. She was starting to have more energy and excitement for the future. She knew there was still much to be accomplished and decided, but she also knew that realizing her future potential was an adventure she could not pass up—with all its uncertainty and ups and downs, she was just about ready to explore the possibilities.

And you can take a few moments and let your mind wander to explore some of your own possibilities. Listening to yourself in a different way, tuning into your own unique experience and allowing that to develop in a variety of ways (*pause*) even more fully (*pause*). And when you are ready you can reorient back to the present, bringing with you whatever is important for you now.

(To be continued)

CHAPTER 7

Stage Four: Empowerment and Evolution of the Sexual Self (Part B)

Part B of Stage Four marks the survivor's foray into the final healing stage. Not that the process of healing ever quite ends, but, like a river, it is an ever-flowing life stream, which allows the survivor to gradually increase the quality of her life over time—taking those steps toward becoming a "thriver." We identify a thriver as a survivor who has emotionally worked through her sexual abuse to the point that she is successfully able to sustain a healthy, thriving lifestyle that has transcended mere existence, freeing her to ally with healthy others. From this point on, we will identify those courageous individuals who have reached this final healing stage as thrivers.

In this chapter, we will track the thriver as she progresses toward a more integrated sense of self, to encompass her final lost part of self—her sexual, creative self. In many ways, this healing stage presents the most challenges, as the thriver reframes her sexuality from its initial enmeshment with the abuse to its reintegration as a natural, beautiful part of self. Once the sense of her sexual self is freed from the fetters of shame and embarrassment, the thriver may even be ready to connect with a healthy other, where she has the opportunity, over time, to build a healthful sexual relationship. When the thriver reaches out to a healthy other and dares to be in an intimate relationship, she is, in a sense, exorcising her guilt and shame—as these are the feelings that come into play when she takes those first steps toward soliciting support within a significant relationship.

The thriver often finds herself connected with the larger community through her link with the Feminist Movement, where the messages she has absorbed in the course of her healing echo back to herself—freedom of speech, equal pay, and equal rights for women and children. The group venue also offers the thriver ample opportunity to increase her awareness of societal and political messages to women and therefore can be an entree into further exploration of feminist perspectives. Once the collective feminist consciousness has been raised in the group, each member participant can begin to exercise her own choices around incorporating new awarenesses into her own unique lifestyle.

At this stage, life for the thriver is filled with more hope; she is able to shift her backward glance from the past to a more future-focused one, and in so doing, she develops the ability to plan ahead with a new sense of optimism. In addition, at this stage, the thriver undergoes the gradual process of phasing out the therapist's voice, so that she can listen and more clearly attend to her own strong inner voice—making that shift to finding a safe place for herself outside of the therapeutic circle.

This chapter will therefore include the following substages:

   I. Acknowledging and Reintegrating the Sensual/Sexual Self: Retrieving Creativity
   II. Rejoining Society: Creating Safety in the Present to Promote a Positive Future Focus
   III. Transforming the Fragile Alliance: Building Strong, Healthy Partnerships

Following our discussion of these substages, we will present Metaphors, Exercises, and Rituals, which will help the client reinforce and anchor the healing tasks that challenge her at this juncture.

I. ACKNOWLEDGING AND REINTEGRATING THE SENSUAL/SEXUAL SELF: RETRIEVING CREATIVITY

Part B of Stage Four represents a major turning point for the thriver, as she is now more able to accept all parts of the self as being valued by her as well as those parts that have been a source of pain, guilt, and shame. Up to this point, as a result of the healing work that she has completed from Stage One through Stage Four, it is now the therapist's role to encourage the thriver to connect with the valued parts of herself that she may have developed as a child—for example, a particular athletic or academic ability—and with the recollection that she had the capacity to survive whatever traumas she had no choice but to endure.

More tangible proof for the thriver can be available through photographs of herself as a child, where she has the opportunity to clearly see, for example, that the little girl had a nice smile, strong hands, intense eyes, and so on. Her appreciation of that child can link the adult thriver back to that innocent time in her life in such a way that a true reintegration of those lost parts of self can take place. In turn, this can bring about the revelation that the abused child she once was was not an ugly monster but, rather, an innocent being who had limited choices.

The sensual/sexual self is usually the most difficult part to retrieve because of the negative associations with the sexual abuse. In this, the final stage of healing, the thriver has hopefully broken through and initiated the process of overcoming her body shame and is beginning to accept her sexuality as an integral part of her identity—linking and grounding her to her mortal human self. The reintegration of the sexual self can come about more easily if the thriver has successfully overcome self-blame for the abuse and has directed her anger at her offender(s), which was described in Chapter 6.

A further integral aspect of the healing process is when thrivers feel ready to reconnect with their bodies through touch, which assists them in making healthier connections to their physical/sensual self. Bodywork, a process that identifies energy flows and blocks in various parts of the body, is often the treatment of choice for a survivor who is feeling a sense of safety around reconnecting with her physical self. Bodywork is a technique that requires special training, and, as a result, it is important for you, as her therapist, to refer your client to someone who is properly certified.

In addition to using bodywork as a healing tool, practicing meditational exercises such as Yoga and Tai Chi are helpful ways for the thriver to reconnect with her sexuality. One particular Eastern healing practice involves identifying and working with the various "chakra" points on the human body. Chakra means spinning wheel and is the Sanskrit word given to the vortices that control the flow of energy throughout the entire body. The seven chakras or energy centers form a matrix that supports physical, emotional, mental, and spiritual life. By separating her sexuality from the abuse and making it her own, the survivor can reclaim the child self through a renewed connection with her creativity—a part of her that was not safe to develop before, during, and following the abuse. As the survivor taps into and explores her creativity via the metaphorical healing stories (as we have illustrated throughout the stages of recovery described in this book), she is able to gradually give herself permission to reclaim her sexuality from her offender(s) and, finally, make it her own.

Sylvia, a 48-year-old survivor of periodic sexual abuse by her estranged biological father, delighted in the opportunity she provided herself when she chose her favorite fragrant bath oil—Patchouli—to bathe with. By immersing her body in the fragrant bubbles, she felt she had a new sense of control over what her body could feel like and smell like. This became a weekly ritual that continued to connect her with her sensuality and sense of choice in an ongoing way.

At this final stage in her recovery the thriver's newly developed imagination can lead her back into her sexuality, where she can begin to connect with her sensual self in a healthful way, perhaps for the first time in her life. Rather than further intellectualizing the reconnection process to her sexuality, we have found the meditational exercise entitled "Restoring and Balancing Intimacy and Sexuality in Relationship to Self and Significant Others" in the Metaphors, Exercises, and Rituals section of this chapter provides the thriver with an opportunity to explore and take better care of herself sexually so that she does not continue to further place herself at risk for revictimization.

Helena, a 36-year-old survivor of ongoing sexual abuse by multiple offenders when she was a child, returned to school to complete her high school diploma, whereupon she was required to complete a series of creative writing assignments. On paper, Helena was able to tap into and express her innermost thoughts in an extremely creative way. This ability was frightening to her, as it linked Helena back to the memory that academic achievement was one of the few areas of her life where she received acknowledgment that she was "okay" and not stupid—very different messages than the ones she had been receiving at home. As a result, it was important for Helena, with the support of her therapist, to explore and make the distinction between returning to school to please herself or returning to please her parents. Helena ultimately decided to withdraw from her high school program until she reached clarity around this pivotal issue. Taking time away from school proved most valuable for Helena, as she discovered that she was, in fact, responding to the child's message within her: Going to school at this particular time in her life remained a desperate attempt to please Mom and Dad—an impossible task.

As a result of this revelation, Helena felt, for the first time in her life, that she could make her own choices, which freed her up to create a daily routine that contained some extremely appealing, creative activities including Tai Chi, massage therapy, and working a few hours a week at a residential drug and alcohol program. Helena found that as she shifted to giving herself permission to make choices, the chronic physical pain and discomfort she had been experiencing in her lower back and pelvic area, since she began her recovery from the sexual abuse, began to gradually dissolve until she could reconnect healthfully to those parts of her body she had previously identified as being blocked.

Once the thriver can overcome and conquer the abhorrence she has had with her own body as a result of the abuse, and with her feelings perhaps more intact than ever before, she can safely reclaim her sexuality and relate to herself and others in a more intimate way. This sense of her own ability to maintain her safety can only come about if she has created secure and clear boundaries around her sexuality, as we discussed previously in Chapter 6. Making distinctions between past negative patterns of intimacy and new healthier forms of intimacy is an exercise that needs to be done first with self and then, when ready, with a partner, which we will explore in the section on "Transforming the Fragile Alliance: Building Strong, Healthy Partnerships" (see pp. 193–196).

II. REJOINING SOCIETY: CREATING SAFETY IN THE PRESENT TO PROMOTE A POSITIVE FUTURE FOCUS

It is now time for the thriver to take a leap of faith from the safe womblike environment of individual therapy and survivor groups into the real world, where pedophiles and perpetrators of all varieties exist. An excellent method of bridging the gap between the outer therapeutic circle and the real world is the "buddy system," in which thrivers who have successfully completed a substantial portion of their healing can team up with survivors whose journey to recovery has just begun. The buddy system serves a dual purpose, as it gives the veteran thriver an opportunity to reinforce and recognize the tremendous gains she has made in her own healing process as she passes the message to the fledgling survivor that recovery and healthfulness are possible.

Susannah had been attending counseling sessions for 5 years when she decided that it was time to deal with the painful memories of long-term sexual abuse by her swimming coach that took place during her youth. She was successfully able to mourn the loss of a safe childhood and, at the same time, to celebrate the inner strengths that assisted her in getting through the trauma. During the course of the healing process, Susannah conquered her feelings of intimidation by authority figures and was able to stand up for her own personal rights in a variety of settings, which included having the courage to approach the faculty advisor at her university program to discuss what she felt was biased grading by a professor; working on a committee on campus to organize chaperons to accompany women walking alone across campus to evening classes; and, in addition, reporting to her local child protection agency a neighbor, whom she observed leaving three young children alone in the house for many hours at a time. As a result, when Susannah felt personally ready, she put in a request through her counselor for a "buddy" which resulted in her connection to a woman named Lila, who had just begun looking at the impact that a sexually abusive school teacher had had on her life.

As could be expected, Susannah had a great deal to offer in the way of support to Lila, as she had successfully learned to deal with authority figures. She could use her influence, in a small but significant way, to affect social change and to contribute to the healthful functioning of her community. Susannah encouraged Lila, who had been a long-time member of a local society for the rights of children and youth, to give an impassioned speech to 50 members, urging them to strike a task force to work on identifying offenders in their community and making the list available to the public. When other members of the society readily agreed with Lila, she felt she had triumphed on both a personal and community level, which, in turn, gave her the courage to continue to speak to her beliefs.

Another way for members to bridge the gap to the outside world is to continue to meet after the group therapy program has officially ended in order to maintain the support so vital to their ongoing healing. A number of survivor group members have made this choice. Due to increased awareness of sexual abuse issues there are groups of survivors in many communities now who meet regularly to share their experiences and continue to advocate for other survivors. One particularly cohesive group that we worked with recently, which had been together for a full year, decided that they would assume an advocacy role with one another so that when some of the members were dealing with issues of a contentious nature in their lives, they would bring their concerns to the group, taking on supportive roles with one another and consulting with a professional when needed. The adventures of "Hush—Part Five" at the end of this chapter describes such a group and helps to seed the endless possibilities of continuous growth beyond the therapeutic circle.

> Michelle, a 22-year-old survivor of childhood sexual abuse, who had been attending group therapy for 6 months, would spend her time away from the group listening to music alone in her apartment, as she did not feel ready to face the outside world where her perpetrators lurked. A metaphorical story ("Womb with a View") and subsequent exercise/ritual that helped her to overcome her fears of the outside world and to break through the "safe" womb she had created for herself by maintaining contact only with her individual therapist, survivor group facilitators, and other group members can be found in the final section of this chapter. As a result of working through this crucial aspect of her healing, Michelle began to manifest clear signs of becoming hopeful about her future for the first time in her life. This was indicated through a developing ability to plan ahead, restoring her own personal ambition, a crucial aspect of self taken away during the course of her abuse that could now more safely be retrieved and reclaimed.

At this point in her healing, there is more hope for the future and an ability to plan ahead and set new goals. The thriver is now more aware of her remarkable internal resources, and a stronger inner core is developing. As one strong voice, the thriver discovers she can make a significant contribution to creating a safer place for herself and other women and children.

Becoming involved in the Feminist Movement can be a positive shift towards channelling anger in a healthy way, and, in so doing, benefiting other women and children. In a societal sense, connecting with the Feminist Movement is a way for the thriver to continue to keep in touch with her own strong inner core and to express herself with a newfound sense of freedom and purpose. This message of freedom and equality flows between self, group, and society, where the thriver is connecting with her thoughts and asserting her equality in a group setting, and in a more global context, through feminism. Her own strong individual voice and the collective feminist voice reinforce the right to equality both personally and within a societal context. As a result, the collective feminist voice gives the thriver a stronger sense of support in the real world, so that she is able to take the risk of expressing her genuine self—that is, her whole self—without having to conceal key aspects of her identity. By becoming actively involved in child advocacy groups, the Feminist Movement, or some other association that is involved in the lobbying for women and children's rights, the thriver can begin to assist in creating a safer niche for herself and others previously identified as victims so that future planning can be made possible.

III. TRANSFORMING THE FRAGILE ALLIANCE: BUILDING STRONG, HEALTHY PARTNERSHIPS

A particular survivor group that we facilitated, whose members had worked together for some time, successfully reached the turning point in their healing, where they could shift their focus to an outward one and begin to reexamine their intimate relationships from a health-oriented context. Within the group were three women who were particularly vocal about this recent awareness and the new choices they realized they could begin to initiate within their respective partnerships:

Colleen, a 47-year-old married woman with two school-age children, was sexually abused by her father, uncle, and brother for a period of 10 years; Betsy, a 34-year-old woman, had been living with the same partner for the past 3 years and had only recently disclosed her past sexual abuse to her partner—which radically changed their relationship; and Donna, a 29-year-old woman, had made the conscious decision not to be partnered while she took time out to rethink personal values and boundaries.

Betsy brought to the group her experience of having difficulty over the years with her partner in requesting his support when she felt vulnerable; each time she attempted to reach out to him, feelings of shame and self-doubt began to emerge. This difficulty was most poignantly felt by Betsy following disclosure of her childhood sexual abuse to her partner. As group members discussed Betsy's situation, it became clear that her feelings of shame and lack of entitlement were linked to the relationship with her father in particular. He would impose his sexual needs onto her 9-year-old body and cry on her shoulder when he felt sad but would walk away when Betsy gave any indication that she needed his unconditional affection. As a result, she got the message that the only way she could feel any sense of self-worth, at the time, was to fulfill the sexual/emotional demands of her father, and then later, her husband.

Once Betsy disclosed her past sexual abuse to her partner, she began to avoid reaching out to him for emotional support for fear that she would be rejected, which would then reconnect her to her original pain of not being loved unconditionally. While Betsy was struggling to reach out for support from Jed, her partner, he revealed in a couple's therapy session that he felt he had to play a guessing game with Betsy—as he desperately struggled to determine what her needs were. This became an exercise in frustration for Jed, as he felt that he was a failure in his attempts to please Betsy, which translated into feelings of inadequacy on his part.

At this particular therapeutic stalemate, the counselor intervened by making the suggestion that Betsy and Jed work on building trust by checking out their feelings with one another on a regular basis, so that they both could create confidence around making requests to one another. Consequently, they developed an acceptance around the very real possibility that saying "no" to a request made by the other partner, when appropriate, was as healthy a response as saying "yes" when appropriate.

The result of the nature of the relationships that Betsy and many other partnered thrivers find themselves in is a tendency within the relationship to create distance, and to feel threatened and undeserving. This particular struggle with relationships is really one in which the thriver endeavors to disengage herself from the isolating tactics of the offender, so that she can eventually enjoy healthy intimate alliances. Unfortunately, the thriver often takes herself through a series of physically and emotionally abusive relationships with others before she begins to realize that she can connect with her right to make healthy different choices.

Until she began the process of recovery from her past sexual abuse, Donna found herself losing control over her behavior with her partner, and, as a result, began, in her own words, "spinning off her axle." She found herself, for example, having a strong reaction to something as minor as her partner brushing a hair from her face—feeling that there were no warning signals that would provide her with some preparatory time for her reactions. This behavior on Donna's part would place her partner in the position of feeling like every move he made would be unacceptable, which resulted in his withdrawal from any attempt to initiate emotional, physical, or sexual contact with her.

As a result, Donna made the conscious choice not to be partnered at the time because she felt it was "too dangerous" for her. A number of other group members concurred with her: Many believed that while they were focusing on their recovery, they felt it was healthier to build a stronger self prior to entering into further intimate partnerships.

When in therapy 10 years ago, 47-year-old Colleen first began to explore the effects of the sexual abuse perpetrated by her father, uncle, and brother; she felt that she would never overcome her fear of sharing sexual intimacy with a partner. However, after 5 years of therapy, Colleen had a sense that she was ready for intimacy but secretly hoped that her therapist would suggest further self-examination. As she shared her experience, Colleen acknowledged to the group that she was looking for an excuse to avoid the risk of reaching out and connecting. With the support of her therapist, however, Colleen realized that life was about relationships, and that by working on friendships, she was building confidence and preparing herself for the next big step into a deeper level of intimacy—that is, with her lifemate.

Colleen shared with the group that over the years she and her partner have continued to work on building awareness of the impact of the sexual abuse on their relationship, and as a result, discovered that Colleen's way of maintaining her independence and control in the relationship was by being disagreeable. The need for control is one of the most common struggles that occurs for the partnered thriver, as often the only other experience of intimacy the thriver has had has been with her offender(s), and by being agreeable in that relationship, she was abused.

Prior to her relationship with her husband, Colleen shared with the group that as an adult she had had a number of relationships with men that had failed, because giving in to her partner's request, however small, meant that she was giving up her power and control to her offenders, which resulted in a great deal of conflict between Colleen and each of the people she chose as partners. As a result of a number of these unsuccessful relationships, Colleen made the conscious choice to forego further intimate involvements, until she was ready to include a significant other in the decision-making process. Over the course of individual, group, and couple's therapy, Colleen has come to realize that she is not necessarily giving her power and control away when she is being agreeable with her partner, and that part of maintaining her sense of self within the relationship is taking the time out to consider both her own needs and choices and the needs of her partner in order to nurture their compatibility.

Agreeing to disagree, at times, was a helpful suggestion made by the therapist who was working with this couple, which assisted Colleen and her husband to accept and celebrate their differences, instead of insisting that there was only one correct approach or solution. As a result of identifying the aforementioned common themes for partnered thrivers, the writers and group members co-created a metaphorical story and follow-up exercise to assist survivors in dealing at a deeper level with the remnants of their abuse, entitled, "The Blooming Cactus," and the exercise that follows this story (found in the final section of this chapter).

Keep in mind that it is important to normalize some of the issues that come up for partnered thrivers as those typical of being in an intimate relationship, by making distinctions between the issues in the relationship that have to do with past sexual abuse and those that are connected to common relationship problems. Indeed, it is reassuring for thrivers to have the awareness that they are not alone in their struggle to strive for intimacy with their partners.

As important as it is for thrivers in a group to celebrate the differences between members, it is equally vital as a therapist to be accepting of the thrivers' personal definitions of success. For some thrivers, the fact that they have broken away from the grasp of their offender(s), become independent, and established a safe place for themselves in society can be considered a major triumph. For others at this advanced healing stage, connecting with a healthy, viable, intimate other is not only a possibility, but a realistic goal that can be attained.

METAPHORS, EXERCISES, AND RITUALS

RESTORING AND BALANCING INTIMACY AND SEXUALITY IN RELATIONSHIP TO SELF AND SIGNIFICANT OTHERS (MEDITATIONAL EXERCISE)

The following meditational exercise provides the survivor with an opportunity to rethink her relationship to her sexuality—to move toward creating a more respectful link to her own body and to significant others with whom she has chosen to enter into an intimate alliance. As you go through this exercise with your client, remember to pause after each question, providing her with an opportunity to consider new possibilities as she quietly responds to herself.

TAKING SOME TIME NOW to breathe fully and deeply. With each inhale taking in safety and respect for your sexuality and with each exhale letting go of any old messages that may have been blocking the path to a healthy self-image—allowing for new future possibilities. Inviting yourself, now, to consider learning how you can extend yourself to others in a way that still maintains your own integrity in a more respectful manner. Taking special care to pay attention to and look after your own needs—creating the opportunity and space in your physical body to allow this to occur while allowing yourself the time now to ponder these questions that you can ask yourself gently and respectfully.

Considering now, which parts of your body house the abuse and the feelings that accompany it: the pain, anger, shame, rage, sadness, grief, and loss. What is it like to live and experience being you? How do you experience your sexual self? What emotions do you experience in connection to your sexuality? How fluid are they? How do you make things happen in your life? When has your personal power flowed through you easily, willingly, and happily? How can you connect with your inner core to fire up your energy to empower yourself? What can you do for you? Does love come easily into your core being? Where is the center of your compassion for yourself? How can you integrate self-compassion and love with your sexuality? How would it be to reacquaint yourself with your body in a more accepting way? How often do you communicate with yourself? How have you anchored yourself and connected yourself to others? Is it safe to allow others into your life? What is it that you would want to be different about how you allow others into your space now? How have you allowed intimacy into your life? What does it mean to have an intimate relationship with yourself? How has your abuse blocked your ability to be intimate with yourself?

Remembering to breathe.... How has your abuse colored your understanding of intimacy and having a respectful relationship with your sexuality? If you were to identify the shape and color of those blocks to intimacy, what would they look like and sound like and would they have a certain texture, taste, and odor? Utilizing, now, your newly found personal power...imagining shifting those blocks, transforming them into an opportunity to rebuild intimacy into your life. Imagine, now, giving yourself the power to shift the abuse so that it occupies only the smallest corners of your body...actually shrinking the abuse as it moves further away from your inner core and closer to the outer extremities of your body.

Remembering to breathe. What is it like to have the abuse experience occupy a smaller space in your body? How would you wear your newly found intimacy? What would it look like, sound like, feel like, taste like, and smell like to you and to others? How would you create a circle of intimacy, surrounding yourself with respectful, honorable others who respect and honor you? Once the circle has been created, how would you anchor yourself to yourself in a way that would allow you to safely and comfortably connect to those significant others? And is there one special other that you would choose to connect with even more intimately than the others? How could you share yourself more openly with that intimate other? Imagine now what it would be like to show yourself to that intimate other. Imagine now what it would be like to share yourself with that other...to experience the physical, emotional, and spiritual feeling of coming together with that beloved other. Creating the boundaries and the safety that you need to be able to achieve that intimacy, comfortably, when ready. Taking in a deep full breath and on the exhale, letting go now of what might no longer belong.

How would you like to communicate your sexual needs and preferences to this intimate other, your partner? Is it safe to get in touch with your own body sensations while you are intimate sexually with your partner? What is it like to voice your sexual boundaries and preferences to your intimate other? What is it like to hear the sound of your own voice respecting the sensations that are being voiced by your body and then, further, carrying out the wishes of your body's need to be respected by you and your partner? Wandering through your body, taking stock of any new awareness you may have, now, of how to stay in touch with your body's requests while maintaining your integrity when you enter into sexual intimacy with a chosen other. Remembering to breathe, freely and deeply. That's right.

Does your intimate other respect the boundaries you have created around your sexual relationship with him/her? If so, how do you personally experience this person's respect and honoring of your sexual self? If not, considering, now, what actions you would take in order to enter into a healthier, more respectful alliance with your sexual self. When will you know you are ready? Remembering to breathe. Writing down any important personal images to self-discovery that you may have, now. Is there any new information you now have about yourself since embarking on this journey of self-discovery? Taking some time, to ponder and wander where you might go from here equipped with this new information. Feeling your load lighten, now, unburdened from the past, stepping into the future with a new relationship to sexuality, creativity, and vitality.

⌘   ⌘   ⌘

"THE BLOOMING CACTUS"

In this final healing stage, the writers have identified a key developmental turning point for the thriver, that is, the ability to connect with healthy others in meaningful, caring ways. This particular metaphorical story was developed for members of a survivor group who were at the point in their recovery where they were feeling hopeful about the possibility of repartnering or partnering with healthy others for the first time in their lives. These members had been successfully able to identify the pitfalls of former intimate relationships that had been fraught with dishonesty, insensitivity, and, in some cases, physical, emotional, and sexual abuse. This particular group of thrivers were beginning to add the following phrases to their vocabulary: "I deserve to be treated with respect" and "I am now able to give myself permission to be loved and cared for unconditionally in an intimate relationship."

YOU CAN TAKE SOME TIME NOW, to just take some nice, big deep breaths, taking in what you need and letting go of what no longer belongs…noticing that what may have been comfortable before, no longer fits as comfortably—like an old jacket that now feels too tight in the shoulders and across the back. It almost feels as if you have perhaps outgrown your old clothes and that now it is time to don new threads that make allowances for your new growth.

And now that you are feeling a greater sense of comfort in your own skin, you can make any further adjustments…while you listen to a story about an attractive flourishing cactus. That's right…taking some time to focus.…

There was once a beautiful cactus that lived and thrived in the Painted Desert. This particular cactus was deep green in color, with a very strong, tough, exterior, exuding fans of sharp yellow spikes in rows that appeared almost armorlike in their protection of the skin. At the very top of the cactus was a soft cushiony part arising from its interior, with spikes encircling it to protect the soft top from any encroachers.

The top of the cactus was a very important part, as this was where the cactus absorbed sunshine and water and carefully stored it so that when the earth was dry and parched, the cactus could utilize its own cool store of water from deep within its inner core, in order to continue to grow and flourish. That's right....

And when the desert was flooding, the cactus was able to transform the heat absorbed from the sunshine to keep it strong and able to weather any storm.

It just so happened one day there was a blinding sandstorm that came over the desert.... Although the cactus was able to remain rooted and steadfast, she had become temporarily blinded, experiencing difficulty seeing clearly until the storm passed, so she didn't notice that another less hardy cactus uprooted from another part of the desert had been transported by the wind, landing directly next to her.

The beautiful green cactus automatically took pity on the newly arrived cactus and began to share her inner reservoir of heat and water with the other cactus.... But it didn't seem to matter how much of her resources were shared with the other cactus, as the new arrival had difficulty transforming the resources so that it could grow strong enough to begin to rely on its own ability to maintain itself.

The green cactus began to realize that it didn't matter how much of herself she shared with the other cactus, it was never enough to enable the other cactus to begin to utilize its own resources. The green cactus began to feel depleted as her own supply of energy dwindled, and she felt weak and tired.

Then, one day, the strong desert winds returned, and because of its weak roots, the other cactus, which had maintained its livelihood by relying solely on the green cactus, was swept up by the wind and transported far away.

Once again, the green cactus with the strong exterior flourished, as she utilized the sun and the rain, transforming these elements into her own resources to rebuild herself and reconnect with her many strengths. She felt a renewed sense of self...and, this time, the cactus began to truly appreciate her abilities to transform the resources around her into healthy parts of herself, that's right.... realizing that each part had to be nurtured in order to feel whole, centered, and rooted. Just then, something quite wonderful began to happen—the green cactus began to grow between her spikes the most exquisitely colored blooms: a magnificent sienna red! The green cactus was amazed and thrilled, as this was the very first time that her blooms had surfaced and opened themselves up to take in the nurturing warmth of the sun and the cool relief of the rain.

A yellow cactus that had been growing and flourishing fairly close by, and had been the subject of the green cactus's admiration for some time, began to notice the green cactus, as she proudly displayed her newly acquired sienna red blossoms! Isn't it nice to know that inner growth can also be noticed on one's exterior?... And you can give yourself permission, now, to sit back, noticing and admiring your own growth that you have worked so hard to acquire.

Over time, the green and yellow cacti became good friends, appreciating one another's strengths and abilities, and sometimes when either required some extra nurturing, a small supply would be shared between them. There was always a respect for each cactus's need to utilize its own inner resources in order to maintain a healthy self before sharing with the other. In this way, both the green and yellow cacti could respect and honor themselves, which allowed them to maintain a healthy, caring relationship with one another.

⌘ ⌘ ⌘

THE BLOOMING CACTUS RITUAL

In order for the advancements and progress of your client to remain anchored and become a genuine, integral part of the self, it is essential to follow this metaphor with a daily ritual that she has devised herself, perhaps with your help. This ritual needs to be something the thriver can do for herself that reflects her own unique healing experience. This ritual can be created right after you have told the story of "The Blooming Cactus" so that the essence and richness of the metaphor does not get lost. You may find the following phraseology a helpful way in which to encourage and seed the thriver's own thought processes.

A ND, NOW, YOU CAN take some time to honor yourself in some special way just as the green cactus was able to do.... That's right, allowing yourself a moment or two of clock time just to concoct your own unique brew of self-respect and love...creating an opportunity to celebrate yourself each day in some special way.

Just as the green cactus was able to recognize and enjoy the yellow cactus, you can appreciate even more the healthy links you have successfully forged with healthy others. Now, more than ever before, you can realize the possibilities of future intimate alliances and partnerships—even more comfortably and even more confidently.

"WOMB WITH A VIEW"

This metaphorical story is wonderful to use with thrivers who have done considerable individual and group therapy and are preparing to reenter society with a greater ability to make distinctions between potential abusers and healthy others than prior to their recovery from sexual abuse. It is here that the therapist can assist the client in making the transition from a limited circle of contacts, that is, therapists and other survivor group members, to taking that brave step to reaching out beyond the therapeutic circle. This includes perhaps connecting in some way with various women and child empowerment groups such as the Feminist Movement and child advocacy groups, in addition to ultimately connecting, perhaps for the first time, to healthy others.

This metaphorical story was co-created by the therapist and the client Michelle (mentioned earlier in this chapter) who, after five years of intensive individual and group therapy, was apprehensive about taking that all-important step back into society, beyond her therapist and other survivors she had met all with whom she had developed meaningful connections.

Keep in mind that as you read this metaphor, you, as the therapist, may want to change some of the details. For example, Berthie, the Danish babysitter, is meant to resemble the thriver's relationship to her therapist; however, if your particular client was sexually abused by her babysitter, this would not be a very useful symbol to use! This metaphor is about the inner strengths and courage the thriver has discovered and developed, with the assistance of her therapist, as life skills she can take with her and use so that she can exercise healthy judgment independently.

A S YOU ARE SITTING THERE, you can take some time to just experience the air around you and the closeness of it...and the comfort that closeness provides. There is something safe and secure about the vantage point you are at, right here, right now, that allows you to look past the windowpane to the world outside.

At the same time as you focus on the coziness of the room, you can also listen to a story about a friend of mine called Noni, who learnt a very special lesson from her Danish babysitter Berthie.

You see, when Noni was a small child, every time her parents would go out on the weekend, they would employ a babysitter to look after her. Noni had had several babysitters over the years, but her favorite one was a young woman with golden hair named Berthie.... Noni loved

Berthie, for she hailed from Denmark and had a special way of speaking that was different from anyone else she had ever heard before.

A special Danish word that Berthie would use to describe coziness, comfort, and security was "hyggelig"—"hyggelig" described exactly how Noni felt when she was with Berthie—happy, warm, loved, secure.... And when Berthie held Noni close, and they looked outside through the windowpane at the snowflakes falling to the frozen ground, Noni would wonder to herself what it would be like to go for a sleighride with Berthie, holding her close and keeping her warm, and what it would be like when they returned to the warmth of the fire inside and Berthie would make her hot chocolate with marshmallows floating and melting on the top.... You see, Noni was not allowed outside of the house too much, as her mother and father felt that the world was a bad place, so they restricted their daughter's movements....

When Berthie was looking after Noni, she used to tell her wonderful stories about life in Denmark. One particular story Noni loved to listen to was about how the Danes celebrated Christmas, as it was very different from anything she had experienced in her family. In Denmark, Christmas presents were opened on Christmas Eve, and, most wonderful of all, there was a very special rice pudding that the Danes would eat for dessert, which tasted so delicious that the children would request a second helping...so that the adults always made sure there was plenty of the heavenly concoction to go around!

Sometimes when she was baby-sitting Noni, Berthie would bring over her favorite records for Noni to listen to.... When the music was playing, Noni would just close her eyes and imagine a soirée of musical notes dancing to the rhythms of the sweet melodies they were playing...so freely and easily...that's right. Often Noni would imagine those musical notes beckoning her to glide with them down the streets...laughing out loud as they jumped back and forth on the sidewalk...treasuring the time she had to be with her own thoughts and feelings.... It was also very freeing to know that she had choices of her own to make.... "Maybe, just maybe, someday I will be able to exercise those choices," Noni thought as she laughed out loud!

Then, on one particular weekend, when her parents went out for the evening, a new babysitter arrived called Margianne! "Where's Berthie?" thought Noni, "Where's my Berthie? Why is she not here to look after me?" Noni found herself feeling very sad, and she felt the tears streaming down her face....

The next day she asked her mother why Berthie had not been there to look after her, and her mother explained that Berthie had found a

204 § RECLAIMING HERSTORY

full-time job and would no longer be available. At that very moment Noni felt like the earth below her had fallen away, and she was free-falling downward with no safety net to catch her.... She had no idea when or where she would land and if she would ever find her feet again.

That night Noni dreamed that Berthie was holding her close as they sat next to the hearth, where she could feel the warmth of the fire turning her cheeks a delightful shade of pink. Just at that very moment in her dream Noni began to hear Berthie with her thick Danish accent whispering the words…"hyggelig, hyggelig, hyggelig"…and, just then, in the dream, Noni could see herself getting out of Berthie's lap, finding her feet, and then, visibly growing taller and taller, as she walked away from where Berthie was sitting.... Waving goodbye, she took the hyggelig with her as she opened the window, stepping out to the other side of the pane to the steep roof directly below. She cautiously made her way down to the ground…crawling in some of the bumpier parts and scaling the flatter parts of the roof, until she reached a tree with very strong branches, where she slept that night until morning broke and she could find her way more easily....

Once the sun began to rise, Noni scaled down the tree, landing on her feet as she hit the ground with a thump! Just then, Noni woke up from her dream with a start, thinking that this would be a special day for her.... She realized she would probably not see Berthie for a long time, or, maybe never again.... But Noni knew deep in her heart that she would carry the hyggelig feeling that she got from being with Berthie around with her for the rest of her life.

Years later Noni became fairly independent of her family and, when she was old enough, she moved away and found her own place to live. It was a bit scary in the beginning to turn the lights out at night and know that she would be all alone until morning, but after living alone for a while, she began to exercise the choices she had only dreamt of so longingly as a child. However, putting those choices into practice was something entirely different when it came to actually taking those first steps outside of her cozy place, away from the familiar into the unknown. It was terrifying and yet exciting at the same time that Noni could actually give herself permission to go to her favorite coffee shop for a cappuccino or meet a friend for Thai food (her favorite!) and a movie. Noni realized just at that moment she had created a hyggelig living space just for her…up from where she could look outside the pane—it was her window on the world. She had created that comfort and security all by herself! "Well done, Noni!" she exclaimed to herself. "What an accomplishment!" Noni thought as she felt the pride growing within her.

It became easier over time for Noni to sort out the hyggelig people from the others—for hyggelig people respected the personal boundaries Noni had created over time for herself and did not intrude into her space unless she gave them her permission. But, most important of all, Noni developed a respect and trust for herself...enough to make healthy choices—even in the real world.... She realized at that moment that she had really moved beyond the pane, and she could feel the self-doubt that she had carried with her for so long slowly melting away, as it was being replaced gradually with a deep love, trust, and respect for self.

FOLLOW-UP RITUAL FOR "WOMB WITH A VIEW"

This is a key turning point in the thriver's recovery from sexual abuse, as she is more than likely reaching the end of her individual and group therapy, which means that she is spending minimal time in the therapist's office and more time pursuing her life outside of the safe, therapeutic circle she developed for herself over the years. As a result, this ritual has been devised to assist the thriver in taking her learnings and healing into the real world, where she may initially feel vulnerable and apprehensive. This ritual passes the message to the thriver that "You can do it on your own and you can do it well!" An additional suggestion that you may want to make to the thriver at this juncture is that she can use her own voice to tape record the process involved in performing the ritual in order to promote further individuation from the therapist and develop an intensification and deepening of self-trust.

YOU CAN TAKE SOME TIME, now, to experience identifying and letting go of something that you have perhaps stored for a long time in a particular corner of your body, that you have deemed now as unhealthy.... It may be experienced by you as a particular pain in your neck, shoulder, or back...or perhaps a chronic sense of knots in your stomach...or somewhere else in your body.

It is now time to take on something new...something that is unique to you and only you.... I'm not sure what that might be...perhaps, you may concentrate on providing a warmth to a part of your body that has always felt cold...or you may give yourself permission to untie the knots in your stomach and experience the soothing sensation of having a relaxed, flexible intestine for the first time in your life! And isn't it amazing how wonderful it feels to have the power to make an adjustment in your body no matter how small....

Now, you can contemplate what a relaxed neck or back or an untied stomach may free you up to do.... You now can experience the freedom to do and feel what may have only been a dream to you up until now...and how wonderful that feels to consider how this newfound freedom can open up all sorts of new possibilities for you.... And isn't it nice to know that you can now plan ahead?... Perhaps, deciding to pursue a hobby that you have always wanted to take the time to focus on... or learn a special skill.... The possibilities are endless!

"HUSH—PART FIVE" (STAGE FOUR, PART B)

Part Five of the "Hush" chronicles, the concluding chapter of the story, symbolizes how far the thriver has come in her healing. This final Hush story provides the thriver with the message that self-transformation is a process that continues throughout life and does not stop when the formal individual and group therapy sessions have reached their conclusions. Rather, it is more important now, than ever before, that the thriver can hear and dialogue effectively with her inner wise voice, since the therapist, who is assuming a lesser role, will not be as available to coax it out of its hiding place from deep within.

If you recall, we left Hush with a new sense of energy and excitement about the future—ready to explore the many possibilities that lay ahead of her.

HUSH CONTINUED TO experience a strong sense of family with the other group members—so much so that at the final sessions led by Eidolon, the discussion turned to future plans of continued contact. Eidolon observed: "I can see that you are very close to one another, and that although you haven't always seen eye to eye on different issues that have surfaced over the course of this group, you have learnt to really enjoy celebrating and respecting one another's differences of opinion." As she was listening to Eidolon, Hush suddenly had an idea: "Once our groups with Eidolon are over, I would like to continue to have contact with all of you." "What a wonderful idea!" exclaimed Raye. "Yes, we seem to have an inspiring influence on one another—I wonder if it would be possible to meet with one another further, perhaps at each other's homes," said Crystal as she opened up the topic for the other members to consider. Dot continued with further suggestions: "We could be one another's advocates whenever an issue comes up for one of us that we may be struggling with...we could use our strong collective voices to provide the support we may need along the way as we try out what we have learned."

The group members agreed that it would be wonderful to continue to be there for one another after they bid farewell to Eidolon, as they practiced standing on their own.

The day had finally arrived when it came time for Hush, Crystal, Dot, and Raye, to say their goodbyes to Eidolon. They had planned a special celebration to honor their graduation.... It was a perfect spring day as they carried their hampers up the mountain to a special grassy plateau with a little stream running through the middle. This time, the mountain climb did not seem so steep as the group had discovered a path of lesser resistance...so that they enjoyed their climb, and by the time they reached the grassy plateau, they were dancing and singing with one another.

Hush felt the pride welling up inside, as she observed how far she and the others had come in their healing.... The mask-making seemed to be a major turning point for all of them, thought Hush, as she watched how Raye seemed to be stretching her outer limits, by taking the initiative to engage in lively discourse with the others...no longer hiding her sadness over past losses but, rather, wearing her feelings more comfortably. Hush's gaze then turned to Dot, and the anger that had been noticeable on her face before was now beginning to soften into a broad, genuine smile, exuding a vitality that seemed to come from within, as she danced...making creative rhythmical movements with her body. Hush noticed that Crystal, too, seemed more comfortable in her own skin, as the past visible signs of tension had dissolved into a relaxed confidence.

Just at that moment Eidolon suggested that Hush, Crystal, Dot, and Raye stand before the stream and peer down at their reflections in the water.... Hush gasped as she gazed at her own reflection..."Was this really her?" Hush had always carried a low self-image, as she viewed herself in her mind's eye as an unattractive, weak lynx.... Now, however, as she peered into the water, she caught herself looking confident, with the corners of her mouth turned upward in a smile.... She also noticed that she had grown taller, and that her coat had become shiny and her fur had taken on a brilliant caramel color. Hush closed her eyes as she began to experience that funny feeling in her body again. The others began to feel it too—as they made the necessary adjustments, both physically and emotionally, to match with the startling changes they had discovered as they peered at their reflections in the stream.

As the group sat with her in a circle for the last time, Eidolon whispered, "Now that you know how far you have all come in your healing, it is time for me to bid you farewell, and encourage you to continue to do and feel what is working for you both now and in the future." Hush and the others felt a deep sadness well up inside of them, as they waved goodbye to Eidolon, watching her until she disappeared down the other side of the mountain....

Amazingly, just at that moment, Hush felt a certain calm come over her, as she began to contemplate her future...remembering how Kit had reassured her that her backpack contained all the tools she would need to cope.... Now, she could add the new tools that she had recently fashioned to further enhance the quality of her life. What an exciting prospect! Hush watched as the sad faces of her friends transformed into visions of hope and future possibilities. They then said so long for now to one another, agreeing to meet in two weeks time at the new home Hush had recently established for herself on the mountainside.

Two weeks seemed to pass very quickly, and it seemed strange to be meeting with the others without the presence of Eidolon. The group sat in a circle in Hush's living space and began to brainstorm about the issues they wanted to deal with in their meetings together. Raye, Crystal, Dot, and Hush agreed that they all appeared to be struggling in different ways with fitting into their rather new self-images...this seemed to be a good place to start.

Raye opened up the discussion by talking about her experience of looking for a new place to live.... After searching for some time, she had discovered that there was an empty beaver dam made of tree logs that she thought would be a perfect place for her to take up residence. However, just as she was moving in her possessions from Eidolon's place to her new home, she noticed two beavers arguing ferociously on her doorstep.... As Raye drew closer, she could hear them fighting over whose dam home it was.... Raye described how she calmly stepped up to where the beavers were standing and said in a firm voice, "I have been searching for a home for some time, and this is where I want to be. I am just in the process today of moving in my possessions, and it's a nice feeling to know that I have finally found a place of my own." The beavers stared at Raye in disbelief, as they never imagined the possibility of a mountain lion living in a beaver dam! "Well," one of the beaver's explained, "we need to talk this over with our specially appointed housing committee before we can allow you to move in—you see, any beaver-built dam that has been abandoned can be lived in by other beavers, but a mountain lion...we don't know if that is possible." Raye felt the anger welling up inside of her, as she listened to the beaver's rationale, but, this time, instead of blowing up and losing control, which would have backfired anyway, she took a deep breath and firmly stood her ground, as both beavers agreed that she could live in the log house until a decision had been made by the housing committee.

Hush took the initiative as she stretched out her paw to congratulate Raye for her ability to stand up to the beavers without losing control and, at the same time, maintaining her position. "Well done," the others chimed in. "We are so proud of you!" Hush encouraged Raye to continue to stand up for her rights in the way that she had been doing.... Here she was...negotiating her rights without getting angry and out-of-control...this was proof of the incredible transformations Raye had made!

Dot and Crystal had decided to share accommodations for a while after leaving Eidolon's home. They discovered a beautiful cave, where the natural rock formations within had been fashioned over time into soft, smooth beds, on which they could lay their heads and feel safe.... The entrance to the cave even had a door, so that if someone wanted to visit Dot and Crystal, they would have to knock first to gain entry. Dot and Crystal shared with the group that they were learning, through experience, how to share their living space with one another in a way that respected each other's need for privacy and quietude...recognizing that there would be an ongoing need to maintain an open dialogue with one another on the subject.

Hush discussed with the group a dream that she had had where she observed herself stepping out of her own skin...she could feel the sensation of shivering as she shed her old coat...the coat that had absorbed her pain and shame...as she felt the sensation of letting it go...that's right.... She described how she really felt ready to do that now, more than ever before. And, then, like magic, as Hush peered at her reflection on the water's surface, she watched as her new skin and fur began to grow...taking on a coat that glimmered and shimmered in the spring sunshine...expressing in a meaningful way her multifaceted self. Just at that moment, something clicked for Hush...the dream was a true reflection of all the work she had put into healing her wounds, and now she could reclaim her new life in a way that was genuinely hers!...She truly had become a strong lynx....

Raye, Dot, and Crystal beamed, as they listened to Hush's triumphant dream...feeling encouraged that they, too, would be ready to turn that all-important corner one day soon.

The friends agreed that the group they had formed independently of Eidolon was a comfortable, safe haven in which they could continue to grow over time, both individually and together.... They looked forward to future group meetings with each other...excited about sharing all the healthy changes each one of them would continue to make in their lives—now and in the future.

PART III

SELF-CARE FOR THE THERAPIST

CHAPTER 8

Tracking the Evolution of the Sexual Abuse Therapist

So much has been written about treating survivors of sexual abuse, but not until recently have sexual abuse therapists acknowledged the need to develop a certain set of practices to assist them in dealing emotionally and mentally with the traumatic stories imparted to them on an ongoing basis. It seems appropriate to warn therapists who are just starting to work with survivors of sexual abuse that they should proceed with caution: they need to set clear professional boundaries around their caseloads from the outset, so that they can follow a preventive path, rather than choosing the path of least resistance by attempting to impress and please colleagues and supervisors with an overwhelming collection of sexual abuse cases. For therapists who are reassessing their positions mid-career as well as seasoned clinicians, we encourage you now, if you have not already done so, to put into practice a secondary preventive plan before you develop a terminal dose of empathy malaise as a result of having carried an unvaried large caseload of trauma survivors for far too long in your clinical practice.

In this chapter we will identify and track the developmental stages of sexual abuse therapists, by describing the various issues that they face during the following phases of their career:

Stage One: The Quest of the Fledgling Therapist—Trying to Do It All
Stage Two: Proving Self—Acquiring Skills
Stage Three: To Be or Not to Be a Therapist—That Is the Question!
Stage Four: Choosing to Stay—Assuming a Balanced Perspective

Following our discussion of these substages, we will present Metaphors, Exercises, and Rituals, which will help the therapist incorporate self-care practices as a key part of their regular professional routines.

We hope that our identification of the common pitfalls that you may encounter and our suggestions about how to stay on track will help you to cope during the trying times and also help to support you in your professional development.

STAGE ONE: THE QUEST OF THE FLEDGLING THERAPIST—TRYING TO DO IT ALL

As is natural in any developmental process, doing and experiencing are crucial to understanding, making sense of, assimilating, and accommodating new experiences and environments. However, as the neophyte therapist begins his/her career, there is often a tendency to take on anything and everything in a quest to acquire knowledge and skills as well as to fulfill one's need to prove oneself and assuage self-doubt. This often results in the fledgling therapist going in many directions at once and taking on and often inundating oneself with too many new challenges and sometimes naïve and unrealistic expectations of personal capacity and boundaries.

The new therapist has been learning, training, and meeting academic and licensing requirements for many years; therefore it is only natural that when many of the hoops have been successfully maneuvered, there is a resurgence of energy and curiosity for this new phase of life and career. On the upside, since the fledgling therapist is generally open to new ideas and experience, his/her energy level is high. Without appropriate boundaries, however, the therapist at this stage may be too eager to take on the responsibility for "fixing the client" and may do too much of the work in the therapeutic relationship.

Self-care at this point in time may seem unnecessary as the excitement and novelty of one's new position takes hold. If one is beginning a job in an established clinical environment, there is often an implicit message, both internal and external, that "paying your dues" is a required element of initiation into the professional "real world." When one is starting a private practice, saying "no" is often next to impossible because every potential contact may result in much needed "business."

At this point, one's therapeutic work and perspective are still evolving and there is often some philosophical angst in relation to one's personal experience and belief system as it relates to one's work and view of therapy and how that affects practice with clients. This can be a valuable opportunity to take stock of one's beliefs and values in relation to self and work. As supervisors of many graduate students, we utilize this opening to begin a process of self-inventory in order to gain awareness and insight into how presenting issues and sexual abuse—and family violence issues in particular—affect one's view and approach to therapy; we also try to ascertain their impact on the therapist's personal history and present life.

In our experience, dealing with trauma and toxic content at this time can be both fascinating and disturbing. However, because one does not usually have prolonged experience and exposure with such content, it may be easier initially to maintain a safe distance from experiencing trauma vicariously. As the therapist becomes more specialized and saturated with the details of the clients' stories of abuse, he/she is challenged to examine his/her own values and beliefs surrounding these issues. Inevitably, this will lead to the reexamination of one's belief systems and cognitive schemas as they relate to this disturbing material. Some therapists with traumatic histories of their own may be more affected by such content earlier on in their careers and may take steps to care for themselves accordingly. Others may disregard early warning signs and go full steam ahead, believing that they should be able to deal effectively with such reactions if they are to be "a good therapist."

By and large, this is a time of high energy, expectation, and self-discovery and in the process of acquiring knowledge and skills, one may lay the foundation for future work habits and patterns that can lead inadvertently to vicarious burnout and traumatization. We can all benefit from more training and information early in our careers concerning the importance of pacing ourselves, the need for establishing clearer personal and professional boundaries, and the ability and practice of saying "no" without feeling guilty or judged by self and others.

STAGE TWO: PROVING SELF—ACQUIRING SKILLS

Following the initial stage of the therapist's career enough skills have been acquired in order for the helper to begin to feel fairly competent and confident in his/her work. However, the therapist often maintains the mind-set from the fledgling stage that perpetuates a continued need to prove self by adding more cases to what is already a demanding, heavy caseload. It is key at this point for the supervisor to assist the relatively new therapist-incumbent to regulate and vary the cases, so that he/she has an opportunity to begin skill-building in a number of different areas, for example, couple counselling, school problems, and adolescent issues. In addition, the therapist may discover, after working with a number of different types of cases, that the issue of sexual abuse arises during the course of the therapy, and he/she has a choice to refer the case to an experienced colleague or to tackle the case with supervisory assistance. It is important to point out that working with survivors of sexual abuse may be contraindicated for the skill-building therapist, if the helper is a sexual abuse survivor and has not had an opportunity yet to be in his/her own therapy. This is where the continued support of a supervisor/consultant is crucial, so that the survivor-therapist does not fall between the cracks and continue to work with sexually abused clients, a detrimental situation that could result in a blurring between the issues of the therapist and those of the clients. Once the therapist who is also a survivor of sexual abuse has had an opportunity, through therapy, to work through his/her abuse, he/she can return to counselling survivors (with the proviso of ongoing supervision/consultation), better equipped to make distinctions between client issues and his/her own.

If, however, the supervisor and other experienced colleagues are not aware of the therapist's needs at this particular career juncture, the fledgling therapist, whether or not he/she is a survivor, often continues to prove his/her worth and competency in a tangible way—by taking on more and more challenging cases. It is at this professional juncture, when the therapist is taking on cases to gain the admiration of colleagues and increase his/her skill level rapidly, that the symptoms of empathy malaise may begin to manifest themselves, possibly somatically or behaviorally, even though these reactions may be just outside of the helper's conscious awareness. For example, the therapist may begin to feel tired when waking up in the morning after a supposedly good rest or may feel exhausted as a result of working long hours at the office, seeing one stressful case after the other, without a break. The therapist's weariness may also be due to certain dreams and/or obsessive thoughts, in which he/she is featured as the traumatized victim, with safety and security compromised and threatened in some way.

However, even though the therapist may be feeling one or more of the above-mentioned symptoms, he/she—who is still very much needing to prove self—may remain dissociated from these warning signals, willing to go to any lengths to maintain professional credibility. The acquisitive therapist often is in rigorous competition with colleagues, turning supervisory/consultative sessions into opportunities to prove to other staff members that he/she is more reliable, knows more, and is more competent than the others. Herein lie the seeds of future difficulties, where the therapist may gradually begin the process of decreasing consultation time with colleagues through such unconscious behavior as double booking so that the competitive element increases and the cooperative aspect begins to diminish as the therapist, accordingly, becomes more isolated in his/her practice.

If the therapist has chosen the private practice route, there may be a tendency, in order to build up his/her reputation in the community, to take on most of the referrals received in order to ensure that the referral sources are not at risk for drying up. In the environment of private practice, the therapist often works in isolation, where ongoing collegial input and support is not received, which accordingly places this private practitioner at even greater risk for empathy malaise. We will demonstrate in the following section, that is, "Stage Three: To Be or Not to Be a Therapist—That Is the Question!" the therapist's more marked tendency towards professional isolation: As a result of working in a competitive environment, it may not be safe for the therapist to expose struggles and vulnerabilities with certain challenging cases, for fear that his/her competency will be brought into question.

Apart from the competitive/appeaser aspects of the acquisitive therapist's clinical development, he/she is in the process of growing his/her own style of therapy, reflecting a comfortable blend of personality and professional skills. The ability to absorb new information regarding ways of intervening with clients increases dramatically, for the therapist is now far enough along in his/her career to apply more sophisticated counselling methods, and early enough in his/her career to be open to embracing and integrating new learnings into the clinical practice. At this time, the therapist may start making distinctions between cases and show a particular preference for certain types of cases. This is also a time when the therapist is attempting to incorporate all of the different models of therapy that he/she was trained in, trying in some way to blend the voices of mentors and other authority figures that have been a part of his/her education and clinical training: This becomes a struggle, as it is difficult and exhausting to please everyone. As a result, the therapist's own brand of therapy does not begin to emerge until he/she is ready to let go of the voices of mentors, as will be described in the next two stages of the helper's career.

STAGE THREE: TO BE OR NOT TO BE A THERAPIST—
THAT IS THE QUESTION!

As the therapist travels along his/her career path and continues to evolve therapeutically, there generally comes a time when the warning signs of overload become all too apparent. Prior to this the therapist has been taking on more and more, integrating various techniques and theories into a personal framework for doing therapy. In building a caseload, whether by choice or not, the therapist inevitably has to deal with issues of trauma and abuse. Many clients, on entering therapy, may identify other issues as the focus of therapy and later in the course of treatment identify or feel more comfortable unveiling issues of trauma, family violence, and sexual abuse. Therefore, even if one has tried to steer clear of working specifically in the area of sexual abuse, some cases evolve into this arena. In time, therapists may find themselves working increasingly in this area. Whether we have consciously identified interest in specializing in these issues or have developed our practice and reputations as therapists to a point where we are constantly in demand, we may begin to take on too much as we are validated and needed more and more. After several years of working at a fast and demanding pace, therapists may begin to experience serious signs of personal stress as it becomes more and more difficult to separate from the constant demands of work and its often toxic content.

The temptation of feeling needed, validated, and indispensable may be a by-product of coming to terms with our own self-doubt concerning how effective and competent we are as therapists. This is a profession where tangible quantifiable results are all too fleeting. One of the reasons we enjoy doing group work with survivors is that we can see visible positive changes in most participants from the beginning of the group to the end. However, with some more difficult and complex cases a clear, positive outcome is not always evident or possible. Some clients may leave therapy before any tangible positive change has been achieved.

Since there is no real scientific definition of what therapy is and how to do it, as therapists we are often driven toward the attainment of positive outcome by our own insecurities or unrealistic expectations. This may take the form of expecting a significant transformation in our client that is not consistent or achievable within the client's potential. In this way, we may be imposing a view of health or healing that may not be an appropriate or even a desirable outcome from the client's perspective. Therefore, we may be doing therapy according to our own hidden agenda based on our own issues and beliefs rather than checking out the client's expectations and goals that fit his/her vision of a more positive future. This can lead to disillusionment and burnout for the therapist as well as frustration and pressure for the client.

McCann and Pearlman (1990) speak about countertransference in the context of vicarious traumatization and suggest that therapists' own issues, beliefs, insecurities, experiences, and memories (perhaps of their own trauma) are triggered by the traumatic content of their clients' histories. This can often lead to overidentification with clients' victimization and therefore the myriad of effects that trauma survivors experience may also be experienced by therapists. McCann and Pearlman broaden the old definition of countertransference to include the effects on the therapist's own cognitive constructs, which can impact and also alter the therapist's individual beliefs about life, feelings, and personal relationships.

Thus, the therapist dealing with trauma survivors may struggle with redefining and realigning his/her beliefs, expectations, and assumptions about the world in general and specifically regarding issues of trust, safety, power, esteem, and intimacy. This in turn can reflect one's work therapeutically and may result in disillusionment, fatigue and dissatisfaction, the clouding of therapeutic focus, and the loss of perspective in how one views clients either consciously or unconsciously.

It may be at this point that the helper decides that the work is too virulent and its effects too immobilizing to continue. Self-doubt and exhaustion may eclipse the original excitement and creativity with which the fledgling therapist entered the therapeutic domain. Some therapists may ask themselves, Is this really what I want to do? We view this type of juncture as an opportunity to take stock of self and career by examining the process that led up to the current state and then making new choices about how the situation can be richer, more fulfilling, and less overwhelming.

In our experience of observing and discussing these issues with colleagues, there is often a sense of increasing isolation as the therapist lives through personal distress and burnout. It is much like the "secret" dilemma of the abuse victim; her guilt and shame keeps her from seeking help. As competent therapists we are often too hesitant to seek help ourselves as we sink into the quagmire of vicarious trauma. We often struggle with the notion that to be seen as proficient therapists, we cannot expose our own vulnerability or difficulty in dealing with personal issues that are triggered by our clients. There is often a concern that seeking personal consultation and therapy ourselves may mean that we are deficient. How can we be good therapists if we can't get our own act together?

This notion is often enhanced by competitive work environments and peers. If we cannot openly discuss these issues with our peers, the result may be to go underground and become secretive with our own issues and conflicts, which inevitably isolates us and adds to the pressure we feel.

Because there is little, if any, protocol in dealing with these issues, we feel it is important for the therapist to create his/her own individually relevant self-care plan. When we can identify and acknowledge problem areas within ourselves and our work, we can plan strategically to combat these often paralyzing issues that block our energy and creativity in doing this work. Therefore, vicarious traumatization can be used and transformed into an experience of being more in tune with ourselves both personally and professionally. As we let go of the need to please others and listen to our own needs and personal style of working, we can thus continue to evolve and self-actualize.

In the next section, "Choosing to Stay: Assuming a Balanced Perspective," we identify ways and means of designing a personal self-care plan. In the final section of this chapter we present specific metaphors, exercises, and rituals that can serve as guidelines and examples of dealing with the effects of overload and toxic material.

STAGE FOUR: CHOOSING TO STAY—
ASSUMING A BALANCED PERSPECTIVE

If the therapist manages to survive the above-described Stage Three, we say to them BRAVO! and welcome to the trials and tribulations of being a sexual abuse therapist! These therapists are now more acutely aware of their boundaries, having perhaps been pushed to their proverbial limit in Stage Three. Now there is a more conscious awareness about when they are about to violate one of their own boundaries, for example, by taking on just one more challenging case that is going to tip the scales and wreak havoc on physical health and emotional balance. These therapists can now say "NO!" comfortably to one, two, three, or more extra heavy cases and not feel guilty. This is a tremendous feat, as they may be risking disdain or flack from colleagues about not adequately pulling their load at work.

For therapists in private practice, the ability to say "NO!" comfortably to taking on more cases presents even more of a challenge, as the willingness and discipline to do so often comes solely from oneself. In order to combat the isolation and potential blurring of boundaries, we highly recommend that private practitioners become involved with other professionals on a consultative basis so that they can receive regular, ongoing support to implement healthy boundaries between their clients and themselves. If the private practitioner perseveres with setting clear professional boundaries, he/she is free to gain a healthier perspective as new, inspiring, and creative skills are acquired. The previous competitiveness may have interfered with taking the time out to train further through workshops and conferences, blocking the much-needed opportunity to continue to acquire new skills in order to keep work fresh and creative and avoid further empathy malaise. The therapist is interested now in sharing knowledge, skills, and questions with other colleagues, keen to get their support and their opinions, for it is no longer as important to please them or to prove credibility. Even though this is the last stage we discuss in this book, it is not the final one, as even the well-seasoned therapist can still learn and build on his/her already acquired rich skill level.

In terms of the way in which evolved therapists work with clients, we see them as defocusing from the gory details of the sexual abuse, so that the vicarious traumatization they may have been more vulnerable to previously is not as intense; these helpers focus in with their clients more on the emotional, visceral impact of the abuse. This shift in clinical approach equips such therapists with the ability to continue working in the area of sexual abuse and can free them to become more creative than ever before in their therapeutic interventions—We have found that utilizing the metaphors, rituals, and exercises precludes us from the tendency to "fix" our clients, and rather, allows us to enter into a co-creative process with them. This process also begins to shift the therapeutic relationship to a more equal plane, where the client assumes a more active role and personal investment in her own healing, thereby allowing for a less burdened, happier, more optimistic therapist!

The attitude of the therapist is key to the survivor's healing, for if the therapist is feeling bogged down by the gravity of the case, he/she may transmit this to the survivor-client in the form of hopelessness, thereby sabotaging the healing process. The co-creative process creates a sense of hopefulness for both the therapist and client, freeing them to draw more deeply from their own inner pools of resources, and in so doing, keeping the work fresh, flowing, and viable. It is at this juncture that the therapist becomes increasingly confident about his/her clinical skills, returning to the fold as it were, so that he/she can begin to share expertise with colleagues, rather than withholding this knowledge or using it as a competitive weapon against other therapists.

Whether in private practice or as a therapist in a counselling agency or other professional setting, the need for ongoing peer consultation, where clinicians have a regular opportunity to debrief, helps complete the transformation from a competitive to a more cooperative working environment. This, in turn, contributes to setting a healthier tone for the agency, freeing staff to provide quality care to their clients, without the stress of constantly having to watch their proverbial backs with one another. In addition, regular consultation with colleagues creates a working environment for the private practitioner where there is more assurance around developing a healthy, boundary-conscious practice.

At this stage, the therapist may be taking on more than just the responsibility as a front-line counsellor—for example, the therapist may be ready to assume a supervisory role with student interns in training and/or a consultative one with colleagues. In addition, the helper may be taking on more administrative duties, where he/she becomes involved in grant writing and interfacing with other agencies/institutions within the community, in which a representative/advocacy role on behalf of the agency is assumed. As the therapist embraces both a clinical and community perspective, this allows him/her to appreciate the bigger picture, where he/she can see that direct service to clients is only one way in which therapists can ensure that clients are the recipients of state-of-the-art care. Seeing the broader "macrocausal" perspective can also shift the previously competitive nature of the therapist's relationship with colleagues to a more cooperative one, where each clinician becomes a valued member of the team and in the clinical community as a whole.

Throughout the course of their careers, therapists may revisit a number of the stages previously described, where they repeatedly reach the point of spreading themselves too thin—taking on much more than they can cope with and destroying that balance that they may have worked so hard to maintain. It is at this point that the helper needs to pull back—taking off responsibility rather than taking on more. This is where a self-care plan becomes vital—a plan the therapist can always revisit when he/she connects with the warning signs of forthcoming empathy malaise. A self-care plan involves internal mechanisms that will consciously alert the therapist to the warning signs of stepping beyond the boundaries. Earlier on in professional development, the symptoms of empathy malaise are dissociated from conscious awareness; the therapist now has the ability to recognize that stomach knots, dark rings under the eyes, and heaviness of the shoulders are an indication that he/ she is pushing the outer clinical limits. In our experience, it is a tremendous relief, and a freeing sensation, for the therapist to consciously hear him/herself saying "NO!" to taking on more work—followed by the statement, "In order to take care of myself, I need to decline from taking on that extra load." At the end of this chapter in the section on Metaphors, Exercises, and Rituals, we have constructed a self-care plan especially tailored for the sexual abuse therapist that can easily be implemented at any given point in the therapist's career.

Feeling comfortable in one's own skin is the hallmark of the seasoned therapist—knowing that one does not have all the answers and solutions to the issues presented by clients and that one's sense of wonder and thirst for learning are still very much intact. Becoming comfortable with ambiguities, anxiety, and helplessness are what experienced therapists have been trained to deal with throughout their careers—these are the keys to longevity and success. It is at this career point, when helpers truly trust their clinical abilities, that they can put the voices of mentors, teachers, supervisors, and theories aside and allow their own voice to emerge—one that speaks with experience and a wonderful inner wisdom that frees them to be impactful, effective therapists.

METAPHORS, EXERCISES, AND RITUALS

TO PROMOTE SELF-CARE AND RESTORE BALANCE IN THE THERAPIST

Introduction

In the process of writing about vicarious trauma, self-care, and toxic content in therapy, we have become more aware of the abundance of media coverage concerning toxins contaminating our environment. Countless articles and news items barrage us daily with information about pesticides, secret government testing, oil spills, and so on. The message seems to be that we are defenseless, vulnerable, and unable to restore balance in our world. Advertising is increasingly saturating our consciousness by telling us that it is necessary to detoxify our bodies by taking vitamins to counteract the pollutants in our environment. Many treatments are available to scrub and purge our insides, boost our immune systems, and help us slough off the outer layers of skin that have been contaminated by the global desecration of nature. Are we trying to cleanse and renew our environment, our bodies, or our souls?

People are turning increasingly to alternative forms of medicine, especially Chinese medicine, and to Eastern philosophies and practices such as Tai Chi and Yoga, perhaps to help counteract their overwhelming reactions to the exponential rates of change we all face politically, socially, economically, and technologically. With all of this continually going on around us, it makes perfect sense to detoxify and cleanse our inner vistas so that we can be more balanced and resilient to better deal with the chaos and everyday stressors in our lives.

In this section of Chapter 8 we have incorporated some metaphorical meditations, exercises, and rituals that are a combination of Eastern practices and Ericksonian techniques for the purpose of helping you, the therapist, to cleanse and balance your mind and body: As such, this material is meant to act as a guide to assist you in the creation of a personally relevant path of self-care. The metaphors, exercises, and rituals have been created with the intent of addressing the various issues previously discussed in this chapter. The content reflects our orientation and style and represents the tip of the iceberg in terms of the topic and realm of self-care alternatives. It is meant to be a starting point in the awareness and process of personal care.

HEALING, RENEWAL, AND BALANCE (GUIDED MEDITATION)

The following guided meditation is intended to assist the therapist in assessing, clearing, and rebalancing both the body and the mind. The method employed follows the ancient chakra system of accessing consciousness via the seven chakra points or centers of energy and consciousness within the body. This theory is based on the understanding that beliefs in the mind affect the body in its behavior and structure. Therefore, the systems or schemas in which we think affect our behavior and perception which, in turn, affect how we approach our everyday life and future. We are thus involved in a self-perpetuating cycle that can be used to our advantage if we are in tune with our minds and our bodies.

One of the previously identified dangers of working with trauma survivors is the often contaminating effect it has on the therapist. Therefore, being able

*to relax, meditate, and rebalance one's own body and mind becomes vital to
sustaining the creativity and energy needed to do this work.*

*We recommend that you make a tape of this or any other meditation or
metaphor that is personally relevant so that you can hear and experience this
process in your own voice. Many clients and colleagues have found this to be
an effective and personally intimate way to experience this process.*

AND YOU CAN BEGIN by being in touch with your breathing. Taking some slow, easy breaths into your body. Adjusting to any position that is comfortable for you. Being aware of the rhythm of each breath and how that sounds inside, as your breath travels into your lungs and spreads throughout your entire body, nourishing you and linking you to the earth and to your own center like a stream connecting to a river, connecting to the ocean. Your body is the vehicle which connects you to the physical world and contains all of your thoughts and memories, past and present. All of your accomplishments, pain, resources, and potential. Breathing as deeply and as comfortably as possible, just notice how it feels to be in your body right now. Noticing any of those tight and tense places, allowing yourself to sense those areas of your body where you hold the tension and stress. Taking a moment to ask yourself which parts of your body hold onto those painful stories and feelings? Listening inside to your own intuitive voice, smelling your own scent. Tasting what it's like to be you. Breathing as deeply and as comfortably as possible.

As you are gaining awareness and comfort inside, it might be interesting to be aware of the area of your perineum, your legs, the base of your spine, and allow yourself to think about how you have survived in your life so far, what has it been like to live and experience being you? How have you anchored yourself, connected to yourself and others? Just allow yourself to take a moment and be in that area of your body, imagining it bathed in a clear red light, permeating that area at the base of your spine and letting any symbols and images that seem relevant to select themselves or be known to you now (*pause*).

And continue up your body to the area of your lower abdomen, your reproductive organs. Breathing in as deeply as possible and thinking about and feeling your sexuality. How do you express your sensual self? What emotions are connected to your sexuality? Take a few moments and explore these emotions. How fluid are they? Imagine as fully as possible what it would be like to allow their expression in a way that is safe and satisfying to you. Just allow your mind to wander and wonder about that. Allowing any images or symbols to flow like fresh spring water through that part of your body. Thinking about how it would look to drench these organs in a beautiful orange color. What textures or symbols or scents might be there—just allowing yourself to experience that even more fully (*pause*).

Moving up your body a little bit further to your solar plexus, the seat of your personal power and will, and just thinking about that area of your body, feeling it and sensing it, how do you utilize your own intuition to take care of yourself? How do you make things happen in your life? Think of times when you have felt powerful, when has that power flowed through you easily, willingly, happily? How can you connect with your inner core to fire up your energy to empower yourself? Feel that energy flowing up and through you from your feet to the top of your head. What can you do for you? From you? How would it be to image a beautiful yellow light permeating that center of you? A sunny light cleaning and warming your core. Just take a moment and experience that even more fully—allowing any images or symbols to surface from your core into consciousness (*pause*).

As you breathe in and out, allowing your own comfortable rhythm and pace to emerge, imagine and sense that area around your heart and chest. Your back and your front, your left side and your right side. Sensing your circulatory system, pumping oxygen and blood throughout your body. Thinking about feeling and hearing from deep within your own ability to love self and others. Does love come easily into your core or being? For what does your heart long? Where is the center of your compassion to yourself? How can you balance your love with your will? Your compassion with your antipathy? (*pause*) As you continue to breathe, listening to your own breath circulating throughout your body, with each breath you take in, wouldn't it be interesting to imagine a beautiful shade of green entering your body through your lungs and saturating that area around your heart, lungs, and sternum, letting any images or symbols that seem relevant to you to emerge, being aware and in tune with that part of your body for as long as you wish to (*pause*).

And let yourself move up even more to that area around your throat, listening to the sound of your inner voice. How do you listen to your inner self? How often do you communicate with yourself? What would you like to say to yourself about your life right now? What truth about yourself could you voice at this time in your life? Whom in your life do you want to speak your truth to? Listen to those sounds within and hear and feel what they are saying to you. What color might those sounds be? How would it be to imagine a beautiful shade of blue passing through that area of your throat, front and back, relaxing your neck and inspiring your own emerging voice and creative spirit (*pause*).

Moving up even more to that area located in the center of your forehead; this is the center of your imagination and creativity. Intuit what you need to carry out your creative ideas. Is there anything blocking you from fulfilling your vision for your present and future? What is your image of tomorrow? What insight into yourself might help you realize your full potential? Ask your unconscious mind to help you sort through your ideas and experience, to help you identify and sense your own personally relevant focus for your imagination and creative skills, both personally and professionally. Imagine a shade of indigo spreading through that area around your head, behind your eyes, inside your mind, coloring your view of self, offering insight into any areas which might be temporarily blocked, cleaning your mind of cluttering, limiting thoughts. Clearing out the cobwebs and letting in the light, indigo light. Allowing new patterns to emerge (*pause*).

And you can travel up from your roots, tracing your connection and evaluating yourself, healing and feeling yourself going beyond those limits that may stick you to old ways, hearing, feeling, tasting, seeing, and learning from all those other layers of self. Moving toward that door which can open more possibilities within and without. Moving up to the very top of your head, the seat of your knowledge, personality, and spirituality. That place where understanding stems from. Allow yourself to be in the top of your head in a different way than usual. Understanding yourself in a clearer, more integrated, open fashion. How can you access all that inner knowledge and strength and make it work for you? How can you locate and communicate the answers within yourself to your conscious mind? Ask yourself an important question that is relevant to your life right now (*pause*).

What do you intuit or sense the solution might be? Let your mind wander and drift. What kinds of images or symbols or words come into your mind? How would you know you had the answer to your issue or question if it became known to you? What parts of yourself do you find difficult to accept? What is it like to be with you, in you? Allow yourself to think about integrating those aspects of you that may seem more difficult to accept than others. Like fitting pieces of a puzzle together to make a whole picture. A personal matrix, integrating all those unique qualities of you. Being aware of where the pain and discomfort exists, sorting through what is you and what fits and letting go of other people's anguish, focusing on what is relevant for you. Understanding and thinking in a different way, listening to your own process and realizing there are no absolute truths but being open to a new understanding of self and other.

Think about what it might be like to feel the color violet penetrating the top of your head, entering your conscious and unconscious, coloring your thought process in a way that is both tranquil and exciting. Trusting yourself, being open to new ways of being, safely and intimately with yourself and important others. Allowing an open stream of ideas and creativity to flow like a wellspring throughout your body and mind. Letting go of whatever you need with every exhale of your breath. Holding on to your unique abilities and resources which can help you to regenerate your energy both physically and creatively. Even more.

And you can take a few moments of clock time, or however long you need to be aware of your internal processes, symbols, images, and experience in whatever way is relevant to you now. And when you are ready to reorient back to the present, bring with you a renewed sense of comfort, tranquility, and creativity. It might be interesting for you to ask your unconscious mind to help you answer some important questions. And your unconscious may share these insights with your conscious mind in a variety of ways, today, or in a week, or in a few hours from now; whenever that happens, it's important to know that you can help you experience yourself in a different, more balanced way. It might be interesting to imagine how you might look in a more balanced way. How might you feel and sound? What might you be doing differently? Just allow yourself to ponder and wonder a while longer, as long as you need to. That's right. Giving yourself the opportunity to blossom and unfold. Opening up to all of those unacknowledged possibilities and a different understanding of your own consciousness, whatever path of development that might follow, being more in tune with yourself and your surroundings.

⌘　　　⌘　　　⌘

AN EXERCISE FOR IDENTIFYING AND UNDERSTANDING ONE'S PHYSICAL AND EMOTIONAL NEEDS

This exercise is a continuation of the process in the previous meditation. As we focused on each of the seven chakras and their focal points in the body, there were various questions posed to help identify areas of stress and to uncover significant issues perhaps yet unresolved or perhaps blocking your process of self-actualization.

Using the questions from the meditation listed below as guidelines, reread or listen again to "Healing, Renewal, and Balance" and allow yourself to explore, in writing, or in any other medium (e.g., art or poetry) which areas of your current life warrant further exploration or attention at this time. As you go through the meditation, be aware of any symbols or images which present themselves and draw and/or write about those which are most significant to you.

QUESTIONS FOR SELF-DISCOVERY

- Which parts of your body hold on to those painful stories and feelings?
- What is it like to live and experience being you?
- How have you anchored yourself and connected yourself to others?
- How do you experience your sexual self?
- What emotions do you experience in connection to your sexuality?
- How fluid are they?
- How do you make things happen in your life?
- When has your personal power flowed through you easily, willingly, and happily?
- How can you connect with your inner core to fire up your energy to empower yourself?
- What can you do for you, from you?
- Does love come easily into your core or being?
- Where is the center of your compassion to yourself?
- How can you balance your love with your will?
- How can you balance your compassion and your antipathy?
- How do you listen to your inner self?
- How often do you communicate with yourself?
- What would you like to say to yourself about your life right now?
- What truth about yourself could you voice at this time in your life?
- Whom in your life do you want to speak your truth to?
- Are you aware of anything blocking you from fulfilling your vision of your present and future?

- What is your image of tomorrow?
- What insight into yourself might help you realize your full potential?
- How can you access all of that inner knowledge and strength and make it work for you?
- How can you locate and communicate the answers within yourself to your conscious mind?
- Ask yourself an important question that is relevant to your life right now.
- What do you intuit or sense the solution might be?
- What kinds of images or symbols come into your mind when posing these questions?
- How would you know you had the answers to an issue or question if it became known to you?
- What parts of yourself do you find difficult to accept?
- What is it like to be with you, in you?

⌘   ⌘   ⌘

BALANCING AND HEALING RITUAL

Following along with the self-exploration in the previous meditation and exercise, create a time and a place on a regular basis that fits for you and meditate on any significant issues or images that have been identified in the previous exercise and meditation. We have found that establishing a regular routine of self-contemplation and relaxation can be vital to restoring personal balance at the end of or during the course of a busy, stressful day.

Taking a few easy breaths, as deeply as possible, go through each part of your body and concentrate on releasing and soothing any tense areas, think about releasing them on each exhale. As you do that, it might be interesting to identify a particular color, sound, or image which represents your own inner creative energy. Think about using that color to clear out those tight or tense places within you. If you come up with a concrete image or symbol associated with that tense or blocked area, draw or represent it in some way in order to externalize it. You may want to then do something symbolic to let go of that, in any way that seems right for you.

⌘   ⌘   ⌘

CONTAINMENT, RESTRUCTURING, AND RENEWAL (METAPHORICAL MEDITATION)

The work of the therapist is demanding and ever changing. Each client presents a unique challenge that requires us to connect on an empathic level while simultaneously remaining objective and focused. We must be attached and yet detached. All the while our clients' issues may trigger or unsettle our own personal issues, constructs, and beliefs. Maintaining a healthy balance requires the ability to acknowledge and sort through personal issues on an ongoing basis which may be triggered by or affected by the work we do.

The following metaphorical meditation is intended to help each of us honor our own individual and constantly unfolding process of change, while protecting and shielding ourselves from taking in the traumatic details and material we deal with on a daily basis. Taking on the client's pain and responsibility for change can block or interfere with the taking care of our own needs and maintaining a healthy and creative focus both personally and professionally.

In order to let go of what is no longer helpful or healthy and to accept the challenge of growth, it is important to have a structure with which to contain the change, the chaos, and confusion we often feel in the transition process. A container can help us put new practices into place which can enable us to then let go of whatever is cluttering our inner vista.

This metaphor is intended to help you construct such a container or protective chrysalis in which you can continue your own developmental process in a safe and intimate place within yourself. At the same time, this can act as a shield against the harmful effects of the client's traumatic material.

Once again, we would suggest that you tape this metaphor in your own voice to assist you in experiencing your unique individual process and to benefit from your own healing voice as you enable your clients to do.

AND YOU CAN BEGIN BY TAKING SOME DEEP EASY BREATHS, at a comfortable rate for you, opening up and letting in those easy, comfortable breaths. Connecting to your own rhythm. Feeling and hearing each breath as it enters your body. With each breath there can be a new possibility, an opening, another chance to take in some nurturing and enter a different path of learning and integrating all that is contained within you. Feeling free to adjust your position at any time for more comfort.

And it might be interesting to feel your feet connected to the ground beneath them. Feeling and experiencing your feet in a different way as though they are part of a root system linked to the earth, just as a tree is joined by its roots into the ground. Attached, tapping into all of the energy and life beneath the surface. Such a complex root system taking in nutrients, light, and water and utilizing and transforming the warmth of the sun, natural energy to create each breath of fresh air, the magical slight-of-hand of nature. Impossible yet real. Taking in the carbon dioxide and transforming it, just as you can transform the pain, confusion, and the lost innocence into knowledge and understanding on so many different levels.

And just as a tree is connected to its roots and the knowledge of nature, you have the ability to tap into your own inner source. Allowing information and experience to travel from that source as a river begins its journey, flowing, connecting, and taking a variety of routes, arriving at its destination after negotiating many obstacles and currents. And you can allow yourself to drift comfortably in whatever direction your unconscious might take you and the comfort of knowing that you can tap into that source of inner knowledge, sorting through, taking stock of which way to go from here. Which is the right way for you to turn? What do you need to sort through in order to move ahead on your own individual path? Feel your feet rooted in comfort, with a deep sense of self-appreciation for all you have accomplished so far in your life. Imagine yourself safely connected to that solid foundation, there beneath the surface (*pause*).

And as you experience that sense of attachment to self, it's nice to know that you can create a sanctuary inside of you that can help you feel safe and in touch with your inner world. And wouldn't it be interesting to design that inner space to fit you and your needs. A safe place to regenerate, restructure, and renew your ideas and beliefs. To take in what you need to take in and release whatever you are ready to let go of.

Take a moment to explore inside. How could that sanctuary be? So many possibilities. So many choices. And would it be like a cocoon, comfortably enveloping you with enough space to feel unrestricted yet embraced in comfort, sheltered from the unsettled weather outside? And what would it be like inside your cocoon? What temperature would it be? How would it feel? Would it be furnished with comfortable textures, colors, and sounds? Would it be quiet and tranquil? Would there be music or sounds of nature, the ocean, the breeze, the sounds of birds or a clear stream? Or the sound of your own breathing and heartbeat? Just take a moment to allow that protective, contained place to materialize inside, allowing yourself to explore all the possibilities. Even more (*pause*).

And could that place safe within you have a very unusual protective barrier? Solid and safe but not rigid. A clear boundary yet with enough flexibility to be insulating but accommodating. Contained but not isolated. Allowing in whatever is right for you, whatever you need to add to yourself to become more complete and fulfilled.

A place where you can retreat to, to heal and to learn. To look back to understand and to remember that childlike curiosity and innocence. That spontaneity and excitement for discovery. To look ahead to what is still to come. A place to sit with those frozen pieces that don't know which way to go. A comfortable place to decide which direction to take. To face the obstacles and find the release from those sticky patterns. A place to reinvent yourself, creatively, respectfully, and courageously.

Just as that caterpillar tucks itself away to regenerate and transform itself into a beautiful butterfly, so can you transform that old material into something new. Weaving your own tapestry from all of those threads from your past and your present into your future.

And just let yourself consider the possibilities. The possibility of utilizing that clear protective shield to be present yet removed, visible but invisible. And what color might that flexible boundary be? Would it have a texture, a luminous quality that permeates or diffuses when appropriate? And you could use this shield in a variety of ways for a variety of purposes. To contain and shelter, to reflect and refract, to refrain or persist. So many possibilities.

So take a few moments of clock time or as much time as you need to contemplate your sanctuary and container. To think about imagining and experiencing that protection around you, like a guard allowing in only what is safe or right for you to take in or take on. Like an energy field, protecting and helping you to filter out whatever you need to let go of. Sifting through. Just allowing any personally relevant symbols, images, or messages to emerge (*pause*).

And when you are ready, you can reorient back to the present, bringing with you whatever images, symbols, or tools that can help you create the safety and containment that you need to remain focused and balanced, inside and outside, personally and professionally, in whatever way is right for you.

⌘ ⌘ ⌘

CONTAINMENT AND PROTECTION EXERCISE AND RITUAL

The intent of this exercise and ritual is to practice the skill of maintaining a safe distance from clients' often troubling and toxic content. This can be accomplished by utilizing your ability to access your own tools and resources to shield and protect the self from the intrusive material by imaging a barrier or container within and around yourself.

After reading, or preferably listening to the previous metaphor, "Containment, Restructuring, and Renewal," you can create and practice imaging a contained safe place within as well as a protective shield between the client and yourself, which allows you to be empathic and focused, while simultaneously maintaining a safe distance or boundary.

Rituals can be powerful tools to symbolize significant changes and rites of passage. We encourage you to think about a way to mark or symbolize your own process of self-discovery and self-care—a way of maintaining your own inner balance and beginning to acknowledge your unique needs and individuality as a therapist—a way of acknowledging all that you contribute to others while realizing the importance of taking care of yourself.

One way of accomplishing this might be to create your own symbol of containment as discussed in the previous exercise and to employ that symbol in some significant way on a regular basis as a way of maintaining balance. Perhaps this could be accompanied by some messages of appreciation and validation to yourself that you could repeat or listen to at times of relaxation or meditation.

We recommend drawing this shield or boundary to personalize it and to help yourself become familiar with it and then to practice utilizing this shield as a tool with clients. We have also found it helpful to create a tangible symbol of the shield to keep in the office as a concrete reminder of a protective barrier or to maintain one's distance while doing therapy.

The possibilities are endless and the significance and process of such a ritual can and must be tailored to your own needs, beliefs, and values.

⌘   ⌘   ⌘

"LEANA ON ME!"

This is a metaphorical story especially designed for therapists who are just about to, or already have, reached the stage in their career where they are experiencing empathy malaise and are in search of creative ways in which they can institute self-healing practices. We recommend that you tape the following metaphor, changing any details to better fit the specific issues you are facing as a compassion-fatigued therapist, so that you can hear your own voice, giving yourself permission to take time out for self-care.

THERE ONCE LIVED A BEAUTIFUL DOVE NAMED LEANA. Leana was a special dove in many different ways.... She had a particularly warm heart that was filled with love, and very broad shoulders that encompassed a wide wingspan that allowed her to carry other smaller doves and an assortment of birds on her shoulders when they needed her to rescue them. Leana also had an extraordinary intuitive ability to sense the pain of others. It was uncanny; each time her heart beat a little faster, she knew that she was needed somewhere, and she would fly until the sound of her own heartbeat would transform into the sound of drums, beckoning her to the windows of the homes of people in despair. Leana would answer their cries with food for the hungry, medical supplies for the sick, and alms for the indigent. Leana loved her work and gleaned much joy when she saw sad, despairing faces transform into smiles when she was able to answer their needs in some way.

It just so happened that on one particular winter just before the Christmas season, Leana was frantically busy, answering the cries of those who feared that they would not have enough to give their families for Christmas. Something very unusual began to happen on this particular year that had not occurred before.... Leana began receiving not one call, but many requests from each family...so that she now would fly back on three, sometimes even four occasions, on the wings of need. There were some nights that Leana would return to her nest so late, that she would spend the rest of the night awake thinking of all those in despair, her wings feeling weighted down by the hopes and expectations of others. She then would arise early in the morning, returning to the families who beckoned her to their homes.

It was on one particular morning, Leana noticed that when she spread her wings in preparation for flight, they looked dull (not shiny like they used to), and she felt pain when she began to fly…. Was she spreading herself too thin? But, who had time for such thoughts? She told herself to concentrate on her duty to others, making sure that all the families requesting her help would be happy and fulfilled by Christmastime. Something, however, very strange began to occur…. Even when she visited a family on three or even four occasions, it still didn't feel like enough…. The more she visited them, the more they needed her, and soon the drums that signalled the needs of others, began to pound desperately for herself. The pounding in her heart came to Leana's attention one evening when she was returning home, as she passed by an olive tree that cried out to her, "Little dove, come and rest in my branches, for they are strong and you are tired. Just let go and rest, and I will hold you and keep you safe until morning."

And it was while the dove slept that the olive tree began to whisper her wisdoms into Leana's ears:

> You are a wonderful and giving dove, and there are many who respect and love you. You have forgotten, however, one very important bird who desperately needs your care and support, now; she needs you to send messages of peace and calm—she needs time to be and feel nurtured—she needs to experience personally all the love that she so easily gives to others. And that very special bird is you, my dear Leana. And so that you will always remember to take the time to care for yourself, I am giving you one of my branches to carry with you to always remind you of how important it is to nurture yourself above all else. Every time your feathers come into contact with the olive branch, either by touch, smell, sight, or sound, you will remember to love and honor yourself.

When Leana woke up the next morning she felt rejuvenated…. It was Christmas Day, and as she opened her eyes, she saw the olive branch. Upon seeing the branch, she decided to spend the next few days doing something special just for herself. She flew to her favorite bird pond and had a special bath…delighting in the wonderful feeling that occurred when her feathers connected with the water. She then flew to her friend the olive tree, and settling on its branches, dried her wings in the morning sun. The olive tree smiled as she watched the shine and strength return to Leana's wings. Leana so enjoyed the peace and calm that came over her when she lay on the branches of the olive tree, that she decided to say there for the rest of the day, becoming aware of herself and her own needs for the first time in months. Leana now knew that all she had to do to remind herself of those pleasant feelings was to connect with the olive branch...recalling the wise words of the olive tree.... TO LOVE SELF ABOVE ALL.

Leana began to notice that the better care she took of herself, the more others would respect her and the personal boundaries she created. The families Leana helped, learned from her example, and began to set their own boundaries with one another. Leana was now able to use her intuition to nurture herself, which was both healthier for her and also for all the families she had helped and supported over the years. How happy she felt...recalling that all the love she gave to others, she was now able to return to herself.

⌘ ⌘ ⌘

"SANDY GETS A LIFE"

Here is an opportunity for you to become more consciously aware of the symptoms of empathy malaise that you may have, until this point, dissociated from, in order to continue to cope with an overburdened caseload. This metaphor will help you to go beyond the point of just identifying the warning signs, as you are now provided with the tools to transform the way you practice your art into something that is a co-creative, healing process for both you and your clients. Immediately following this metaphor is a self-care plan that you can begin to institute as part of the way in which you bring to conscious awareness useful methods of self-care.

The needs of clients can be so great, that therapists sometimes get caught in a trap, where they feel compelled to devote even their personal time to the survivors with whom they work. It is at this point that therapists risk tumbling over their own somewhat weakened boundaries, by making themselves available to their clients at any time of the day or night, resulting in a situation where their lives become eclipsed by the needs of others. By presenting with vague boundaries, such therapists set up a situation where the survivor-client becomes confused by what the appropriate limits are and, as a result, the boundary violations experienced with her abuser(s) are recreated in the therapeutic relationship. The ongoing experience of blurred boundaries between therapists and their clients can also be a stress-

ful experience for therapists, where they risk confusing their own needs with those of their clients.

We recommend that if your professional and personal lives have blended into one another, or if you are approaching this dangerous place in your practice, you record this metaphor onto a tape, using you own healing voice, and changing any of the details to tailor the metaphor to meet your needs. Giving yourself permission to listen to this tape on a regular basis will assist you in untangling your own web, hopefully before you reach Sandy's crisis state.

S HE WAS ON THE RUN...not knowing what she was running to or where she had been running from.... She had had flashes of what it had been like before...but were they scenes from her life or somebody else's? She desperately tried to ignore the horrific graphic images in her head, but they kept returning to her over and over again, so she continued to run...hoping that if she moved fast enough, she could leave them behind in the dust. She used to care...far too much for that matter...but nothing seemed to matter now.... So many times she had heard the words: "SLOW DOWN," "TAKE STOCK," "TAKE TIME OUT FOR YOURSELF."... But she had paid no heed, so that now she had reached the point where she was at her lowest ebb—she had reached an emotional place where she had nothing left to give either to others or, more importantly, to herself.

These thoughts continued to flood her mind as she ran into the gathering darkness, as if her feet had a mind of their own.... She could no longer stop herself.... Sandy had finally lost all sense of control.... After running for some time, her legs began to give way from beneath her.... Just at that moment, a huge tree loomed before her as she bumped up against it...causing her to reel backwards and stagger to the point of such dizziness that she fell in a heap on the ground, losing all sense of consciousness....

Over the course of the night, Sandy would regain consciousness for seconds at a time, frantically struggling to move her legs, but continuing to spin her heels in the hard, gritty dirt beneath her...her mind struggling to push away the reality of her circumstance...cold, lonely, isolated. Just before she came to again...that magical place one finds one's self in just prior to waking, an image flashed of being a spectator watching the world swirling past her.... She tried to speak, but no one heard her or seemed to notice her in any way.... Sandy realized at that instant that she had been living a life for some time now, through the pain of others, in which she had become less and less of a participant. But those people she had been living through had all let her down... for she had sacrificed everything for them and their lives seemed to continue on a downward spiral anyway...remaining in their pain.... Here she had thought all this time that she had really been helping them, only to come face to face with the realization that she had been ineffectual.

Sandy continued to dream, recalling what her life had been like before.... She had come from a family where love was conditionally based on academic achievement, receiving the message early on that she had to work extremely hard to receive minimal recognition from her parents. At the age of 18 she left home, unsure of her abilities and potential. She attended university, where she surprised herself by achieving above-average grades, which allowed her to go on to receive a graduate degree in counselling...something she had dreamed all her life about attaining. Sandy had cultivated very few friendships and, at most, had a number of acquaintances that she rarely saw, as she had been so caught up in achieving good grades. When she finally graduated, and began a job as a family counsellor at a family service agency in town, she only realized then that her weekends were fairly uneventful and for the most part lonely.... At work, though, Sandy began to experience the heady rush of being needed, in fact indispensable, to her clients, which resulted in a fairly rapid movement towards booking evening appointments until her weeknights became completely filled.... After all, Sandy had thought at the time, she would rather be at the office seeing clients than sitting at home alone and lonely....

Other staff members at the office began to notice that Sandy never seemed to say "no" to taking on more clients, which made them feel inadequate, as they felt unequipped to carry an equivalent caseload. In fact, it appeared to her colleagues that Sandy was climbing the career ladder fairly rapidly in comparison to themselves, as their superiors, openly impressed with Sandy's conscientious work, began to offer her more and more responsibility.... Soon Sandy was running groups, supervising students, and involving herself in committee work and grant writing. When the compliments were given out at staff meetings, Sandy received a lot of them, creating a situation where the other counsellors began to jockey for position...competing with her for praise and validation from their superiors. Soon Sandy became a compliment junkie.... It was not enough for her to receive praise from the supervisors and other administrators at work; she also began to encourage her clients to phone her at home if they went into crisis day or night...and they began to take her up on her offer to be there for them. It was a heady powerful feeling to be needed so much...Sandy thought at the time....

The red light was now constantly flashing on her answering machine when she would return from work late at night or on the weekends.... By the time she returned all the calls, her free time was all but spent, and when she was finished for the night, she would collapse into sleep, weighed down by the responsibility she carried. Soon Sandy began to ignore the sound of her alarm clock in the morning...shutting it off and falling back into a deep sleep...emerging, eventually, only to find that she was horribly late for work...noticing the looks of disapproval on the faces of other staff members, as she dragged herself through the agency doors. But she still carried on, relying on her adrenaline to get her through her demanding days...trying not to notice the chronic dark circles under her eyes or the constant churning in her stomach....

Sandy had almost forgotten that she had not seen a friend or had a social arrangement on the weekend for almost 6 months! She had no energy or time for herself—that had disappeared long ago.... Then, the inevitable began to occur.... Starting with one particular weekend, late on a Saturday night, when Sandy was sitting alone in her apartment staring into space, the phone began to ring insistently as she stumbled over to pick up the receiver: A client was threatening suicide, and Sandy responded to the young woman's needs by agreeing to drive over to her home. Sandy felt so needed as she threw a cloak over her, readying herself to swoop down and rescue her client from the jaws of fate. She continued to fill her weekends...responding readily to her clients' requests until...her life became so cluttered with the pain and needs of others, that she took her leave in the only way she knew how, by escaping...leaving behind her chaotic, complicated existence without a word to anyone....

As she was reaching consciousness, Sandy opened her swollen eyes to see an old woman looking down at her with a kind face, shaking her head as she watched the young therapist struggling to pull herself up from the gritty ground that had been her sleeping place the night before. The sun was shining strongly in the sky as the old woman motioned Sandy to follow her.... As Sandy began to move her body, she felt pain in her joints and an overwhelming sense of fatigue.... Eventually, the pair reached the old woman's home, where she prepared tea and biscuits and invited Sandy to lie down on an enormous overstuffed ottoman, where she fell into a deep, soothing sleep almost instantly....

As Sandy lay asleep on the ottoman, the old woman began to utter some wise healing words that sounded similar to the following:

You can take some time, now, to just let yourself waft in and out of consciousness...that's right, just giving yourself permission to sit with any uncertainty or confusion you may be feeling right now...starting with your feet and moving all the way up to the tip of your head, tuning into your body, asking each part what it needs in order to heal...making it okay to feel compassion for the parts that are experiencing pain and fatigue...giving yourself permission to take time out for your own healing...letting go of any intrusive thoughts or images.... That's right. Taking some time now to entertain the possibility of taking control back and at the same time inviting a sense of serenity and calm into your life.... Watching yourself take off rather than taking on more.... It's nice to know that you can share your load with others and that it is no longer only your burden to bear.

And as you begin to feel that load lighten, you may notice that you can breathe more deeply and comfortably than before...with each breath taking in what's comfortably yours and letting go of what does not belong...making room for yourself, and slowly expanding into that space...that's right.... Trusting your own internal signals to message to you when you have taken in enough, making any shifts or adjustments in your body to accommodate your own boundaries.... And isn't it nice to know that you can say "NO" when you need to...knowing that the struggles of others need not become your struggle and choosing to share in the solutions rather than becoming a part of the problem.... That's right.... Entertaining the idea of building a life of your own...filling it with healing support and love perhaps in the form of a partnership with yourself and, when ready, with a caring other...filling your life with your own dreams and hopes...knowing that your career will be a part of your life, without becoming your whole life. You may notice, now, that concerns that once seemed so important before are losing their significance, as you replace them with healthier additions. And now, you can slowly bring yourself back to the room...letting go of the burdens of others and gathering yourself up with much love and support....

⌘   ⌘   ⌘

SELF-CARE PLAN FOR THE THERAPIST

Empathy Malaise Signals

1. You can't deal with ambiguity and helplessness.

2. You stopped caring about clients.

3. You tune out clients.

4. You lack interest in the job, and you view it with a sense of loathing.

5. You pressure yourself to radiate wisdom and emotional wholeness.

6. You live vicariously through clients.

7. You feel the need to fix/cure all.

8. You take the emotional burden of your work home from the office.

9. You experience the toxic effects of being a sexual abuse therapist.

10. You are professionally isolated and feel competitive.

Transformation into Self-Care

1. Sitting comfortably with the confusions of others without feeling compelled to take them on.

2. Tuning into own needs will allow you to resurrect your compassion for others.

3. Tuning back into yourself.

4. Varying caseload, taking time to attend a conference, having lunch with a colleague, doing something physical, taking a vacation.

5. Feeling comfortable in your own skin and trusting your therapeutic wisdom.

6. Becoming an active participant in your own life.

7. Accepting that the client will make the necessary healthy shifts when ready.

8. Naming and containing the emotional fallout from clients and leaving these burdens in a secure, lidded box at the office.

9. Putting into practice a method of clearing and making distinctions between clients' issues and your own. (Use exercise entitled Healing, Renewal, and Balance in this chapter.)

10. Seeking out colleagues to consult with, shifting to a more cooperative, supportive way of working together.

11. You are professionally stagnant.

11. Training in techniques that require a more creative approach, resulting in an expanded repertoire of therapeutic interventions; changing jobs.

12. You mistake your own needs for clients' needs.

12. Getting in touch with your own needs through therapy, resulting in boundary clarification.

13. You feel that transformation is taking place in your clients' lives but your own is standing still.

13. Taking healthy risks and adding more adventure to your own life will replenish your compassion for clients.

⌘ ⌘ ⌘

EXORCISING THE NEEDS OF OTHERS: THE DREAM-CATCHER RITUAL (INDUCTION)

In this ritual, with the help of the "dream catcher," you will have a regular opportunity to exorcise the pain, anger, and despair that you may often feel when working with survivors of sexual abuse. According to an Ojibway legend, all dreams, good or bad, float through the air, seeking a sleeping being. The dream catcher's purpose is to catch both good and bad dreams. However, the good dreams know the way to follow the web and slide down the feathers into the owner's head. The bad dreams are also caught, but they are trapped until morning, where the first rays of light cause them to evaporate.

This ritual for the therapist, however, assumes a slightly different function than in the Ojibway legend, as you have an opportunity to tangibly construct, out of materials of your own choice, a net that will assist you in filtering out and making distinctions between clients' feelings and those of your own. Make sure that you have some materials of your choice readily available, so that you can construct your own dream catcher immediately following the trance induction.

You may wish to set aside a consultation meeting and to work together with your colleagues to collectively construct dream catchers in order to experience the support of one another, and in so doing, provide a co-creative opportunity for all. Whether you choose to construct your dream catcher by yourself or with others, we suggest that you tape the following induction in your own voice in a healing, nurturing way, so that you can begin to incor-

porate this ritual into your daily cleansing routine, letting go on a regular basis of toxic material that does not belong to you.

N OW, YOU CAN TAKE SOME TIME to review the day from a safe, cozy place, where you can comfortably distance yourself from others...letting go of what doesn't belong...and giving yourself permission to reclaim what is rightfully yours....

Taking time out, now, especially for you...to create your own dream catcher...choosing the materials that best fit the image for you.... Or, if you have already created your dream catcher, you can focus in on your creation, knowing that you have tailored this catcher of dreams to fit your own needs.... Focusing in on the symbol you have created.... Imagining, now, that you are pouring all the pain and anguish of the work you have completed today into your dream catcher...watching the catcher capture what belongs to you, as it gradually filters out the torment, rage, pain, despair, melancholy of others, like sand ...as it sifts its way to the bottom of the dream catcher, seeping out the bottom into the ground below....

Now, it is easier to make distinctions between what is rightfully yours...and to take hold of what is rightfully yours...letting go of all the rest.... And noticing that when you let go of what doesn't belong to you, your own needs become more accessible to you.... Now, you can take some time, in whatever way you choose, to answer and respond to your own needs.... Taking all the time you need...with a deep sense of self-appreciation.

References

American Psychiatric Association (1994). *Diagnostic and statistical manual of mental disorders* (4th ed.). Washington, DC: Author.

Bandler, R., & Grinder, J. (1975). *The patterns of the hypnotic techniques of Milton H. Erickson, M.D. Vol. I.* Palo Alto, CA: Behavior & Science Books.

Cameron-Bandler, L. (1978). *They lived happily ever after.* Cupertino, CA: Meta Publications.

Briere, J. (1989). *Therapy for adults molested as children: Beyond survival.* New York: Springer.

Butler, S. (1985). *Conspiracy of silence: The trauma of incest.* San Francisco: Volcano Press.

Calof, D. (1993). Facing the truth about false memory. *The Family Therapy Networker, 17*(5), 39–45.

Capacchione, L. (1988). *The power of your other hand: A course in channeling the inner wisdom of the right brain.* North Hollywood, CA: Newcastle.

Capacchione, L. (1991). *Recovery of your inner child: The highly acclaimed method for liberating your inner self.* New York: Simon & Schuster.

Courtois, C. (1988). *Healing the incest wound: Adult survivors in therapy.* New York: Norton.

de Shazer, S. (1988). *Clues: Investigating solutions in brief therapy.* New York: Norton.

Dolan, Y. M. (1989). Only once if I really mean it: Brief treatment of a previously dissociated incest case. *Journal of Systemic and Strategic Therapy, Winter.*

Dolan, Y. M. (1991). *Resolving sexual abuse: Solution-focused therapy and Ericksonian hypnosis for adult survivors.* New York: Norton.

Driver, E., & Droisen, A. (Eds.). (1989). *Child sexual abuse: Feminist perspectives.* London, England: MacMillan Education Ltd.

Durant, M., & White, C. (Eds.). (1990). *Ideas for therapy with sexual abuse.* South Australia: Dulwich Centre Publications.

Erickson, M. H., & Rossi, E. L. (1979). *Hypnotherapy: An exploratory casebook.* New York: Irvington.

Erickson, M. H., & Rossi, E. L. (1989). *The February man: Evolving consciousness and identity in hypnotherapy.* New York: Brunner/Mazel.

Finkelhor, D. (1986). *A source book on child sexual abuse: New theory and research.* Beverly Hills, CA: Sage Publications.

Fraiberg, S. H. (1959). *The magic years.* New York: Charles Scribner's.

Freyd, J. (1993). Personal perspectives on the delayed memory debate. *Family Violence and Sexual Assault, 9*(4), 28–33.

Gil, E. (1983). *Outgrowing the pain: A book for and about adults abused as children.* New York: Bantam Doubleday Dell.

Gil, E. (1988). *Treatment of adult survivors of childhood abuse.* Walnut Creek, CA: Launch Press.

Gil, E. (1992). *Outgrowing the pain together: A book for spouses and partners of adults abused as children.* New York: Bantam Doubleday Dell.

Gilligan, S. G. (1987). *Therapeutic trances: The cooperation principle in Ericksonian hypnotherapy.* New York: Brunner/Mazel.

Gilligan, S. G. (1993). Therapeutic rituals: Passages into new identities. In S. G. Gilligan & R. Price (Eds.), *Therapeutic conversations* (pp. 237–252). New York: Norton.

Haugaard, J. J., & Reppacci, N. D. (1989). *The sexual abuse of children.* San Francisco and London: Jossey-Bass.

Heller, S., & Steele, T. (1986). *There's no such thing as hypnosis.* Phoenix, CA: Falcon Press.

Herman, J. L. (1992). *Trauma and recovery.* New York: Basic Books.

Janet, P. (1886). Les actes inconscients et la mémoire pendant le somnambulisme [Unconscious acts and memory during sleepwalking]. *Revue Philosophique, 25*(1), 238–279.

Janet, P. (1889). *L'Automatisme psychologique* [Psychological automatism]. Reprint. Paris: Societé Pierre Janet, 1973.

Janet P. (1893). L'Amnésie continue [Continuing amnesia]. *Revue Générale des Sciences, 4,* 167–179. Also in Janet, P. 1898b. *Nevroses et Idées Fixes.* Vol. 1. Paris: Félix Alcan.

Janet, P. (1894). Histoire d'une idée fixe [History of an idée fixe]. *Revue Philosophique, 37*(1), 121–163.

Janet, P. (1894-95). Un cas de possession et l'exorcisme moderne [A case of possession and modern exorcism]. *Bulletin de Travaux de L'Université de Lyon, 8,* 41–57.

Janet, P. (1895). Les ideés fixes de forme hystérique [Hysterical forms of idées fixes]. *Presse Médicale, 3,* 201–203.

Janet, P. (1897). L'influence somnambulique et le besoin de direction [The influence of sleepwalking and the need for control]. *Revue Philosophique, 43*(1), 113–143.

Janet, P. (1898a). Le traitement psychologique de l'hystérie [Psychological treatment of hysteria]. In A. Robin, *Traité de thérapeutique appliqué* [Treatise of applied therapeutics]. Paris: Rueff. Also in Janet, P. 1911. *L'etat mental des hystériques* [The mental state of hysterics]. Second enlarged edition. Paris: Félix Alcan.

Janet, P. (1898b). *Névroses et idées fixes* [Neuroses and idées fixes]. Vol 1. Paris: Félix Alcan.

Janet, P. (1904). L'amnésie et la dissociation des souvenirs par l'emotion [Amnesia and dissociation of memories through emotion]. *Journal de Psychologie, 1*, 417–453. Also in Janet, P. 1911. *L'etat mental des hysteriques* [The mental state of hysterics]. Second enlarged edition. Paris: Félix Alcan.

Janet, P. (1907). *The major symptoms of hysteria.* London and New York: MacMillan. Second edition with new matter: 1920. New York: Hafner, 1965.

Janet, P. (1909a). *Les nevroses* [The neuroses]. Paris: Flammarion.

Janet, P. (1909b). Problèmes psychologiques de l'emotion [Psychological problems of emotion]. *Revue Neurol, 17*, 1551–1687.

Janet, P. (1919). *Les médications psychologiques* [Psychological treatments]. Three volumes. Paris: Félix Alcan. Reprint: Paris: Société Pierre Janet, 1984. English edition: *Principles of Psychotherapy.* Two volumes. New York: MacMillan. Reprint: New York: Arno Press, 1976.

Janet, P. (1920). *Introduction to the major symptoms of hysteria.* Second edition. London and New York: Macmillan: Facsimile: New York: Hafner, 1965.

Janet, P. (1928). *L'evolution de la mémoire et de la notion du temps* [The evolution of memory and of the concept of time]. Paris: A. Chahine.

Janet, P. (1929). *L'evolution de la personnalité* [The evolution of personality]. Paris: A. Chahine. Reprint: Paris: Société Pierre Janet, 1984.

Janet, P. (1935). Réalisation et interprétation [Fulfillment and interpretation]. *Annales Médico-Psychologiques, 93*, II:329–336.

Kagan, J. (1984). *The nature of the child.* New York: Basic Books.

Kane, E. (1989). *Recovering from incest: Imagination and the healing process.* Boston: Sign Press.

Kaplan, H. S. (1987). *Sexual aversion, sexual phobias, and panic disorder.* New York: Brunner/Mazel.

Kaufman, G. (1985). *Shame: The power of caring.* Cambridge, MA: Schenkman Books.

Kirschner, S., Kirschner, D. L., & Rappaport, R. L. (1993). *Working with adult incest survivors: The healing journey.* New York: Brunner/Mazel.

Knowles, D. W., & Reeves, N. (1983). *But won't granny need her socks?* Dubuque, IA: Kendall/Hunt.

Kübler-Ross, E. (1969). *On death and dying.* New York: MacMillan.

Laidlaw, T. A., Malmo, C., & Associates (1990). *Healing voices.* San Francisco: Jossey-Bass.

Lankton, S. (1980). *Practical magic: A translation of basic neuro-linguistic programming into clinical psychotherapy.* Cupertino, CA: Meta Publications.

Lankton, S., & Lankton, C. H., (1989). *Tales of enchantment: Goal-oriented metaphors for adults and children in therapy.* New York: Brunner/Mazel.

Levin, R. (1974). *The nervous system.* New York: Anchor Press/Doubleday.

Madanes, C. (1990). *Sex, love and violence: Strategies for transformation.* New York: Norton.

Maltz, W., & Holman, B. (1987). *Incest and sexuality: A guide to understanding and healing.* Lexington, MA/Toronto: Lexington Books.

McCann, L., & Pearlman, L. A. (1990). Vicarious traumatization: A framework for understanding the psychological effects of working with victims. *Journal of Traumatic Stress, 3*(4), 131–149.

Meadows, K. (1989). *Earth medicine: A Shamanic way to self discovery.* Shaftesbury, Dorset, England, Rockport, MA, & Brisbane, Queensland, Australia: Elements Publishers.

Meiselman, K. C. (1990). *Resolving the trauma of incest: Reintegration therapy with survivors.* San Francisco and London: Jossey-Bass.

Middleton-Mos, J., & Dwinell, L. (1986). *After the tears: Reclaiming the personal losses of childhood.* Deerfield Beach, FL: Health Communications.

Mills, J. C., & Crowley, R. J. (1986). *Therapeutic metaphors for children and the child within.* New York: Brunner/Mazel.

Napier, N. J. (1993). *Getting through the day: Strategies for adults abused as children.* New York: Norton.

O'Hanlon, W. H. (1987). *Taproots.* New York: Norton.

O'Hanlon, W. H., & Martin, M. (1992). *Solution-oriented hypnosis: An Ericksonian approach.* New York: Norton.

Rossi, E. L. (1986/1993). *The psychobiology of mind-body healing: New concepts of therapeutic hypnosis.* New York: Norton.

Rossi, E. L. (1990). Psychobiological psychotherapy. In J. K. Zeig & W. M. Munion (Eds.), *What is psychotherapy? Contemporary perspectives.* San Francisco: Jossey-Bass.

Rossi, E. L., & Cheek, D. (1988). *Mind-body therapy: Methods of ideodynamic healing in hypnosis.* New York: Norton.

Russell, D. (1986). *The secret trauma: Incest in the lives of girls and women.* New York: Basic Books.

Sanford, L. T. (1990). *Strong at the broken places: Overcoming the trauma of childhood abuse.* New York: Random House.

Saxe, G. N., van der Kolk, B., Beckowitz, R., Chinman, J., Hall, K., Lieberg, G., & Schwartz, J. (1993). Dissociative disorders in psychiatric patients. *American Journal of Psychiatry, 150* (7), 1037–1042.

Shorten, L. (1994). False memory syndrome. *Canadian Lawyer, 18*(4), 16–20.

Sgroi, S. M. (1988a). *Vulnerable populations: Vol. I.* New York: Lexington Books.

Sgroi, S. M. (1988b). *Vulnerable populations: Vol. II.* New York: Lexington Books.

Steinem, G. (1992). *Revolution from within: A book of self-esteem.* Boston: Little, Brown.

Sykes W. M. (1993). The shadow of a doubt. *The Family Therapy Networker, 17*(5), 18–29, 70, 73.

Terr, L. (1994). Unchained memories: True stories of traumatic memories, lost and found. New York: Basic Books.

van der Hart, O., Brown, P., & Tusco, R. N. (1990). Hypnotherapy for traumatic grief: Janetian and modern approaches integrated. *American Journal of Hypnotherapy, 32*(4), 263–271.

van der Kolk, B. A. (1987). *Psychological trauma.* Washington: American Psychiatric Press.

van der Kolk, B. A., Blitz, R., Burr, W. A., & Hartmann, E. (1984). Nightmares and trauma: Life-long and traumatic nightmares in veterans. *American Journal of Psychiatry, 141,* 187–190.

van der Kolk, B. A., & Ducey, C. R. (1989). The psychological processing of traumatic experience: Rorschach patterns in PTSD. *Journal of Traumatic Stress, 2,* 259–274.

van der Kolk, B. A., Greenberg, M., Boyd, H., & Krystal, J. (1985). Inescapable shock, neurotransmitters, and addiction to trauma: Toward a psychobiology of post-traumatic stress. *Biological Psychiatry, 20,* 314–325.

van der Kolk, B. A., Greenberg, M. S., Orr, S. P., et al. (1986). Pain perception and endogenous opioids in post-traumatic stress disorder. *Psychopharmacology Bulletin, 25,* 121–127.

van der Kolk, B. A., Perry, J. C., & Herman, J. L. (1991). Childhood origins of self-destructive behavior. *American Journal of Psychiatry, 14*(12), 1665–1671.

van der Kolk, B. A., & van der Hart, O. (1989). Pierre Janet and the breakdown of adaptation in psychological trauma. *American Journal of Psychiatry, 146,* 1330–1342.

van der Kolk, B. A., & van der Hart, O. (1991). The intrusive past: The flexibility of memory and the engraving of trauma. *American Imago, 48*(4), 425–454.

Vella, S. M. (1994). False memory syndrome. *National: The Canadian Bar Association, 3*(1), 36–39.

Wisechild, L. M. (1988). *The obsidian mirror: An adult healing from incest.* Seattle: The Seal Press.

Woodman, M. (1985). The pregnant virgin: A process of psychological transformation. Toronto: Inner City Books.

Wylie, M. S. (1993). The shadow of a doubt. *The Family Therapy Networker, 17*(5), 18–29.

Yamamoto-Nading, D., & Stringer, G. H. (1991). *A healing celebration.* Renton, WA: King County Sexual Assault Resource Center.

Zeig, J. K. (1980). *Ericksonian approaches to hypnosis and psychotherapy.* New York: Brunner/Mazel.

Zeig, J. K. (1985). *Experiencing Erickson: An introduction to the man and his work.* New York: Brunner/Mazel.

Zeig, J. K. (1990). Ericksonian psychotherapy. In J. K. Zeig & W. M. Munion (Eds.), *What is psychotherapy? Contemporary perspectives.* (pp. 371–377). San Fransisco: Jossey Bass.

Name Index

A

American Psychiatric Association
(APA), 4

B

Bandler, R., 31
Beckowitz, R., 5

C

Chinman, J., 5

D

Dolan, Y. M., 33, 36, 55, 60, 170

E

Erickson, M. H., 24, 27, 34, 35, 58

F

Freyd, J., 8
Freyd, Pamela, 8
Freyd, Peter, 8

G

Gilligan, S. G., 77, 78, 79
Grinder, J., 31

H

Hall, K., 5
Herman, J. L., 9, 53, 55, 75

J

Janet, P., 5, 6, 9

K

Knowles, D. W., 163
Kübler-Ross, E., 163

L

Lankton, S., 83

M

Martin, M., 51
McCann, L., 219

N

Napier, N. J., 109

O

O'Hanlon, W. H., 51

Subject Index

A

Abandonment, empowerment and evolution of sexual self stage (Part A), 160

Abuse experience, minimization of, visibility stage, 80–82

Alice Sheds Her Shell story, reclamation and reintegration stage, 131–135

Ambivalence, unmasking stage, 52–54

Anger, control of feelings, reclamation and reintegration stage, 110–114

Anxiety attacks, visibility stage, emotional content, 85

Approval needs, reclamation and reintegration stage, 108–110

Assessment, group therapy, 40–42

Attention focusing, therapeutic trance, 33–34

Attic and Drawbridge story, empowerment and evolution of sexual self stage (Part A), 165–169

B

Badge of Courage ritual, visibility stage, 101–102

Badge of Courage story, visibility stage, 97–101

Balance, therapist self-care, 220–223

Balance ritual, therapist self-care, 230

Birthdays, celebration ritual, reclamation and reintegration stage, 146–147

Blaming self, unmasking stage, 56–58

Blooming Cactus ritual, empowerment and evolution of sexual self stage (Part B), 201

Blooming Cactus story, empowerment and evolution of sexual self stage (Part B), 199–201

Borderline personality, dissociation and, 5

Boundaries, therapist self-care, 214–215

Boundary creation, empowerment and evolution of sexual self stage (Part A), 161–162

Boundary setting exercise, empowerment and evolution of sexual self stage (Part A), 181–182

Brain, trauma and, 5–6

Breaking of silence. *See* Unmasking stage

Buddy system, empowerment and evolution of sexual self stage (Part B), social relationships, 190–193